D1253391

LUDWIG JEKELS

———

SELECTED PAPERS

SELECTED PAPERS

by

LUDWIG JEKELS

including two papers
written in collaboration with

EDMUND BERGLER

Essay Index Reprint Series

 BOOKS FOR LIBRARIES PRESS
FREEPORT, NEW YORK

First published in Great Britain 1952

Reprinted 1970 by arrangement with
International Universities Press, Inc. and Dr. Emory Wells

~~150~~

~~J47~~

BF21
J44
1970

INTERNATIONAL STANDARD BOOK NUMBER:
0-8369-1963-7

LIBRARY OF CONGRESS CATALOG CARD NUMBER:
72-117815

PRINTED IN THE UNITED STATES OF AMERICA

ACKNOWLEDGMENT

The author gratefully acknowledges the kindness of *Dr. Bergler* and the editors of the *International Journal of Psycho-analysis*, *The Psychoanalytic Quarterly*, *The Psychoanalytic Review*, and *Complex*, in permitting the reproduction of papers in this book.

JUL 1- 1971

CONTENTS

and
in collaboration with
EDMUND BERGLER, M.D.

THE TURNING POINT IN THE LIFE OF NAPOLEON I.*

As my justification for this paper I think I need only point to the vast number of works already published on Napoleon I. According to F. Kircheisen, the bibliography relating to the Napoleonic era now runs to some 80,000 items and, even so, is by no means complete.

No other period in history can claim anything like so vast a bibliography, a fact which amply demonstrates that the problems and motives at issue are profoundly buried: thus, they either resist our customary methods of historical investigation, however conscientious, or can only partially be brought to light. Historical research therefore should borrow from, or yield to, the methods employed by psycho-analysis which, more penetrative, can continue the task where other kinds of investigation fail.

This paper will confine itself to Napoleon's "Corsican Period", to which Masson, in his introduction to the "Manuscrits Inédits", refers as follows: "These two years require especial study (September 1791 to June 1793)".

I

The island of Corsica, on which Napoleon was born, had groaned since the fourteenth century under the cruel and despotic government of the Republic of Genoa; indeed, continual strife reigned between the Genoese and these island mountaineers, so jealous of their independence. Then, in 1730, the general discontent against the foreign tyranny flared into open rebellion which was to continue almost forty years.

* First published in *Imago*, Vol. III, 4, 1914.

It was a struggle full of sacrifice and abnegation which achieved some temporary successes and was followed with admiring eyes throughout Europe. The Genoese, however, despite their victories and aid from Germany and France, failed to defeat the Corsicans completely and their task became still more difficult when, in 1755, Pasquale Paoli was proclaimed Regent by the Corsicans.

This cultivated, intelligent and energetic man, who assumed the governorship of an island in chaos and decay, now earnestly devoted himself to his new duties. He more or less cleared the Genoese from Corsica,—though they managed to retain some fortified coastal places—and introduced order and good administration while providing his country with a sound constitution. Indeed, the speed with which he so much improved conditions won him the admiration of many of the great minds of his time. Rousseau, Voltaire, Frederick the Great, Montesquieu and others, considered the Corsican Constitution a model worthy of emulation.

When Paoli, however, sought to liberate the remainder of his country from the Genoese, these called the French to their aid and delivered their coastal fortresses to them. Eventually, realising they could never reconquer a territory that was so well armed and organised, the Genoese, on 15th May, 1768, ceded the island to the French in return for a money payment.

The French, however, found their task no easier than had their predecessors. The Corsicans resisted them as ferociously as they opposed the Genoese and heroically opposed the new oppressors. At first, these efforts met with success but, strong reinforcements reaching the French, Paoli was decisively defeated at Ponte Nuovo on 8th May, 1769 and his capital, Corte, was captured.

Paoli fled and found ready asylum in Britain, while his supporters surrendered. Among those delegated to sue for a peace, and occupying a leading position, was Carlo (Charles-Marie) Buonaparte, Napoleon's father, who hitherto had nobly fought for his country's freedom and strongly supported Paoli. These loyalties were wholly shared by Maria Laetizia, his wife, a beautiful and energetic young woman, fired with Corsican patriotism, who, even while pregnant, had fought at her husband's side. Four months after the conclusion of peace, Napoleon was born.

Corsica now had to submit to French rule which, as every-where under the Monarchy in France, was most despotic and cruel. The Corsicans, still humiliated by defeat and still dreaming their age-long dream of freedom, fiercely resented the French tyranny. They no longer rose in arms, but they sought to mend their fate within the framework of their narrow constitution which, until the Revolution, was even more limited than that of the other provinces of France. Suddenly, however, the revolutionary movement flared up in Paris and soon spread over France, whence likewise to the new-conquered Corsica. Thereupon, following a motion submitted by the national-liberal Corsican deputies to the National Assembly, then in power, Corsica was declared a French province with equal rights, and its political refugees were granted an amnesty. Paoli, the national hero, loved and venerated by his country-men, thereupon returned to the fatherland, after appearing before Louis XVI and the National Assembly, and taking the oath of loyalty to France. A deputation of his countrymen ceremoniously met him at Lyons and, on 14th July, 1790 (anniversary of the storming of the Bastille) he disembarked with them at Bastia amid the enthusiastic plaudits of his countrymen. He was then 65. Lucien Bonaparte later des-cribed the crowd, each of which wished to see, hear, and touch the hero back from his twenty-one year exile. When, two months later, public officials were elected under the new constitution, his compatriots, as token of their love, their faith and reverence, unanimously elected him governor of the island and to this task he brought all his probity and gifts.

*   *   *

We shall now briefly consider the relation of the young Napoleon, at this time, to his country and its father, *il babbo*, as the Corsicans called Paoli.

Even Napoleon's worst detractors, his bitterest critics, those who saw him solely as an embodiment of the grossest egotism, agree that, in youth, he was ardently patriotic. Napoleon himself has left so much proof of this in his writings, conversa-tions and acts, that no doubt of this can remain. Even as a child, say his biographers, he manifested the most ardent love for his fatherland. But this is hardly surprising considering

the emotions that surrounded him abroad and at home. No
doubt his mother, loving her country as she did, would have
sung patriotic songs to him in his cradle. According to
Kircheisen: "he grew up half-wild on his rugged island, and
the memory of the fierce battles for freedom still lived on, fresh
and alive in his countrymen's hearts. All about him the little
boy would have heard oaths and threats against the French,
those oppressors of the fatherland". At school, in Autun, his
blood boiled when his French schoolmates uttered the words
"the conquered", by which they designated Corsicans. Then,
inarticulate with rage, he would hurl himself at his tormentors.
The Abbé Chardon relates a scene in which Napoleon, then
nine-and-a-half, at the Military Academy in Brienne, retorted
with flashing eyes to the repeated teasing of his schoolfellows:
"If there had only been four to one, Corsica would never have
been taken, but they were ten to one". "Here at Brienne,"
says Chuquet, "he was very homesick, especially soon after his
arrival. He missed Corsica, its clear skies, the gentle warmth
of its clime. Heartsick for his homeland, deported to the drear
and harsh Champagne, it pained him to think that not for six
years, at least, would he again see his dear Corsica, so deeply
graven on his heart".

In addition to the lives of the Greek and Roman heroes, his
favourite reading was Corsican history; history which glorified
Paoli and belittled the French. And while still but fifteen, he
asked his father to send him Boswell's *A Tour in Corsica*.

Indeed, far from diminishing, his Corsican patriotism increased once he was gazetted lieutenant in the French army.
"In the garrison at Valence" (I quote Kircheisen) "his exalted
sensibility and his feelings became even more inflamed. His
hatred against the tyrants continually increased, irrespective
of the fact that he was a lieutenant in the King's army and in
the service of these very tyrants".

What fiery patriotism we find in his youthful writings:
One has only to read in *Sur la Corse:* "Paoli Colombano,
Sampiero, Pompiliano, Gaffoni! illustrious avengers of humanity, heroes who liberated your countrymen from the furies
of despotism, how were your virtues rewarded? By daggers,
yes, daggers! You modern effeminates who, almost to a man,
languish in sweet slavery, those heroes stand far too high for
your cowardly souls! But look on the picture of the young

Leonardo, the youthful martyr for the fatherland . . ." Or in *Sur le Suicide* where, prey to a melancholic and suicidal mood, he writes: "But since misfortunes begin to come upon me, since nothing pleases me, why should I ensure an existence in which nothing goes right . . . What spectacle will greet me in my homeland? My countrymen in chains, trembling as they kiss the hand that oppresses them". And in *Sur l'Amour de la Patrie:* "Very few believe in the love of the fatherland. What masses of works have not been written to prove how chimaerical it is. Feelings which produced the sublime acts of the Great Brutus, are you then nothing but a chimaera?"

In 1785, after ordering "everything on Corsica the Geneva bookseller had or could get for him" he began, barely seventeen, to write a history of Corsica in two volumes, entitled *Lettres sur la Corse*. Apparently, the following note, made by him, refers to this work: "I am barely of age and already my pen serves history. I know my weakness . . . but . . . I have that enthusiasm which a deeper study of mankind often destroys in our hearts. The venality of age will never sully my pen. I utter nothing but truth. I feel the strength to say it and I see your tears flow as you read this sketch of our sufferings. Dear Countrymen, we have always been miserable". This feeling is strongly expressed in the now celebrated *Lettres à Buttafuoco*, in which he accuses this Corsican-born Field Marshal, who went on loyally serving France, of treason to Corsica: a loyalty which made his countrymen declare him a traitor. "What! Not content with helping to forge your fatherland's chains, you now want to subject it to an absurd feudal system! . . . Ah! son of that same fatherland yourself, had you never felt aught for her then? Ah! did never the sight of her mountains and valleys, her rocks, her trees and houses move your heart?"

These examples, I think, will suffice to prove how deeply, indeed, Napoleon loved Corsica. But this same period of his life—from 1789 to 1793—is rich too in the most daring exploits inspired by ardent patriotism, exploits which aimed at no less than liberating Corsica from the French yoke. And all this while still an officer of the King, to the risk of promotion, of freedom, of life!

What, then, was Napoleon doing at this time when, in 1789, the "Etats Généraux" was convoked, and before which the two Nationalist deputies for Corsica proposed the setting up of a People's Militia, drawn from the young men. It was a motion which entirely accorded with Napoleon's views, for even then, it would seem, he contemplated concentrating in himself every means of ousting the French. And when the government rejected this motion, owing to the opposition organised by the conservative Buttafuoco, referred to above, Napoleon set to preparing a revolution of his own. At Ajaccio, where he had been on leave since September, 1789, he disclosed his plan to the Patriots' Club. It ran as follows: to overthrow the reactionary authorities: to organise a National Guard to capture the citadel of Ajaccio: to drive out the French. Soon he had organised a Civic Guard which, however, resulted in the garrison being strengthened and the Club and Guard being dissolved; the revolt was thus nipped in the bud.

Nevertheless, this was but a temporary check for, whether in garrison in France, or on long and frequent leaves in Corsica, the capture of the citadel of Ajaccio and the expulsion of the French remained the centre of his hopes and feelings. In these three years, we see him surmount all obstacles and seize each opportunity by which to achieve his goal. The vicissitudes of these years, so chequered and eventful for France, were followed by him with the utmost attention and, always in touch with Corsican feeling, he would obtain leave on every occasion which seemed propitious to his plans. These leaves he prolonged indefinitely, indifferent to the consequence for his military career. "In these difficult times the place of honour of a good Corsican is his homeland". This conviction, which he expressed in a letter to the Commissary of War, Sucy, he considered self-explanatory. Careless of his rank or of the oath of loyalty taken a year earlier, we see him in 1792 intriguing to command the volunteer battalion which the National Assembly had raised in Ajaccio, as throughout France. Eventually, by buying votes, issuing false statements and curtailing liberties, he managed to secure his appointment as Lieutenant-Colonel of that battalion. Then, about Easter, 1792, he attempted to seize the citadel and establish himself master of the town, which plan, however, owing to the vigilance and loyalty of its French commander, failed. Only one thing equalled his love of the homeland, and that was his hatred of the French. In proof, we give some examples, taken from his works, excerpts which we shall discuss more fully later. In *Sur la Suicide,* for instance, he writes: "Frenchmen! Not content with bereaving us of all we cherish, you have, besides, corrupted our morals". In *Sur l'Amour de la Patrie,* he borrows every example of true love of the fatherland from antiquity or Corsica, and personifies immoderate ambition solely by French heroes. But the deepest expression of this hatred of the French emerges clearest in his *Nouvelle Corse,* a phantasy of a Utopia on a desert isle: there, every Frenchman is mercilessly killed, because its owner has sworn to do so.

*   *   *

Now let us consider Napoleon's relation to Paoli and the latter's significance to him.

Briefly, Paoli embodied, to him, all that was great, beautiful, noble and wise. As a child, while the tumult of war still raged, he would have heard "Paoli spoken of with reverence and love by his playmates and family". Small wonder that " in his mind Paoli should remain a typically exiled and mighty hero who would one day reappear like the Messiah", as Jung says in *Bonaparte et Son Temps.* And Chuquet writes: "At Autun, as at Brienne, any mention of Paoli would excite him and set him on fire . . . How often this name had struck on his ears as a babe! How often and with what emotion he would have heard the veterans of the war of independence regret they no longer bore rifles, and proudly tell of their blind marches over the mountains, their sudden attacks, their prudent flights, their swift counter-attacks and intersperse these dramatic recitals with praise of their chief and his unquenchable energy! How often, at home in Ajaccio, would he have heard the feeling with which Carlo and Laetizia recalled their collaboration with the great Pasquale! These talks had excited the child's imagination. He yearned for the glory of Paoli. He would not tolerate the slightest criticism from any teacher or classmate, of his idol". In this same scene at Autun, recorded by the Abbé Chardon, Napoleon is said to have made this answer to the following remark: "Yet you had a good general in Paoli?" "Yes, Monsieur, and I want to be like him". Again, on another occasion at Brienne, the little boy cried: "Paoli will return, and if he cannot burst our chains, as soon as I have the strength I shall go to his aid and perhaps together we may free Corsica from its hated yoke". A schoolmate at this time says: "Paoli was his God".

Nor did his feelings for Paoli change while at the Military College in Paris, where he passed his fourteenth and fifteenth years; he continued to praise Paoli to the skies, and always asserted that he wanted to fight at the great Pasquale's side to help and support him. We have an interesting and eloquent proof of his attitude at this time in a caricature, drawn by a classmate, which shows Napoleon hurrying to Paoli's aid. An old professor clings to his hair but the young man walks determinedly away holding a stick in his hands. Under the drawing the following words may be read: "Run Bonaparte, fly to Paoli's aid, to rescue him from his enemy's hands".

The following episode well shows the part played by Paoli in Napoleon's emotive and imaginative life. When, in 1787, after an eight years' absence, he was on leave in Ajaccio, he found that his uncle and guardian, the archdeacon Lucien, had been bedridden for years with the gout. Napoleon, who loved him dearly and wished to relieve his suffering, thereupon thought of writing to Dr. Tissot of Lausanne, a man who was a stranger to him.

The reason for this strange action is revealed in his letter: "You have spent your life teaching humanity and your renown has even penetrated to our mountains. Indeed, the brief but honourable praise you gave their beloved General (Paoli) is sufficient reason to inspire gratitude in all Corsicans". The "praise" in question occurs in Tissot's paper *Traité de Santé des Gens de Lettres*, where he calls deskwork unhygienic and adds: "Caesar, Mahomet, Cromwell and Paoli, greater than them, it may be, doubtless received from their peoples more than human powers". This brief juxtaposition, which gave so high a place to Paoli, was enough to inspire him with full trust in Dr. Tissot.

When he had finished his *Lettres sur la Corse*, Napoleon wished to dedicate it to Paoli and wrote so in the following letter, dated 12th July, 1789, addressed to London.

"General! I was born when the homeland perished. Thirty thousand Frenchmen spewed upon our shores and suffocating the throne of liberty in oceans of blood: such was the hateful spectacle which first struck my eyes . . . You left our island,

and with you our hope of happiness vanished; slavery was the price of our submission. If fortune had allowed me to live in the capital, I should doubtless have found other ways to make our groans heard but, obliged to serve, my only recourse is to publicity . . . If you, General, would deign to approve a work which deals so largely with you, I would dare to have favourable hopes for its success . . . for a time I hoped to be able to go to London to express all you have roused in my heart and to talk together of the fatherland's miseries, but the distance puts obstacles in the way . . . May I, General, convey the respectful greetings of my family. Why do I not say of my countrymen? They sigh in memory of a time when they hoped to be free. My mother, Madame Laetizia, asks me to send remembrances of the years at Corte".

Napoleon's literary works, already referred to and written between his fifteenth and twentieth years, testify as clearly to his veneration for, his admiration of, that remarkable man. For instance, in his *Lettres sur la Corse*, he writes of him thus: "I shall have to speak about M. Paoli whose wise institutions assured our happiness for an instant, and caused us to conceive such shining hopes. He first consecrated those principles on which the prosperity of nations rests. His ability, his fortitude, his eloquence must be admired; amidst civil and foreign wars, he confronted all difficulties. With an unfaltering hand he lays the foundations of the Constitution and even as far as Genoa makes our tyrants tremble . . ."

Again, in his *Discours de Lyon*, he says of Paoli, setting him up as the model legislator: "M. Paoli, who is distinguished by solicitude for mankind and his fellow citizens; who, for a time, restored the glorious age of Sparta and Athens to the midst of the Mediterranean; M. Paoli, who is imbued with the feelings, the genius, which nature only unites in one man as consolation to a whole people, made his appearance in Corsica to focus the eyes of all Europe . . . in his unparalleled activity, his persuasive, his burning eloquence, his penetrating, his fruitful genius, he found the wherewithal to safeguard his Constitution".

In 1790, when Paoli returned to Corsica after the general amnesty, the Bonaparte family were among the most zealous of those present to celebrate his return. Napoleon had himself urged his brother Joseph to accompany the deputation which went to Lyons to meet him, and it was Napoleon too, who delivered the speech of welcome. Jung says: "He is his god as it were . . ." "They all worshipped Paoli. He was the god by whom everyone swore".

Later, we see Napoleon, on leave in Corsica, pay frequent visits to the Governor at his country residence of Rostino. They would take long walks together and discuss social and political questions. Napoleon, on St. Helena, is even said to have said: "Paoli often gave me a friendly tap on the head, with the words: 'You are a true character out of Plutarch'. He suspected I should be someone exceptional some day". Another time Paoli is said to have said: "Napoleon, you've nothing in you of the modern man, you're entirely a man out of Plutarch. Courage! You'll make your way".

*   *   *

This then was the relation of the two men, one twenty-three, the other sixty-seven. Even Napoleon's attack on the citadel of Ajaccio, sometime near Easter, 1792, appears to have clouded their friendship as little as did his revolutionary activities at Ajaccio in the autumn and winter of that year. Between whiles, he had spent four months in Paris, where he had managed to get himself reinstated in the Army and even promoted Captain, in spite of the grave accusations under which he lay.

The ensuing events, which we must now consider, undoubtedly constitute the most puzzling and complex portion of Napoleon's life, as many authorities agree. These, briefly, are the facts.

Early in 1793 France despatched a military expedition against Sardinia, which utterly failed. And when, on 3rd March, 1793, Napoleon returned from that expedition to Corsica, the political situation, in comparison with that of the year before, had radically changed. Louis XVI had been executed on the 21st January, and on the 31st of the same month, war against England had been declared. In Corsica itself the volunteer regiments were supposed to be disbanded and replaced by regular troops. More serious still, Paoli's military and administrative powers had been severely curtailed. These measures, on the one hand, resulted from the machinations of his political enemies and, on the other, from the fact that Paoli, all through his twenty-years exile, had been warmly welcomed in Britain, had even been a pensioner of the British, and made no secret of his liking for that race. Thus, once war was declared, the French government could no longer fully trust him.

In the ensuing weeks the conflict between Paoli and the Convention became so embittered that its Corsican commissaries were given every authority to arrest Paoli at all costs and bring him to Paris (Resolution of the Convention: 2nd April, 1793).

One may easily imagine the consternation which this decree, menacing the very life of the *pater patriae*, aroused in the Corsicans, as lieges of their chief, when it reached Ajaccio on 16th April.

Under the impact of this news Napoleon, about the end of April, drafted an address to the "Club des Amis de la Constitution" of Ajaccio, to be presented, in its name, to the Convention. This warmly defended Paoli and sought to refute the accusations which taxed Paoli as self-seeking and corrupt. "Could Paoli be corrupt or ambitious? Corrupt! And for what reason? To yield Corsica to England, he who never wished to yield it to France, despite Chauvelin's offers, who would have spared him neither titles nor favours! Deliver Corsica to England! Why did he not stay there when he was exiled? Can Paoli be considered ambitious? If Paoli is ambitious, what more could he want? He is a man his countrymen love, a man they refuse nothing: he is head of the army and on the point of having to defend the homeland against foreign aggression . . . It must be at Coblentz that Paoli is thought ambitious: but in Paris, at the very heart of French liberty, Paoli, if people really knew him, would be one of the patriarchs of liberty, a forerunner of the French Republic: so will posterity think and so the people believe".

After which, to strengthen his defence of him, against the senseless accusation of wishing to surrender Corsica to the English, he adds: "Heed my words, silence this calumny and those utterly perverse beings by whom it is used".

Almost at the same time, however, we see him, hitherto so implacably hating the French, in connivance with the Conventions' commissaries Saliceti and Lacombe-St-Michel, doing his utmost to win his rebellious country back to France. With

this purpose, he also made several attempts on the citadel of
Ajaccio, held by the Paolist national guard; this time, however,
to win it for the French. We also see him proposing that the
Corsicans re-swear the oath that bound them to France! In
addition he indicted Paoli before the Convention in a report
entitled: "*The Political and Military position of the Department
of Corsica on June 1st* 1793", in which he said that all those who
had made and supported the Revolution in Corsica and
ardently desired General Paoli's return, had soon come to
see that his boundless ambition demanded they should see
with his eyes and look to him for every decision . . . that he
believed France already lost (it had many foreign enemies at
this time) and was himself preparing to spurn it, also. He
also accused Paoli of removing the regular troops from the
coast and replacing thém by Corsican national guards on whom
he could place more reliance and also of appointing, to officer
them, men whose fathers had fallen, in 1786, in the struggle
against France: men who clearly might feel bitter towards
France.

He also indicted Paoli as responsible for the failure of the
Sardinian expedition: he had pretended he would provide
the demanded troops but had managed to prevent their des-
patch to Sardinia, lest the Corsicans might become French.
The indictment continued: "Since the declaration of war on
England, the whole world has been struck by the affection
with which he praises the generosity, goodness, virtue, power
and wealth of the *English* nation. His plans at *this* time *were
clear*, and all who were *attached* to him, but who *preferred* the
homeland *to* him, *began* to fall away. They had lost their good
opinion of his virtue and only saw a traitor in him. For no
treason is as odious as his. He is plunging his homeland into
civil war, and holds it back from that association with France
which can *alone* create its happiness . . . Can so much perfidy,
then, be part of the human heart? *What* fatal ambition mis-
guides a greybeard, 68 years of age? But it is because there is
virtue and *mildness* in his face, and hate and *revenge* in his heart.
Benevolence shines in his eyes but there is *gall* in his soul: he
has no character, no strength. He is without courage!"

We know that this standpoint of Napoleon's resulted in the
whole of the Bonaparte family being banished and declared
infamous at a gathering attended by all Corsica, and that

after his mother, by a lucky chance, had perilously escaped with her children, the indignant Corsicans burnt down the Bonaparte home and destroyed their vines and property. Thus, on 11th June 1793, Napoleon, with his kin, sailed from Calvi to settle in Toulon, and forever abandoned his two youthful ideals, Corsica and Paoli, "after destroying the latter with his calumnies and insults", says Fournier.

This rupture with Paoli was to have immeasurable consequences for mankind. In Jung's opinion, "its effects were immense for France . . .", it ". . . was destined to be a determinant influence on the history of Bonaparte and of France". This rather underestimates things for its consequences shaped the destiny of the world. *Indeed, this rupture with Paoli was the psychological moment in which the Napoleon we know from history was born and formed,* the Napoleon who sowed terror and anxiety, and kept mankind on tenterhooks for some twenty years but, also, as Fournier says, "the man who everywhere . . ." on the Manzanares as on the Tiber, on the Rhine as on the Elbe, in Naples as in Poland, in Prussia as in Austria . . . appeared as the initiator of a new dawn of a higher social order; the bloody progenitor of immensely significant evolutionary processes".

But now we must ask what motives determined this sudden change in Napoleon's heart, a point on which historical research supplies a far from satisfactory answer. Jung, for instance, does not try and contents himself with saying: "It is indeed difficult to explain how it came about that Artillery Captain Bonaparte, who had so often professed his devotion to Paoli in his writings, and had drafted the Peoples' Club of Ajaccio's famous address to the Convention, could so suddenly renounce his past to become the agent of Saliceti and his co-workers.

To Chuquet, whose meticulous research and findings have become an inexhaustible source to Napoleon's biographers, the position at the time, and the course of events, appeared as follows:

Paoli, having spent twenty years in England under an orderly, disciplined regime, was distressed on his return by the anarchic conditions on his semi-barbaric island. He also disliked the first two Directories which administered the communes, to begin with headed by Aréna, and then by Saliceti. These syndics found the governor's continual complaints a

B

source of exasperation, whence arose strife between them and
Paoli whom, till then, they had adored. The position worsened
when, due to Paoli's influence, no member of Saliceti's party
was re-elected at the elections of December 1792, so that the
new Assembly was wholly composed of members devoted to
Paoli. In addition, they termed themselves "honest", no
doubt to emphasise their difference from their predecessors,
accused of venality and abuse of power.

Doubtless, this was what forced Saliceti into open conflict
with Paoli. Next to Paoli he had been the most popular man
in Corsica which, indeed, owed him much. Had he not, since
1789, been leader of the Patriots' (Paoli's) Party, and was it
not he who, with Césare Rocco, had proposed that the National
Assembly give Corsica an elected Administrative Council and
a Peoples' Militia? Had he not also, in 1789, led the people
of Bastia to revolt, to compel the Assembly to recognise Corsica
as a French province of equal status, and also, were not Paoli's
pardon and recall due to him? Small wonder that the
Corsicans saw a second liberator in him, or that he was immensely popular. But now he felt his popularity threatened,
and especially as the new Directory taxed him with pluralism
of profitable posts as well as of rendering false returns to his
own advantage.

In this struggle between himself and Paoli, a struggle begun
in 1793, Saliceti found strong support in the French government, already suspicious of Paoli's anglophile past. Now,
therefore, that war with England was declared, it sought, on
divers pretexts, to provoke Paoli's departure to France and
thus remove him from Corsica. It would seem however that
Paoli suspected the plot and, conscious of his innocence (he
had always been faithful to France and the Republic), as well
as jealous of his dignity as a French general, he refused to
obey the orders of the Minister of War, and decided to remain
in Corsica.

For his part Saliceti, as Deputy to the Convention, proposed
a number of motions, all of them aimed at Paoli. He asked,
for instance, given the imminent war against England, for
government measures ensuring Corsica's defence, for the
volunteer regiments (devoted to Paoli) to be disbanded and
for regular troops in their place. Again, under pretext of
assuring the security of the ports, he got himself sent to Corsica,

with two other Deputies, as Commissaries of the Convention, furnished with absolute powers.

Thus, civil war became inevitable for, in addition to his own partisans, he commanded some new battalions whose officers he himself had mostly appointed.

Despite the many clashes that followed the Commissaries' arrival in Corsica, it seemed possible that their differences with Paoli might soon have been peacefully arranged. A new event, however, thwarted Saliceti's peaceful intentions for, meanwhile, the Convention had decided on Paoli's arrest, which arrest was entrusted to the Commissaries.

This decree, which everyone, even Paoli's adversaries, judged premature and which, indeed, was later revoked, sprang from an impulsive speech by Lucien, Napoleon's younger brother. Vain and excitable, eighteen, and eager to play a part, he uttered a violent diatribe against Paoli at the Republican Club of Toulon. He says, in his Memoirs, that he had no motive for this speech but, if the historians are to be believed, it came from disappointed ambition, for Paoli had refused to appoint him to the secretarial post which he coveted. This diatribe depicted the governor and his tyranny in the darkest colours and ended by demanding his removal and punishment, with all the rigour of the law.

Meanwhile, after the Sardinian expedition, numerous in-cidents arose between the Corsicans and men of Provence, the latter being greatly incensed against the islanders and Paoli, whom they ended by considering responsible for the failure of the expedition. Aréna too, in Southern France, had aroused strong feeling against Paoli, whom he accused of treacherous plans. It was natural, therefore, that Lucien's accusations should be eagerly seized and promptly conveyed to the Convention by Escudier, Deputy for the Var. The Convention, with Dumouriez's treason fresh in mind, smelt treason everywhere and ordered Paoli's immediate arrest.

When the Commissaries, and especially Saliceti, deeply dis-mayed by this misunderstanding, and "sick at heart" attempted to obey the order, they were confronted with open resistance which soon flared into general revolt. Rushing to arms to protect their "babbo", the mountaineers possessed themselves of the towns, most of which, with Ajaccio, were thus lost to the Republic, for the very citizens had turned against the French and their sympathisers.

As a result, due to considerations set forth by Paoli's friends, and to his own letter of 26th April which calmly and simply explained the position to the Convention, while assuring it of his attachment to France and re-declaring his readiness to leave the homeland once more should his presence cause disturbance, the Convention, on 16th May, decided to rescind its decree of 2nd April. Later, on 30th May, it appointed two additional Commissaries from the mainland to establish order in Corsican affairs, with instructions to avoid force, and to treat the old general with all necessary respect and moderation.

It was too late. The Commissaries, losing patience, and fearful, too, of being compelled to renounce all authority, as well as of possible accusations of weakness, began to employ coercive measures: they dissolved the General Council, replaced the old Directory by a new and sent troops against the seats of rebellion. They also publicly condemned Paoli and, in these ways, greatly increased the general exasperation. On the other hand, the insurrection in Southern France which followed the *coup d'Etat* of 31st May, furnished Paoli, then of the party of the defeated Girondists, with new forces for his own rebellion. He also succeeded, for a time, in preventing the two Commissaries reaching Corsica and, far from believing the decree ordering his arrest rescinded, considered the news a trap, since everything with which Saliceti was connected—that Saliceti whom he was doing his utmost to keep from joining his colleagues—seemed to him suspect.

Before this, however, he hastened to convoke a National Assembly at Corte for 27th May. At this assembly over a thousand delegates from the different communes protested their loyalty to France, their attachment to and confidence in Paoli, and enumerated the wrongs done by Saliceti and his supporters. The deputies, in addition, resolved not to recognise Saliceti and his two colleagues as Commissaries of the Convention, nor to carry out their orders or plans: in addition, the Bonaparte family was declared outlawed.

Almost simultaneously the Commissaries, on Napoleon's advice, attempted to surprise the citadel of Ajaccio, in order to seize the town from the Paolists and restore it to the French.

The attempt failed but all this, plus the measures taken and ordained by the Corte Assembly, directly occasioned the disturbances which led to the destruction and plundering of the houses and estates of the francophile Corsicans of Ajaccio: a fate which, as we know, also befell the possessions of the Bonapartes.

The Commissaries, realising their impotence, decided to separate. Whereas Lacombe-Saint-Michel remained in Corsica to defend the few towns and villages still in French hands, Saliceti and Delcher hastened to France to seek reinforcements. The Convention, having heard Saliceti's report and, inspired by him, on 17th July declared Paoli a traitor to the French Republic and an outlaw; it also indicted certain of his main supporters, with the result that Corsica passed into English hands.

*   *   *

Chuquet explains Napoleon's part in these events, his attitude towards them and his motives, as follows: Napoleon, it appears, like Saliceti, Aréna and Volney, declared against Paoli because the man on whom he modelled his conduct, and whom he had decided to follow, was Saliceti. Before this, in the enthusiasm of youth, he had greatly admired Saliceti, and his youthful writings bear witness to the influence of the latter's works. A closer acquaintance sprang up between them in 1792, in Corsica, and was later resumed in Paris: thereupon followed a correspondence which, in certain passages, reveals marks of a close, though recent friendship.

Chuquet opines that under Saliceti's influence, it would seem that Napoleon finally opted for France once he was convinced that Corsica could never, and indeed, should not, be independent. Thereafter, he eagerly seized every opportunity to testify his loyalty to France, a loyalty which remained unaffected even when the Convention, by its law of 2nd September, 1792, abrogated the hereditary leases to national properties, such as the Boldrini mansion and the Milleti farm, which were held by the Bonaparte family.

Apart, however, from Saliceti's influence, thus postulated as immensely significant, Paoli's own attitude to the Bonapartes would also have contributed to Napoleon's defection. Paoli, apparently, did nothing to prevent it, for he distrusted all

Carlo Buonaparte's sons as offspring of the man who, though originally his warm supporter, had not hesitated to turn to the French, once they were in power, or woo, and receive, proofs of their favour. For these reasons Paoli would distrust Carlo's importunate, devouringly ambitious family, and remain distant and aloof. As to Lucien, he would refuse to appoint him to the secretarial position he coveted, though well aware of his merits, because of a distaste for "fusing with them" as he said, or making common cause with the family. He also disliked Joseph's behaviour while in the Directory and had often made it clear. Napoleon too, was not much better treated by the governor for, when the former presented him with copies of his *Lettres à Buttafuoco*, written in Paoli's defence, the latter is said to have thanked him coldly, while curtly refusing his request for the loan of certain documents needed for his history of Corsica. Furthermore, he had appointed someone else to the then vacant post of personal aide-de-camp, which, according to Chuquet, Napoleon coveted. Also, Paoli's hostility to the Bonapartes was apparently encouraged by Pozzo di Borgo, their sworn enemy.

For all these reasons the Bonaparte brothers turned against Paoli, and, in especial, because Napoleon was still irritated by the failure of the Sardinian expedition and Joseph had failed to be re-elected to the Directory. Neither hesitated, therefore, to attack Paoli at the Patriots' Club of Ajaccio; they accused him of "inquisitorial ambition"; of not loving France and of liking England. They also made him responsible for the failure of the Sardinian expedition, while priding themselves on their connection with Saliceti through whom, some day, they hoped to get their share of power and success.

When the decree ordering Paoli's arrest reached Corsica, Napoleon was eagerly following events at Ajaccio, and the news disturbed him deeply.

He realised at once that war between Corsica and the Republic was inevitable and that Paoli, with his military strength, would prove victorious, at least at first, and that he would proscribe his enemies and confiscate their property. He also realised that the victorious Paolists would hardly spare the Bonapartes and their possessions. Thus, fear of the consequences to his family would motivate his writing the well-known defence of Paoli.

Since this defence, however, would hardly seem to him enough, he contemplated another, and one more impressive. On Masseria's advice, the latter having seized this opportunity to reconcile him to Paoli, he presented a petition to the Ajaccio municipality begging that party differences be ended and, also, that a General Assembly be convoked, at which all citizens would swear their loyalty to the French Republic.

Despite the deep antagonism, even enmity, which divided the Paolist "Société des Amis incorruptibles du Peuple" from the "Club des Patriots"—an enmity which Napoleon himself had largely provoked, since it was he who first opposed the fusion of both, as the Paolists wanted—he now proposed this fusion to the rival factions and offered to deliver his two addresses to them himself.

Rejected by the Société des Amis which refused to discuss the matter, he, nothing daunted, made a direct approach to Paoli, to whom he asked Masseria to write, saying: "Paoli considers me suspect, what should I do to prove my friendship?" Paoli, however, had just intercepted a letter from Lucien to his brothers, informing them, who knew nothing of the matter, of his Toulon speech denouncing Paoli. Naturally the latter scornfully rejected Napoleon's proffered friendship.

Then, late in April, having seen his attempts at pacification fail, Napoleon audaciously attempted to trick the citadel of Ajaccio into surrender, which attempt also failed.[1]

His position in Ajaccio was no longer tenable, especially as Paoli had meanwhile published the contents of Lucien's letter throughout the island. Besides, it was common knowledge that Joseph, his brother, was in Bastia with the Commissaries of the Convention and that the Bonapartes were all intimates of that Saliceti who, as the Corsicans saw it, had caused the Convention to prosecute Paoli, and created the unrest to which this gave rise. Napoleon therefore, to escape the Paolists' rage, decided to leave Ajaccio and join the Commissaries in Bastia, but this he only managed to do by taking a secret route; he thus evaded the gendarmes sent by Paoli to stop him, and it was only the cunning of his guide that saved him from arrest.

[1] Salgues and Arnault even claim that then Napoleon himself posted the municipality's answer on the walls of Ajaccio: "which refuted the reasons that the Convention gave for its decree against Paoli".

In Bastia, he soon succeeded in convincing the Commissaries of the necessity of capturing Ajaccio and organising an expedition against the town. This plan, however, also failed, due to the vigilance of the citadel's Paolist garrison, as well as the loyalty of the population.

Retreat was impossible and so his break with Paoli became final. Then, learning of his family's flight, the destruction of their property and the ban of outlawry imposed by the Assembly on 27th May, the enraged Napoleon wrote his indictment of Paoli. Shortly after he sailed for Toulon, and severed every tie that bound him to his homeland.

*   *   *

If we have quoted Chuquet's views so minutely, it is not only to familiarise the reader with the situation but to avoid a charge of partiality for our own opinions, whether or no they agree with those of Chuquet or of others that shall have our special attention. True, Chuquet's facts are immensely valuable, but there is no doubt they leave much unexplained. This is particularly true as regards the cardinal point of the motives which determined Napoleon's break with Paoli. Chuquet's statement that, having been rejected by Paoli, Napoleon sought to return to Saliceti, seems hardly a sufficient explanation.

In describing this conflict, Chuquet's error lies in attaching insufficient importance to the immense place held by Paoli in Napoleon's affective life; that Paoli indeed, who, for so many years, had been his idol and star. This is a fact which no one familiar with Napoleon's childhood and youth could deny, one which Chuquet himself emphasises when dealing with the earlier period of his life, although he all but entirely neglects it in relating the conflict with Paoli!

If, however, we take the opposite course, it is just as difficult a problem, though otherwise expressed. We still need to know how a man who, for twenty years, has ardently pursued one ideal, can turn and attack that ideal and, in a twinkling, barter it for the friendship, the power, of a Saliceti, who meant so little to him before. Why, only three years before, referring to the possibility of the Republic failing to incorporate Corsica as a French province, he had written: "We should have summoned Paoli, that great man, the object of our enthusiasm, whom 40,000 bayonets and our wretchedness alone could tear from us, and should have said: You, the one man that Corsica trusts, take the helm of the ship once more, the ship you can steer so well. Our love, as unshakeable as are those virtues of yours, has grown with your misfortunes; brigands have ruled us, and our soil is strewn with their victims: nevertheless, they could not humble us. Appear! we are worthy of you still!" And why again, but six months before their rupture, when it seemed that France might restore liberty to Corsica, had he written: "Paoli is all and will be all".

It seems to me that we have here a psychic upheaval so violent that Paoli's negative attitude to the Bonapartes could never alone have produced it. Chuquet does well to note it, but it could never entirely have arisen from this fact.

What clearly shows how far Chuquet ignores the affective significance of the relation between Napoleon and Paoli, is his assumption that the sole motive for Napoleon's apologia of Paoli, was concern for his family and its wealth.

True, Napoleon felt grave concern for his family and their fortunes on learning of the decree for Paoli's arrest: he made no mystery of the fact and it was indeed a factor in inspiring the writing of Paoli's defence. But it would be misconstruing their whole relation to consider the apologia as deriving solely from this, as does Chuquet. It seems to me also that Napoleon's later attempts, referred to above, as well as his earlier efforts at reconciliation with Paoli, bear this out. Also we see that, at need, he could subordinate material advantages to his ideals, as is proved by his continued attachment to France after the latter had stripped his family of their valuable hereditary leases.

Though Chuquet pays little heed to the affective significance of the two men's relation, he commits a grave error in ignoring this factor when dealing with the vicissitudes of Napoleon's nationalism; as when he deserted the Corsican cause to embrace that of France. All we are told anent this is that Napoleon was influenced by Saliceti although, on the one hand, that particular influence is never defined, nor the manner in which it made itself felt, nor the cords which it caused to vibrate in Napoleon's soul to produce this result and, on the other, why that influence became only operative then and not before, or why, if so suggestible, Napoleon did not change his opinion much earlier, say, at the Military College in Paris, or in garrison in France where, surely, francophile influence would not have been lacking.

To my mind, therefore, Chuquet's account throws no light on the strange psychological problem posited by the change in his nationalist convictions. Above all, we must seek to explain how a man who, for twenty years, had nurtured a deadly hatred against France, and who, in the five months following his return from Paris (15th October, 1792, and the start of his conflict with Paoli) could turn from Saul into Paul, and so completely forget his twenty years' past as to sacrifice, without a moment's hesitation, his one-time idol Paoli, for a new love, as most of his biographers testify. F. Kircheisen believes that Napoleon's apologia of Paoli came solely from his love of France, "to which he thought he could render no better service than by recommending that the Convention rescind its decree against Paoli". Yet shortly before this, writing to French acquaintances, Napoleon had referred to France as "your country" and "your nation" and, only a year earlier, had tried to oust the French from the citadel of Ajaccio. Also, anent his stay in Paris, Chuquet writes: "His imagination never rests: it tortures him. His only thought is of his island". Again, at this same time, from Paris, the future Emperor wrote to his brother Joseph: "It now seems more than ever likely that all this will end in our independence". And yet once more, when he was posted Captain, despite a sharp reprimand from the Minister in Paris, he again returned to Corsica instead of rejoining his regiment in the field.

However, there are others, besides myself, who have demanded some explanation here. H. Conrad, the publisher and translator of the "*Mémorial de Sainte-Hélène* (the Life of Napoleon told by himself), asks the same question in his introduction. "The Emperor attached no historical importance to his youth or family. He saw the history of his life as beginning with the first martial exploits on which his glory was founded. Everything which had helped him to become what he was, must disappear: in this, he followed the example of the great Republic which, also, proudly dated its birth from the year I". Nevertheless, it is possible that other motives were at work in Napoleon. It was when in command of the artillery before Toulon that, for the first time, he felt himself French. *And, as a Frenchman, all his past,* until Toulon, must have appeared to him not only as of no historic importance but even, *justifiably, disagreeable to him. For, till then, he had been a Corsican.* That is why this chapter *of the history of his youth should explain how, from a Corsican, he became French.*

Faced by such gaps, which exasperate the historian, we must allow Fournier, who evidently had similar feelings, the merit (though hardly approving his deductions), of entirely ignoring this love of Napoleon's for the French as the motive for his rupture with Paoli, and of attributing his *volte-face* to purely egotistic factors such as his boundless ambition and despotic nature. These, to him, were the motivating forces which impelled Napoleon "to stop being Corsican without ever being able to become French". It is an explanation however, which for many reasons, I personally find inadequate and unsatisfactory.

For, if we leave aside the problem in question; namely, whether an ambition as boundless as was attributed to him could be the dominant psychical factor and one incapable of further reduction or, whether that ambition was not in fact a complex psychical manifestation and one which could be reduced to other factors, we still have to explain why, just then, it appeared so intensely, and why in that shape and no other.

I think we may also be misled by accepting this explanation of ambition, in view of what he had written some eighteen months earlier, in 1791, in his *Discours de Lyon* where, after some general remarks on violent passions, he goes on to say "Has adolescence passed? Has that same youth reached the age of virility and is ambition now enthroned in him? Pallid ambition, with wild eyes and eager gait, sudden motions and bitter laughter? Crimes to him now are but play, cabals a means; and lies, calumny, slander but arguments, rhetorical turns. Does he finally grasp the helm of State? The nations weary him with their homage".

Again, in another passage he says: "But ambition, that immoderate and ever-unsatisfied yearning to gratify pride or excessive desires which led Alexander from Thebes to Persia, from the Granicus to Issus, from Issus to Arbela, from thence to India; ambition, that made him conquer and lay the world waste in order not to content it, that ambition burns him with the same fire; in his frenzy he knows not what path to let it take; he raves, he threshes about . . . Alexander imagines himself a god, imagines himself a son of Jupiter, and also wants to make others believe it . . . I sought happiness and found only fame". Again in *Sur l'Amour de la Patrie* he says: "No doubt our souls are inflamed by tales of the deeds of Alexander, Philip, Charlemagne, Turenne, Condé, Machiavelli and so many other illustrious men whose guide, throughout their heroic careers, was human esteem: but what emotions master our souls confronted by Leonidas and his three hundred Spartans! They do not go into battle, they race to their deaths because of the fate that threatens their fatherland".

Such national sentiments seem to me sufficient to warn us against attaching too much importance to the motive of ambition.

Besides, we need only remember that, after his flight from Corsica, Napoleon went back to the Army as a mere Artillery Captain and that neither by France, nor her supporters, such as Saliceti, was he offered or given any promotion; that, during this time, his kin were forced to live in the village of Lavalette, since life in Toulon was too dear for them, and that later again, at Marseilles, they passed through a period of extreme poverty. It was only after his heroism at the seige of Toulon (whose capture was mainly due to his efforts), that Napoleon was elevated to higher rank and his family's circumstances began to alter. It will thus be seen that the motive of ambition less than ever can explain the facts.

To the two questions we are now considering; namely, how and why Napoleon, being Corsican became French and, why Napoleon broke with Paoli, no biographer has so far provided a completely satisfactory answer. Yet these questions are in many ways connected and must be answered, if we are not to leave, what was perhaps the most decisive period of his life, hid in impenetrable veils.

The failure which all such attempts have so far met with will hardly surprise us, if we remember that they were wholly confined to exploring Napoleon's conscious life whereas, as we have every right to suppose, the determinant influences must be attributed to the *unconscious* portion of his psyche. We shall now attempt to examine this unconscious portion or, at least, present a general outline of it; for, given the vast extent of the subject, no other treatment seems possible. Victor Hugo, also, recognised the forces at work in Napoleon, when he wrote: "Bonaparte was the huge somnambulist of a shattered dream".

II

If we are to attempt a psycho-analytic enquiry into Napoleon's life we shall find our task made easier by the stores of adolescent phantasies and childhood memories available. These may be found in his own compositions, written between 1786 and 1793—that is, between his seventeenth and twenty-fourth years—compositions which have now been restored after their theft and sale by Libri.

These youthful works, as all his biographers affirm, indubitably reveal the influence of two writers: Rousseau and Raynal. At this time (1785-1792), Napoleon almost, as it were, worshipped Rousseau, whom he considered the deepest, most penetrating of philosophers: there is hardly one of his works which he does not consider beyond praise. This markedly rationalised love is not difficult to explain for Rousseau, in 1762, in his *Contrat Social*, had written: "In Europe there is still one country capable of legislating: namely, Corsica. The valour and constancy with which this brave nation has succeeded in regaining and defending its liberty indeed deserve that it be taught to preserve it by some sage. I suspect this small isle will one day astonish Europe." Also, was it not Rousseau who had expressed the ardent desire to pass the rest of his days in Corsica? Besides, he regularly corresponded with Paoli.

Napoleon's second literary model, the Abbé Raynal, was

no less friendly to Corsica and in his *L'Histoire Philosophique des deux Indes*, eloquently castigates the avarice and perfidy of the Genoese as Corsica's oppressors, while predicting an end to French rule and the re-establishment of a national government.

For reminiscences of Napoleon in youth, we must be grateful to the indefatigable zeal of his biographers who, during the Consulate and Empire, were already ransacking every source. And here I wish to emphasise the authenticity of all the material to be henceforth quoted. Even historians like Chuquet and Masson who, so critical towards so much other traditional material, never hesitate to sacrifice the legendary and romantic where historic truth is at stake, accept it as authentic.

With this material then as my basis, we shall consider his conflict with Paoli in the light of all that Napoleon wrote at this time.

Taking the first of his writings, his apologia of Paoli, the following passage seems to me worthy of special attention. *"He is . . . on the point of having to defend the homeland against foreign aggression"*.

Now this word "foreign" occurs very frequently in Napoleon's writings at this time and, almost always, with a hostile emphasis which far exceeds what the word itself implies as the normal antithesis of what belongs to ourselves.

In other passages again, his countrymen's oppressors, the Genoese and French, both so intensely hated, are called "foreigners" by him. He even, as in his *Lettres sur la Corse*, equates "foreigner" with "enemy" as when, telling of the Genoese-Corsican thirteenth century wars, he relates how a Genoese woman who was raped, pleads to Sinucello della Rocca, the Corsican leader, "I am a foreigner and your enemy". (*Lettres sur la Corse*, Masson et Biagi, p. 408.) But other parts of this work, too, convey the strength of the negative feeling with which this concept was charged, as when, on page 416 for instance, he speaks of "foreign aid", and terms it a "rash step" that will "cost the fatherland dear" ; or when he particularly stresses the fate of Corsicans doomed to a "foreign clime". (*Lettres sur la Corse*.)

This attitude towards foreigners, whom one must always be "against" and never "for", who must be kept at a distance, of whom one must never make friends or allies and whom, in fact, he had never known other than as enemies; this attitude that, in its contrary aspect, reveals itself in his *Souper de Beaucaire*, as his profound aversion to civil war which, as Kircheisen writes: "never had Napoleon's sympathy", and his utter condemnation of it, to my mind, stems not only from the clan-psychology particular to the Corsican, as many authors observe, but also from personal roots. In any case, this hatred of foreigners established itself very early for, according to a well authenticated account cited by Coston, Napoleon, while still First Consul, expressed himself as follows in one of his many talks with M. de l'Eguille, his history professor, in 1784, at the Military College in Paris, whom he always treated very graciously during his frequent visits to Malmaison:

"Of all your lessons, those which left the deepest impression on me, dealt with the rebellion of the Connétable de Bourbon. But you were wrong to tell me that his greatest crime was warring against his king, his real crime was that he came to ATTACK THE FATHERLAND WITH FOREIGNERS".

In his second work, his indictment of Paoli, we also find a passage that demands our closest attention, a passage which culminates in this reproach: "He has prevented her (the fatherland) uniting with France".

I have already shown how bitterly he still hated France when his conflict with Paoli broke out, and Chuquet is fully justified in stating: "Lieutenant Bonaparte remained Corsican, Corsican in heart and soul, Corsican from head to heel. At this period, France's future monarch, the man who will hail it by the name of 'Great Nation', and take the motto 'France first and foremost' as his guiding principle, is not a Frenchman: he despises the French whom he will later esteem above all other nations and proclaim the first nation on earth: he rejects this title of Frenchman, which he will later declare the finest on earth". But where Chuquet errs is that his hatred for the French did not date solely from this period; it was far older than that, almost as old, indeed, as he himself.

Chuquet also tells us that Napoleon was hostile to France even at the Military Academy in Paris, and openly expressed his enthusiasm for Paoli and his wish to join him in his fight for Corsican independence. There, as earlier at Brienne, he boasted how all Europe admired Corsica's resistance to France, and condemned, just as at Brienne, this war which a great nation had inflicted on a small people, which opinions led not only to strife with his superiors, but with his schoolmates. Barely nine when he entered the school at Brienne, and seeing a portrait of the Duc de Choiseul, the statesman who tore Corsica from the Genoese merely to hand it to France, the child, nowise intimidated by his strange surroundings, hurled passionate abuse at the Duke. Many other such demonstrations are told of his childhood. In especial, I should like to remark on a scene which is related by Coston and other biographers, for it throws a valuable light on Napoleon's affective trends; a scene which provides a base for our psychological enquiry into his personality, and thus will help us solve our problem. This passage relates that, when about nine, Napoleon was invited to dinner by his headmaster. There, being teased about Corsica, as usual, by one of his teachers, he replied: *"Paoli was a great man: he loved his fatherland and I shall never forgive my father, who was his adjutant, for helping to unite Corsica to France. He should have followed his fortunes and succumbed with him"*.

If we ignore what these words show; namely, that his father's and Paoli's images, in part, oppose each other in his psyche, we have only to compare his blame of his father, *"He helped to unite Corsica to France"*, with his blame of Paoli fifteen years later, *"He has prevented Corsica uniting with France"*, to realise that both reproaches, however opposite they seem, are in fact the same, and that only a single phenomenon appears before us, although in two different guises.

In the light of this parallel, the outlines of Napoleon's personality, so far hazy and unclear, suddenly take on definition and we perceive the tremendous contrast between Napoleon before, and after, he had broken with Corsica. Now it becomes possible to understand how from francophobe and anglophile he became francophile and anglophobe; how the accuser of Alexander the Great became his most passionate admirer; and how his unbounded admiration for Rousseau gave place to disdain, so that he called him a prattler and fool. With this insight we see how the Jacobin and egalitarian, the scourge of kings, could take command of the Army of Italy, surround himself with kingly pomp, become First Consul, then Emperor, and imagine himself almost God.

We also observe the same contrast between the two

Napoleons, one of whom in his *Réfutation de Roustan*, proclaims that religion is baleful to the State, places Appollonius of Tyana far above Christ, detests the Church and becomes a Freemason, while the other, in a talk with Wieland, claims that "Christianity is a philosophic system second to none, a system through which man is reconciled with himself and which, at the same time, ensures order and peace in States in the same degree as the happiness and hopes of individuals". That other also refuses to be crowned without the Pope's benediction, insists on the Pope's own presence at Fontaine-bleau and begins his last will and testament "I die in the Apostolical Roman Religion in the bosom of which I was born".

*   *   *

We are thus able to reduce Napoleon's conflict with Paoli to the following terms:

"attack the fatherland with foreigners" and

"he helped to unite Corsica to France".

Here a psycho-analytical interpretation seems indispensable, our opinions being so much at variance with those of the non-analytical world which would rather attribute political than sexual understanding to a child. We, on the other hand, consider that, in early life, the child has no abstract affective representations and that its psyche, only aware of concrete images, uses abstractions solely as substitutes for its concrete representations. Our analytic task will therefore be to seek those original representations. In effect then, what is meant by the following terms: "the fatherland or homeland" (i.e. Corsica) and "France" (i.e. foreigners).

As already indicated above, and as our quotations show, Napoleon's ardent and unappeasable love for his Corsican fatherland recurs almost incessantly in his writings of this time. This *leitmotiv* appears in manifold forms; it is discussed, examined and analysed from all points of view; even its justification is repeatedly analysed and investigated. Whether it be in an historical essay on Corsica, or the brief effusions of a suicidal mood, or a parallel between love of the fatherland and boundless ambition for glory, or the *Dialogue sur l'Amour*, or the *Discours de Lyon*, always we see him recur to the father-land, however far-fetched the reference may be. Thus, it is

c

impossible not to feel that we there see before us a powerfully
over-determined representation, a representation especially
strong because so deep-rooted in the unconscious. Chuquet
himself refers to it with a naivety that owes nothing to psycho-
analysis: "Thus, Lieutenant Bonaparte breathes nothing but
love of his little island. He seems a stranger to all other
passion and he might say, like the character in one of his
stories *I drew my life from Corsica and therewith a tempestuous love
for my unfortunate homeland and its independence*." (*Nouvelle Corse*.)

Here, clearly expressed, no longer in symbols or in parable
form, is what I have often noted in analysing neurotic patients;
namely, that the fatherland is a cover representation for the
mother, and that love of the fatherland, strictly speaking,
signifies love of the mother. This reciprocal equation indeed,
Fatherland-Mother, was well known to the Ancients for we
read in Herodotus (Erato 107): "Meanwhile Hippias, son of
Pisistratus, had led the barbarians to Marathon, having the
preceding night seen the following vision in his sleep. Hippias
fancied that he lay with his own mother. He inferred therefore,
from the dream, that having returned to Athens and recovered
the sovereignty he should die an old man in his own country.
He drew this inference from the vision".

To prove that the representation "fatherland" is unconsciously equated with, and has the same affective origin as,
the representation "earth", whose maternal significance has
become a commonplace to the psycho-analyst, I need only
point to Dietrich's "Mutter Erde",[1] Julius Caesar's dream[2]
and the Tarquinian Oracles,[3] from which we perceive the
significance of the German expression, "Vaterland", indicating
the domain of the father (or father's land), as enabling us to
see how the shift in the representation Land-Earth comes
about.

[1] "Mutter Erde", Ein Versuch über Volksreligion von Albert Dietrich,
Berlin 1905, Teubner.
[2] Otto Rank, *Inzest-Motiv in Dichtung und Sage*, p. 237, Suetonius relates:
Chap. 7: "Furthermore, when he was dismayed by a dream the following
night (for he thought that he had offered violence to his mother) the sooth-
sayers inspired him with high hopes by their interpretation, which was that
he was destined to rule the world, since the mother whom he had seen in his
power was none other than the earth, which is regarded as the common parent
of all mankind". (Trans. J. Rolfe: Heinemann.)
[3] Livy, I, LVI. That man shall hold supreme sway in Rome who first
kisses his mother (osculum matri tulerit) which Brutus interpreted to mean
mother-earth. (Terram osculo contigit, scilicet quod ea communis mater
omnium mortalium esset.)

I would add that in Slav languages, for instance, no reference to the element *land or earth* occurs in the word by which the fatherland is represented, this being replaced by the suffix *zna* or *na* to the noun father, to denote something that belongs to him.

The metaphors so frequently encountered in Napoleon's writings as, for instance: "In the bosom of your fatherland", in *Sur la Corse*; or, as to Cimon's son, "Athens, to him, is ever both mother and fatherland", in *Sur l'Amour de la Patrie*; or, "It is the feeling which binds the son to the mother, the citizen to his fatherland", in *Discours de Lyon*; are figures which plead strongly in favour of such interpretation, as also does the high-flown imagery of the letter to Buttafuoco, "Ah! son of that same fatherland yourself, had you never felt aught for her then. Ah! Did never the sight of her mountains and valleys, her rocks, her trees, and houses, her meeting places where your childhood's games took place, move your heart? And when you came into the world, she bore you in her bosom, she nourished you with her fruits; and when you came to the age of reason, in you she placed her hopes, and honoured you with her trust. She said to you: 'My son, you see the wretchedness of my condition . . .'"

We shall now put this analytic key to the test; to prove it, as it were, by certain of his youthful writings.

Let us take his essay, *Sur l'Amour de la Patrie*, which he wrote at eighteen (27th November, 1787), while on a short trip to Paris to attend to family matters, and which was composed in a mental condition of which he himself offers the best description: "I am barely at the dawn of the passions and my heart still throbs with the revolution which this first knowledge of men creates in our thoughts . . ." To understand these words, as well as what follows, we must note that Napoleon wrote this essay five days after he had passed a night with a prostitute; thus, after his first sexual experience, of which we have his faithful account in *Rencontre au Palais Royal*. But it is not only the analyst, seeing the world through the prism of sexuality, whom this coincidence strikes, for his biographer Gertrud Kircheisen, who cannot be· said to be similarly prejudiced, also notes it with her feminine intuition. She says: "It would, however, be a mistake to imagine that Napoleon noted this event in his life because it had left an indelible impression. The mention of this haphazard encounter with a woman is due much more to his bent, or rule, of noting the critical events in his life, than to any inner emotion or feeling. Napoleon's heart was too full of love of his fatherland, for any other feeling, even sensual, to find a permanent place there. From this adventure in the Palais Royal he took away quite different feelings, though not without a struggle. He tries to suppress all physical feeling so that only the emotion of patriotism may remain, the sole true emotion to his thinking.

Five days later, on 27th November, he addressed a *Monologue on Patriotism* to a lady he does not name. Can he have been so ingenuous as to suggest, thus anonymously, his belle of the Palais Royal? It would be very possible".

Yet even without these citations it would be fairly easy to establish that both love and sexuality had now become acuter, more urgent problems for him; to the point indeed of making him, in his *Rencontre*, go so far as to accost the "creature of sex"; he who so deeply felt the odiousness of her condition that he had always considered himself sullied by even a glance. In this essay *Sur l'Amour de la Patrie*, he compares his times with those of Sparta and Athens. Whereas then, love of the fatherland was the ruling passion, love alone rules in his day; these two passions must be incompatible, since they were opposite in their effects. For when a people is enslaved to love, patriotism suffers; which is why so few believe in it in his day. Now, if we attribute these reflections personally to Napoleon, given his state of mind as expressed above and, if we substitute him for the populace, then Sparta and Athens would signify no more to us than his happy childhood and all this would merely express the fear that intercourse with women would deprive his mother of his love. In other words: a conflict had arisen between his erotic past and present.

We have other proofs to support this interpretation. A little later, in this same essay, he disrespectfully and aggressively apostrophises the modern woman. "But you, who now chain men's hearts to your chariot wheels, that sex whose whole merit is contained in a glittering exterior, reflect here upon your triumph (i.e. in Sparta), and blush at what you no longer are". Whereupon, as models and examples, he refers his contemporary women to the heroines of Sparta.

Now there was one such heroine with whom he was only too familiar; namely, his mother Laetizia, whom one of his biographers (Chuquet) describes thus: "A man's heart dwelt in the frame of this proud, untiring and courageous woman. In the last days of Corsica's independence she accompanied her husband amid the woods and mountains. For news of the army, she often left the craggy rocks, in which the women had a sure retreat, to venture where the men were fighting. Bullets whistled about her, but her only thought was her husband's danger and Corsica's salvation. She was then big with Napoleon and she carried her child, she said, as happily and serenely then, as she later bore him in her arms. Such was this Laetizia's past and reputation that Paoli compared her with Cornelia, mother of the Gracchi: small wonder that such a mother should become a heroine to her young son!

Thus, this ostensibly critical essay dictated by the pure enthusiasm and bathos of youth (if we ignore other interpretations to which we shall return later), may be seen as a mighty struggle against the mother-complex, which seems to be fighting for very life. The irruption of puberty which, as we saw, irresistibly urged the young man to the opposite sex, and naturally leads to the loosening of ties with the mother, unleashed a violent conflict in his unconscious. The very fact that he asks whether, in general, love of the fatherland actually exists (or whether it is not indeed a passion for glory), reveals that the trend to detach himself was at work in his soul, and that the mother-complex was sufficiently undermined to inspire this emphatic question. Amid these oscillations, the mother-complex sometimes appears very clearly as when, for instance, he contrasts Themistocles who, with Persian aid, would doubtless have conquered all Greece had he not refrained, saying: "Oh my son, we shall perish if we do not perish", with the exploits of such Frenchmen as Robert d'Artois, the Duc d'Orleans and Condé who, in their vainglory, "did not blush to lay waste the regions that gave them birth". This, indeed, clearly expresses the need to renounce that incestuous desire of the mother which, gratified, will lead to certain destruction.

The struggle for and against this complex provides the latent content to everything else he wrote in the next four years. Sometimes this mother-complex is symbolised by *the earth*, as in the *Discours de Lyon*, which he offered as a prize-essay on the theme: "What truths and what emotions are most important to instil in men for their happiness" where, as Chuquet notes, under cover of social and political reforms, Napoleon "unburdened his soul" and "let his heart overflow". He does this, too, when he cites the young man who, after his childish follies, attains the age of dawning passion: "His vigorous arm, in concert with his needs, demands toil: he glances around and sees the earth shared by a few". Continuing, he apostrophises those who ordain the social order, who consider it enough to show him documents as titles to land; whereupon the young man, greatly angered, vociferates in his rage: "What! are those the title deeds of such gentry? Mine are more sacred, more irrefutable, more universal! They renew themselves in my sweat, they circulate with my blood, they are written in my sinews, my heart; indispensable to my existence and, above all, to my happiness!"

This heart's-cry clearly reveals the powerful libidinal charge which the representation "earth" held for Napoleon, and indicates how little of its intensity his libido had yet lost.

*   *   *

Our deduction of Napoleon's strong mother-fixation, derived from deciphering these symbols, seems to me wholly confirmed by what we know of his erotic life. It is less visible in his relation to his mother which, so far as I can judge from the relevant literature, shows no more than a filial affection, though one of very unusual strength, we must admit. We know, and shall often turn to it later, that he was a most attentive, devoted son to Mme Laetizia; a son who tirelessly strove to make life as easy and agreeable as possible for her and who, on St. Helena, said that, at thirty, she was "as lovely as one of the Graces". At whatever stage of his prodigious career we study this relation, always and everywhere we see proofs of the tenderest solicitude for his mother: "His first thought is for her", says Masson. It was only the way that unchanging feeling was expressed which varied with his different circumstances. For his mother he was always ready to sacrifice time, money and patience, as much when a poor second-lieutenant as when a captain.

He helped her to exist from his meagre pay, and assisted her in her heavy burdens. And when he was ruler of a vast empire, concocting gigantic schemes, he endowed her with millions and himself saw she had that honourable place which was her due at his rigidly ceremonious court. He himself appointed her residence, her retinue, and placed the Sisters of Charity under her charge, to provide her with occupation. He also himself chose the wall-coverings for the Palace of Pont-sur-Seine which he presented to her and always lent a patient ear and respectful indulgence to the often illfounded grievances and complaints of the insatiable and perpetually discontented old lady.

We see the influence of the mother-imago on Napoleon's love-life more clearly still where its effects are almost compulsive: he cannot love, nor marry, except by propping himself up, as much as possible, on this imago of the mother.

A clear indication of this strong fixation—the precocious desire to marry—frequently occurs in his youthful writings and, in particular, in his *Discours de Lyon*. At twenty, at Auxonne, the young Lieutenant had already thought of marriage: he is even said to have asked for Manesca Pillet, a wealthy timber merchant's step-daughter, in marriage.

Where we clearly observe this complex at work is in the episode concerning his sister-in-law's sister, Desirée-Eugenie Clary, who was later to marry Bernadotte, King of Sweden. Napoleon, twenty-six, poor, a brigadier-general relieved of his command and so without any means of subsistence, had won the ardent love of a sixteen-year old girl who was rich and who, in one of her letters, had written "My life, in short, is yours". Napoleon took this love affair very seriously and, after their relation had lasted more than a year, with many letters passed between them, suddenly decided to marry. Thereupon, with all his impetuosity, he urged his brother Joseph to take the necessary steps. "I burn to have a home. The affair must be settled or broken off!" Well, it was broken off: the last word had been said. "The Hymn to Desirée thenceforth disappeared from Napoleon's letters". Why? His biographers do not know. They assume that he did not really love Desirée, that he had sought her from purely interested motives. None of this is true, and we agree with G. Kircheisen when she says: "Yet Napoleon had loved Desirée" for the young girl's letters are full of a confidence she is loved in return and, also, Napoleon is distressed whenever her letters are late; not to mention the proof given by his efforts to see that she makes a good marriage, once he himself has married another.

It is clear then that his affection for her was great. But the object of that affection, according to our deductions, lacked what was essential to enable his love feelings to attain that culmination in which no happiness was possible unless the woman became his. What that factor was becomes clear if we consider Napoleon's subsequent love objects. For, immediately after Desirée, he turns to Mme Permon—a widow with two children and a friend of his mother's—whom he asks in marriage. Next, his attention is attracted by Mme de la Boucharderie, also much older than himself, and then, a year later, he becomes enamoured of Josephine de Beauharnais, a widow too who, like the women cited, was far older than himself—seven years in fact—and whom he immediately marries, although she has two children.

This, then, is the compulsive factor in his life; namely, that the woman shall have reached middle-age: a factor which is also remarked by G. Kircheisen, who says "It seems that Napoleon felt principally attracted by women much older than himself". This, according to Freud, is the surest indication, because least masked, of an incestuous mother-fixation.

*   *   *

We must now seek the original source of the affective significance of the factor "France" or rather "foreigner", and reduce it similarly to its factual origin; in other words, there must have been some "Frenchman" whom the small Napoleon suspected was united to his mother under his father's aegis; or, more clearly expressed, whom he supposed was in a sexual relation to his mother.

Now, while he was a child, such a Frenchman had indeed existed; a man who, thanks to his official position and connection, then and later, with the Bonaparte family, was excellently fitted to dominate the boy's imagination and awake his jealousy and suspicion. This was Count Louis Charles René de Marbeuf, Governor of Corsica and Lieutenant-General of the French Forces; a man with power of life and death on the conquered island. Thus he was well placed to stand for all that was French, and even France, in the child's eyes.

A close intimacy had developed between the Governor and Carlo Buonaparte's family. When the island was finally occupied and peace was restored, Carlo, tired of the war and financially straitened, did all in his power to support the French and, in return, strove to derive every possible advantage from them; money, positions, titles.

In consequence, we find the Governor, during Carlo's life, concerning himself greatly for Carlo's family and, later, perpetually helping his widow. Not only did he personally do all he could, but he made his nephew, then Bishop of Autun and later, Archbishop of Lyons, help too. Thus, if we follow the vicissitudes of the family at this time, we meet these dignitaries almost on every occasion. It is General Marbeuf who holds Louis Bonaparte at the font; through his influence Joseph and Lucien gain bursaries to Autun, Marianne-Elisa is able to enter St. Cyr and Fesch, Napoleon's half-brother, is admitted to the ecclesiastic seminary at Aix. Finally, he procures Napoleon admission to La Flêche and, when these arrangements are changed, to Brienne. Under the influence of Marbeuf, Napoleon abandons his original plan to enter the Navy in order to join the artillery. Besides all this, Marbeuf was always trying to help Carlo Buonaparte in financial ways, in view of his chronic money difficulties. Again, thanks to Marbeuf, Carlo is repeatedly elected deputy of the nobility, a post which bore a salary. Through Marbeuf, too, he obtained a liberal subsidy to plant and maintain certain mulberry groves. Furthermore, the governor supported Carlo in his lawsuit against the Jesuits; a lawsuit to recover an estate, Milleli, bequeathed to them by a relative.

Given Marbeuf's place in the Bonaparte family, and considering that, according to Jung, Carlo was "Always away, utterly absorbed in his pleasures and efforts to materialise his dreams of wealth", as well as Laetizia's youth and beauty, it need not surprise us, therefore, that public opinion should suppose there were amorous reasons for the governor's interest in this family or that it should reach the same conclusions as the small boy. Coston says: "Spite here indulged itself in finding another reason".

Kircheisen, like Masson, reports gossip to the effect that
Mme Laetizia was accused of being "more than a friend" to
the old Marbeuf, but adds that her upright character, so
truly Corsican, would alone warrant the absurdity of such
rumours; in any case, she was no frivol and her beauty would
have aroused more admiration than desire. My own impression is that some of these suspicions persist in the order
which proscribed the Bonapartes after the break with Paoli.
In it we read: "The Bonapartes were born in the filth of
despotism: they grew up under the eyes and at the expense
of a Pasha (Marbeuf) accustomed to luxury".

Be that as it may, what matters here is to show that the
small Napoleon, like others, had sufficient grounds to induce
a belief in a liaison between Marbeuf and his mother; one
that was tolerated, if not encouraged, by his father; and that
he had some justification, at least, for forging a phantasy
which, as we know, has all the validity of a real occurrence.
That this indeed was so, that this was the true significance of
his blame of his father; namely, that "he helped to unite
Corsica to France", is clearly shown by something he said at
a much later date, when, speaking of what he had felt during
his first leave in Corsica, after an absence of eight years: "My
happiness would have been complete if two loved men had
not been absent, my father and Count Marbeuf, whom we
lost on 20th September (i.e. five days before his arrival), and
whom my family long mourned".

This juxtaposition of Marbeuf and his father, with equivalent affect, confirms not only our sexual concept of the words,
"He helped to unite Corsica to France", but makes it probable
that, given this phantasy, Napoleon would feel somewhat
unsure which of them was his father. This doubt found its
legislative projection in that article of the Civil Code which
states: "Investigation of paternity is forbidden".

In the light of this phantasy, however, Napoleon's reflection,
cited earlier, anent the Connétable de Bourbon; namely, that
"his real crime was coming to attack the fatherland with
foreigners", signifies in terms of the unconscious that the
mother must not be brought into sexual contact with strangers.
We need only recall that, in their ignorance, many children
imagine that the sexual relation consists in a fierce battle in
which the woman is hurt. In this way such children manifest

their sadistic leanings; trends we can hardly deny the young
Napoleon. Thus, the condemnation intended for the Connétable de Bourbon would exactly correspond to condemnation
intended for the father.

We are now in a position to resolve other problems as for
instance, why, in his work *Sur le Suicide*, written at seventeen,
he talks of taking his life, because "his countrymen, loaded
with chains, tremblingly kiss the hand that oppresses them";
i.e. because of something which had existed all his life and to
which he had had plenty of time to grow accustomed. "Frenchmen", he exclaims, "not content with ravishing from us all we
held dear, you also corrupted our customs. The present aspect
of my fatherland and our impotence to change it, is thus a
fresh reason to flee a land *where duty would compel me to praise
men that virtue should make me hate*. When I reach my homeland,
what appearance shall I wear? What language speak? . . .
My life is a burden to me, because nothing gives me joy and
everything fills me with misery. It is a burden to me because
*the men with whom I live and shall always probably live, have customs
as different from mine* as moonlight is different from sun-
shine".

Clearly, one consequence of this phantasy, as regards
Napoleon's sexual life, would be to cathect the idea of
adultery so powerfully that it would seem a sin, a crime.
We see this clearly in his youthful writings, particularly in his
Discours de Lyon, full as it is of passionate invective against
celibacy and those celibates who, for reasons of State, should
be prevented from repairing to other men's wives in order to
satisfy their sexual desires. Now Marbeuf, as it happened,
was a bachelor, and only married when 72, in 1784. Napoleon
was fifteen at the time.

In any case, this complex reveals itself, in my opinion,
in a curious error in his *Mémorial de Sainte-Hélène*. In this
he relates how, at twenty-five, when a general of Artillery in
the Army of Italy, he was guilty of gravely irregular conduct.
To please a pretty woman, Louise Turreau de Lignières, the
young wife of the People's Representative, he had sacrificed
several men to prove his gratitude for favours received. "I
was then very young, proud and happy in my little success.
So I tried to show my gratitude by every attention in my
power. You will soon see how far abuse of power can lead

and on what human fate often depends. For I, I am no better than others. Walking with Mme Turreau near the Col di Tenda, on a lovely September morn, in the midst of our positions, I suddenly thought I would play a little at war, in front of her eyes. I ordered our outpost to attack. True, we were victorious but, of course, there could be no question of result. The whole attack was pure phantasy . . . and yet some men were left on the field of battle. Whenever I think of it I blame myself bitterly".

Gertrud and Friedrich Kircheisen dispute the precision of this recollection; firstly because, given his character, he was incapable of such levity and again, because, according to Mme Turreau, although this skirmish did take place, it was in no wise ordered through love of her and, thus, from a frivolous wish to please her. Moreover, F. Kircheisen very plausibly shows that Napoleon's memory is in error, both as to the date and place. For M. and Mme Turreau did not reach Nice from Paris until the 21st September or reach the army until rather later. Also, it is unlikely that the combat took place near the Col di Tenda, for this pass had been taken some months before, so that the event which Napoleon cited probably occurred on 26th September, during the attack on the Union redoubt near Vado.

In my opinion, the solution of this problem should present no difficulty for, exactly as when analysing neurotic remorse, let us admit that the feeling of self-reproach is justified and only question its content, though carefully keeping in mind what Kircheisen asserts. That is to say, we shall assume that this indubitable affect of reproach relates to something else, and that its apparent content only here rises to the surface in substitution for another content. Thus, the true meaning of this self-reproach will not be difficult to guess if we consider that, on one hand, Napoleon accuses himself of having done something wrong to please a woman and, on the other, as we learn, that during this very year he is said to have maintained adulterous relations with four women (Mesdames Carteux, Ricord, Saliceti, Turreau). It need not therefore surprise us that "some men were left on the field of battle". And this is the Napoleon who, three years before, in his *Discours de Lyon*, "demanded that adulterous bachelors be denounced before the whole community".

In effect, he was punishing himself, by thus recounting his sins to his faithful companions.

Our interpretation is somewhat confirmed by this phrase in the account: "the attack was pure phantasy", for our experience in interpreting dreams justifies us in treating this phrase as an allusion to the unreality of what he related. It is a hint to the reader to read between the lines.

Per contra, the words "abuse of power", seem to me to indicate the origin of his aversion to adultery, and the conflict to which it gave rise; for it was abuse of power of which the powerful Marbeuf was accused.

Doubtless, to this same source, we must relate his characteristic meticulousness about "appearances", as respected his own marriage. Unlike his predecessors on the French throne, he never had an official mistress, and his private amours were always indulged with the greatest discretion in his private apartments at the Tuileries. This, however, did not prevent him from freely confessing his infidelities to his wife and even, at times, relating his amorous adventures to her.

* * *

This phantasy of his, it is clear, determined his whole attitude to women. It made him require, as a condition of loving (to quote Freud), the infidelity and degradation of the woman. The women he loved must be faithless, as was his mother. This condition was especially strongly determined in his unconscious.

We can readily observe this in his behaviour to Josephine. Hardly had he married the beautiful Creole, whom he loved so passionately, though she was credited with numerous amorous adventures during her first marriage (or because of them), and though she had been the mistress of Barras (or because of it), than he was obliged to depart for Italy, to take command of the army there. From Milan he wrote her stormy, passionate letters, full of ardent desire, imploring her to join him. But since that ingrate, absorbed in the manifold pleasures of Paris, delayed to appear, the unhappy spouse, but a few months married, said to Marmont: "My wife is ill or unfaithful to me".

She did deceive him, in fact; if not then, at any rate

somewhat later for, when she eventually reached Milan, she stayed on alone, after their short time together, once he had left for Verona to meet the enemy. In Milan, she began a liaison with a subordinate officer named Charles, which soon became the subject of gossip. Napoleon's relatives, always ill-disposed towards Josephine ("la vieille", as they called her), eagerly seized this occasion and openly hinted at her conduct to him. Nevertheless, we find no trace of these crushing revelations in any of the letters he later wrote her. They breathe the same ardent love and desire as his earlier letters except that, now and then, a note of bitterness creeps in, provoked by her indifference and silence.

Even when the conqueror, covered with glory, had hastened to Milan to lay his success at her feet and clasp her, whom he so ardently loved and desired, in his arms; even when, then and there, he can no longer doubt her deceit (she is at Genoa with Charles), he spends the night bemoaning his fate but, next day, clutching at her lame excuses, sends her forgiveness and thus ends his letter: "I once more open my letter to send you a kiss . . . oh, Josephine! oh, Josephine!" Then, for all revenge, he is content to find a pretext for removing Charles from the Officers' List. What is certain is that her infidelity in nowise affected his feelings for her for, a year later, we read in a letter sent her by Berthier: "My attachment to you is so great that I should certainly tell you if Bonaparte had the least rancour against you. This I swear to you; no, he has nothing against you. He loves you, he adores you".

Two years later, when Josephine, during his Egyptian campaign, established herself with that same M. Charles at Malmaison, for a veritable idyll of cloudless happiness which lasted some weeks, a fact his relatives and friends hastened to report, he does indeed complain in his letters to Joseph and friends; then, when he is again in Paris, he cuts himself off from one and all, Josephine included. Nevertheless, after he has sulked for a space of three days, he yields to his stepchildren's entreaties and seems to forgive her entirely. One cannot but think that this lapse, so tragic to many a husband, was quickly forgotten by him for, soon after, Malmaison became his favourite residence, although that was where he had been betrayed. Later too, when they were living

together, we have nothing whatever to show that her faithless-
ness in any way clouded his husbandly feeling. True, his first
ardour may have cooled, but that is an occurrence common to
all marriage, where affectionate friendship replaces passion.
In any case, the well-informed were agreed that the marriage
was exceptionally happy, that Napoleon was an easy-going
and deferent husband and that, always and everywhere, he
thought of her. He continued to load her with costly gifts
after being with other women, he always loved to return to
her; it made him glad and happy that she was his. The
proof is his words to Roederer: "If I did not find peace and
content domestically, I should be a most unhappy man".

Confronted by this kind of reaction, I believe we are
justified in assuming that Napoleon's phrase: "Adultery is
nothing special: a question of a convenient sofa: an everyday
matter", merely represents a way of degrading and generalising
this voluptuous concept of the unconscious to render it com-
patible with consciousness, and thus avoid a conflict.

Nevertheless, as already stated, this unconscious demand
for infidelity was required solely of the woman he loved for,
where his heart was partly or wholly untouched, he relentlessly
demanded fidelity and purity in the woman. Thus it was
with Marie-Louise, for whom he felt nothing that we could
call love. Yet, though her extreme youth, her education, her
frigidity, should have rendered her free from suspicion, he
had her carefully watched. No man could enter her apartments without the Emperor's permission. A lady-in-waiting
was ordered to be present at her lessons, another must be
with her day and night, and no one could reach the Empress's
sleeping-chamber except by passing through the bedroom of a
court-lady. He blamed her severely in a letter for receiving
Cambacérès when in bed, and justified this kind of behaviour
by saying: "The Queen of a great empire must be above all
suspicion". His biographers, meanwhile, uncertain how to
interpret all this, leave it at that.

All this to us, however, smacks of rationalisation, especially
if we note his severity in this regard to women for whom he
cared little, or was more or less indifferent. Here are some
examples according to G. Kircheisen. He, personally, forbade
the Court to Mme Visconti, mistress of Berthier, his intimate
friend, although by rank and birth she was fully entitled to

attend it. Appearance at Court was also forbidden Talleyrand's wife, simply and solely for being the latter's mistress
before their marriage, a marriage, by the way, to which the
Emperor personally compelled him. Again, he would not
allow a monument to be set up in honour of the great Agnès
Sorel, because she had been the King's mistress. Yet again,
how contemptible was the ingratitude with which the Consul
and Emperor treated the charming Mme Tallien, so dear to
all Paris as "Notre Dame de Thermidor" and as "Government property". Surely he owed her gratitude for the hos-
pitality she once showed the penniless, dismissed general, and
for the new uniform she once procured him. In spite of her
many appeals, he ruthlessly forebade her presence at Court.
Even earlier, he had charged Josephine to have nothing to do
with this woman, who was indubitably her best friend. Later,
as Emperor, he even allowed Mme Tallien to be described as
a *loose woman* in the official Police Record! And all because
this highly distinguished woman had led a somewhat chequered
amorous career before she married, irreproachable though she
became after her marriage.

Nor did the "Grand Emperor" hesitate to have Mme
Regnault, whose boudoir he branded as "the worst disgrace
in Paris", denounced to her husband. And indeed, he never
pardoned his brother Lucien for marrying a certain Mme
Jouberton, by whom he had had an illegitimate child, and
did all in his power to break the marriage.

But also we find a strongly determined factor in him which
is closely linked with this *prostitute* or *infidelity complex;* namely,
contempt for the loved and faithless woman. But this factor, too, is
likewise transposed. Napoleon's scorn of women is well known:
not only did he scorn those whose lives were not irreproachable,
but also those whose lives were above reproach, women with
the entry to his straight-laced, frigid Court; in a word, he
despised them all. Women trembled before him at his Court,
because of his way of embarrassing them with wounding and,
at times, brutal questions. He would ask unmarried girls how
many children they had or how long they had been pregnant.
He blamed plain women for being ugly, often criticised their
gowns, and openly referred to their amorous adventures.
This contempt for women found brutal expression in his
well-known episode with the famous actress of the Comedie

Française, Mme Duchesnois. The First Consul had given her a rendezvous in his private apartments but, being busy, made her wait: when she complained, he had her undress and, later, merely sent her away without any apology, despite her wait of some hours, half naked and shivering with cold.

No gifts of mind or intelligence could prevail against this contempt. On the contrary, such qualities in a woman were likely, since they threatened this complex, to inspire a greater aversion on his part. The fates of Mme de Staël, whom he banished from Paris, as also of Queen Louise of Prussia, and many others, are a clear proof of it.

"He was only weak towards one, towards Josephine", says Gertrud Kircheisen. It was simply because she fulfilled the one love-condition he demanded: unfaithfulness in the woman. His feelings towards her, as always in such cases, were so adjusted, that those contradictory emotions which could exist side by side in his unconscious without conflict, were displaced upon other women by his consciousness, and it is only consciousness which can create and respond to contrast. We can now understand why he demanded fidelity and virtue from women to whom he was indifferent, while at the same time despising them with the scorn which his unconscious attached to the love-object.

The immense affective importance of this phantasy in his life, as also the correctness of my interpretation, will be demonstrated if we consider a strange characteristic of the young Napoleon, and one reported by all his biographers: Coston, Chuquet, Fournier, Kircheisen, etc. This appears to have first manifested itself during his schooldays at Brienne; that is, between his ninth and fifteenth years. To quote Chuquet: "The headmaster had shared a large piece of ground between the pupils, to be worked and cultivated as they pleased. Bonaparte decided to participate, forced two of his schoolmates to give up their share to him and made a garden of the ground of which he was master. He used the money he got for trivial outlays to purchase some wooden stakes, whereupon a strong palisade resisted entrance to his little domain . . . There Bonaparte spent the time dreaming or reading and woe, relates a schoolmate, woe to him who, from curiosity, malice or jest, dared trouble him in his repose! He would

D

rush out furiously from his retreat in order to repulse them, no matter how many".

Let us add another scene, also noted by all his biographers, but this time quoted from Kircheisen: "In his last year at Brienne, he provided an example of that egotistical rage which made him oblivious to anything others might suffer, when unforeseen happenings prevented him doing what he wished. Every year the school celebrated the feast of St. Louis in honour of the King, on which day the pupils were left completely free. To their intense delight, every boy over fourteen was given some gunpowder for use in the firework display set up a few days before. Joy prevailed; for weeks before the holiday all the pupils were awaiting this event with feverish excitement. What astonished everyone was that the young Napoleon, whose last holiday this would be with his schoolmates, appeared more morose and inaccessible than ever. He did not leave his hiding place all day, but remained there absorbed in his books and atlases. Was it that the future republican henceforth refused to join in a festival to honour the King? Perhaps it may only have been a caprice? We know nothing of the feelings which animated Napoleon, in this respect, at the time: in any case, for some reason or other, he showed some repugnance to sharing the general joy. One of his neighbours, in the garden next to him, had put up a set piece made by himself, which he wished to let off for his friends. These boys collected in the small garden at about nine and, greatly admiring, arranged themselves round their schoolmate's achievement. Suddenly there came a terrific bang: some sparks had dropped into the canister of gunpowder which, carelessly, had been left open. A huge panic took possession of the boys, who sought to escape as fast as possible . . . In their confusion, some climbed the fence which separated Napoleon's garden from his neighbour's and so doing flattened some of the weaker stakes. At that moment, Napoleon, foaming with rage, takes an axe and hurling himself on those who disturb his quiet, drives them back towards the blaze. What cared he for his schoolmates' misfortune? One single thought filled his mind; they had torn him away from his studies, they had violated his sanctuary".

Surely this symptomatic act is immensely eloquent to those with eyes to see! If we strip it of its symbolic disguise, we shall see that it expresses exactly the same thing as "to attack the fatherland with foreigners", or "he helped to unite Corsica to France": that is, that no one must be allowed to approach the mother and that one must possess her, entirely, oneself.

To convince even the most sceptical reader of the justness of this symbolic interpretation, we have but to cite the following passage from F. Muller-Lyer's *Phasen der Liebe*:[1] "*According to Napoleon, a woman's children belong to the husband, even if some other man begot them: for the woman belongs to him precisely as whatever grows in a garden belongs to that garden's owner*". Thus, Napoleon went on considering Hortense and Eugene as *Josephine's fruits*.[2]

* * *

The surprise occasioned by Napoleon's morose and inaccessible behaviour at this time, behaviour which seems to have puzzled his familiars then as much as, later, it did his biographers, will vanish when we recall its connection with the King, and that King, Emperor and, in general, all authority, are typical symbols of the father and that this typical symbol would have been greatly magnified by these celebrations for, as Chuquet testifies, a large transparency of Louis XVI, supported by Justice and Truth, and bearing the inscription "A Louis XVI, notre père", had been erected over the main gate. Thus Napoleon's behaviour, so singular that day, indicates his hostility towards, and estrangement from, his father: feelings we have already noted in the condemnation we quoted earlier.

These, however, are not the only indications, for his writings, like his letters, provide eloquent proof of this state of mind. I need only recall the passage from the *Discours de Lyon* already cited, which so clearly expresses a libidinal displacement from the mother to the earth and possession of it. In this tale, the young man, stripped of his rights and full of bitterness, goes for protection to his father, who consoles, helps and comforts him. Yet, of that same father he also says in another passage: "My father calls me from the bosom of the other life" (his own father had been dead some years), to warn him, urgently,

---

[1] Albert Langen, Munich, p. 24.
[2] Masson, *Napoléon et sa famille*, Vol. I, p. 142.

against that avarice and striving after great possessions which
always brings misfortune. He then cries out: "Never let
yourself be carried away by avarice or violent passion". Now,
when we read that this young man, "whenever his soul is
open to anguish or untrammelled desires, hastens to his father's
venerable ashes in order to revive the taste for simplicity and
duty" and, if we strip this phantasy of its symbolic content,
can we not then see Napoleon, as it were, struggling against
the father's age-old prohibition relative to incestuous desire
for the mother?

Masson claims that the "father's death" (24th February,
1785), "did not affect him so painfully as to make him express
his anguish in cries. That may do for women. He took it
like a man, the soldier he already was. As a small child, they
were together but little, and in the last six years he had seen
him but once, for an hour. He could hardly, therefore, feel
that affection for him which, above all, is formed by habit
and daily impressions".

All his biographers agree as to the strangeness of the condo-
latory letters he wrote to his mother and uncle Lucien on this
occasion. Chuquet speaks of them thus: "Napoleon's grief
was immense when he learnt of his father's death. It is not
expressed in his letters as naturally and spontaneously as
might be expected. The tone is dignified but rather frigid,
ceremonious, solemn. They are too careful, too affected, these
lines by a sixteen-year-old child".

Again, seventeen years later, we find traces of the same
state of mind when, in 1802, the First Consul rejects the
Resolution and Petition of the Municipal Council of Mont-
pellier to erect a monument to his father, who died when
passing through that city, as to the man to whom the world
owed his great son. Napoleon's reasons for this refusal sound
rather flat: "Forget it: let us not trouble the peace of the
dead; leave their ashes in peace. I also lost my grandfather,
my great-grandfather; why is nothing done for them? This
leads too far".

It was because he knew his brother's attitude that, without
his knowledge, Louis Bonaparte saw that their father's body
was exhumed and reburied at Saint-Leu, and there had a
monument raised to it.

His love for his father, however, was no less intense than

his estrangement from him. Indeed, it was so intense at times as to make him abandon his own ego to be at one with the father, to identify with him and, also, to be the father himself. We need only read the letters which the fifteen-year-old boy wrote to his father and uncle Paravicini about his elder brother Joseph's affairs, to realise how much the father he was. How affectionately, solicitously, and in what detail does the boy discuss "What advantage will the family gain?" That was his password, indeed!

After his father's death "his one thought is to earn some money to help his kin" (Kircheisen). When a second-lieutenant at Valence, barely seventeen, worry about his kin overwhelms him on his first leave; indeed, he always got Joseph to report regularly about their desperate straits. Neither then, nor later, does it occur to him that Joseph, his elder, should more properly support the family. On the contrary, as though a matter of course, he takes on all the family burdens, however onerous and diverse they be. He helps to get Lucien into the ecclesiastical seminary at Aix and prolongs his leave at Ajaccio to help his kin with his pay. At Ajaccio he takes infinite trouble to get the question of the interrupted subsidy for the mulberry groves settled, and makes a special journey to Paris to take it up in the right place. "He neglected nothing to get his rights respected and in this showed the same perseverance and tenacity as his father: he does not readily accept refusals, he is far too much Carlo's son" (Kircheisen). So well does he defend his family's interests that he achieves a qualified success. But this not contenting him, he turns to Versailles, secures an audience with the Finance Minister, Brienne, and petitions him to grant a bursary to Lucien. And all this when barely seventeen! Back at Ajaccio, we see him valiantly aiding his mother and writing all sorts of petitions for her: he is "her advisor and interpreter in dealing with the authorities and gives himself infinite trouble to lighten her fate".

His sisters and brothers also bear witness how much the father he felt, how much they saw him as such. Joseph, for instance, says: "When Napoleon spoke, you had to give way and we all of us obeyed him". Lucien, in his Memoirs, relates: "There was no discussing with him, the slightest criticism annoyed him and he was angered by the least opposition".

Even Joseph did not dare answer him back. His sister Marianne-Elisa states this still more openly when, wishing to leave St. Cyr, she says in her request to him: "Having known no other father than my brother . . ."

As a poor lieutenant at Auxonne, when no bursary could be got for his younger brother Louis—that Louis who later became King of Holland—he took him to live with him at his own cost. He imposed great sacrifices on himself to provide for Louis from his meagre lieutenant's pay, and have him carefully brought up and educated. He was as proud of him as only a father could be of his child, and wrote: "Surely he will become the best of us four".

After the flight from Corsica, it was he alone, then Captain Bonaparte, who supported his all-but destitute family, meagre though his resources were. And shortly after, when, refusing to be transferred from the artillery to the infantry, he drifted about Paris, a general struck off the active list, bitter at heart and without means, and in despair with himself and his life, his chief concern was still the happiness of his family. "Though hopeless and unhappy", writes Masson, "where his family is concerned, he is no longer the same. Then no effort repels him, and nothing is too much trouble to him. At this time he gives so many proofs of devotion to his kindred that any doubt as to the intensity, the depth and power of his feelings becomes impossible". I can only agree with Masson when he terms such solicitude paternal, for only the intensest paternal feeling could have made him write as follows to Joseph: "You know, I only live for the happiness I prepare for my kindred. If my hopes are favoured by the good fortune which never abandons my undertakings, I can make you happy and satisfy your wishes".

After his rise to power, from the 13th Vendémiaire, not only was there no slackening in his solicitude for them but, indeed, an increase. As head of the Army of the Interior, overwhelmed with toil, month by month he sent large sums to his family and still found time to ease the way for some and assure the future of others. Now he obtains useful recommendations for Joseph, or gets some high position for Lucien, or helps Louis in his army career, or gets little Jerome into a boarding school in Paris and follows up his scholastic progress.

He himself best describes these activities when he writes: "I can do no more than I am already doing for all".

According to Masson, to serve his kindred, he must have shown a diligence, a patience, a purposefulness which would indeed be astonishing if we had not already seen him at work; if we did not know what efforts he had made for them since the death of their father".

Yet it was not the father's duties alone which he took on himself, he also arrogated the right to decide the fate of his brothers and sisters, a prerogative he extended over the most intimate, most private parts of their lives, as we see if we look at the marriages or love affairs of Marianne-Elisa, Jerome and especially, Lucien. The sharp reprimand sent Pauline after her marriage to Borghese well illustrates this point. Pauline was discontented with Rome and apparently longed to change it, and her husband, for Paris. Whereupon Napoleon, though busy with State affairs, wrote to her thus: "Love your husband and his family, be considerate, adapt yourself to Roman habits and be certain that if, at your age, you let yourself be led astray by evil counsels, you can no longer count on me. As to Paris, you can be sure you will find no support there and that I shall never receive you without your husband. If you quarrel with him, it will be your fault and so France will be forbidden to you; you will lose your happiness and my friendship". And Masson adds: "Nevertheless, although he blusters, he is not as savage as he seems" for, almost simultaneously, he writes about this business to his uncle Fesch, in a letter full of solicitude and affection. "And", continues Masson, "in his affection for his kin, in his perpetual indulgence for their worst misdeeds, in his illusions about them, in his zeal to carry them to the highest places, regardless of all save the blood-ties that unite them, he is just like a father who makes us feel that the flaw in his reason nevertheless does credit to his heart".

And how that paternal feeling always throbbed in his heart! Even during the catastrophic reverberations of his fall, and when he had signed his abdication at Fontainebleau, all he finds to say to Caulaincourt is: "Arrange things so that my family have everything they need: it is all I ask".

*   *   *

Among all his predecessors on the French throne, as among all other historical personages, Napoleon admired and venerated no one so much as Charlemagne.

Whenever he could, he paid him homage. He dedicated the magnificent monument in the Place Vendôme to him, erected a statue in his honour at Aix-la-Chapelle and paid special reverence to his relics when visiting that town.

In big things, as in small, Charlemagne was his model and example; he insisted that the Pope, personally, consecrate him, and had his coronation robes modelled on Charlemagne's. The quarterings he assumed were those attributed to Charlemagne and, at his coronation, he bore the old imperial insignia of crown and sceptre and sword. Again, most of the titles which he conferred on his dignitaries, were similarly borrowed from the Holy Roman Empire of Charlemagne.

Like him, Napoleon had his Dukes and Counts and, though he created Barons and Knights, it was because those degrees existed in Charlemagne's Empire. And when, even before he had concluded his second marriage, he got the Senatus Consultum of 17th February, 1810, to confer the title of King of Rome on the son for whom he hoped, what further proof do we need to show how perpetually the traditions of Charlemagne's Empire haunted him?

His dream was to make his Empire identical with Charlemagne's but, beyond this, there were times when Napoleon designated himself by the name of Charlemagne, as when he says, for instance: "I am Charlemagne because, like him, I unite my crown of France with that of Lombardy and because my Empire borders the East". Or when he writes to Cardinal Fesch, his ambassador at Rome: "Say that I am Charlemagne, your Emperor, and that I wish to be treated as such".

Masson, from whose book *Napoleon chez lui*, we take these details, explains this attitude of his as arising from the great significance he inclined to attach to the principle of authority which he represented and its demonstration, which principle lacked its most natural, most powerful support; namely, a line of ancestors before him on the throne. It was for this then, that he would choose Charlemagne for his model and example, since the analogies in their fates were so great. No more than Charlemagne had Napoleon any hereditary right to the succession; like him he had founded a new dynasty, and the whole nation had elected them both. Napoleon, too, had his eyes turned towards that Italy which he had conquered twice and he, too, considered his Empire incomplete so long as he could not unite the French, and the nations of the Spanish peninsula, under his sceptre. He, too, had seen the Germans of the East revolt against the principle he represented and he, with his paladins, had suppressed that rebellion. Which was why, presumably, he resolved to link the fourth dynasty to the second, and to turn Charlemagne into his "august predecessor".

This is the opinion of Masson. As for ourselves, who well know what seemingly strange and far-fetched forms the unconscious chooses for expression, and especially its way of finding analogies in sounds that but slightly resemble each other, we shall recall that his father's name (in French) was Charles-Marie and express our conviction that such a complete identification with Charlemagne surely cannot be wholly attributed to conscious thought but must, indeed, in some degree, derive by way of assonance from an unconscious identification with his father. In proof, I once more quote the reasons given by the Senatus-Consultum cited earlier: "Napoleon abstains, in the early days of his glory, from entering Rome as a conqueror. He waits to appear there as a father. He wishes there, a second time, to be crowned with Charlemagne's crown".

This was because, to the child's psyche, which survives in the unconscious, the father is not only Emperor and King but also, always, "Great".

III

We have now depicted the young Bonaparte's psychical condition up to the period so far dealt with. It comprised an intensely powerful mother fixation and the attitude towards the father which corresponds to that fixation; an attitude composed of those contrary love and hate feelings known as "ambivalence" which is so often met with in the psychology of the neuroses.

This psychical condition was the factor which left his soul free to a number of possibilities. If reality frustrated him, neurosis might result but, on the other hand, if reality gratified his wishes, a sublimation of the greatest value might come into being.

The proof is that, given the immense burden which, as we have shown, weighed on his soul, a predisposition to neurosis was already present in him. Nearly all the descriptions which his biographers trace of his youth, indicate to the initiate a neurotic childhood and adolescence. Coston for instance notes that, even at school in Autun, Napoleon was morose and absorbed, spoke to nobody and took solitary walks. Jung gives the following portrait of him at this time: "What a child! A savage, ruled solely by instinct. With his pallid complexion, bristling hair, small size, piercing gaze, and 'sickly' appearance . . ." after which he adds: "Solitary he was, solitary he is, solitary he will remain".

This introverted and completely asocial nature, a nature which his biographers explain by his nostalgia for his Corsican fatherland, and which he himself admitted later in saying he had always been melancholic, became still more marked during his stay at Brienne. Condemned one day to a punishment he must have keenly resented—that of eating his dinner, kneeling, in sack-cloth, at the refectory door—he evaded the ordeal, when the moment came, by a fit of vomiting and violent hysterics.

All his biographers also agree in noting Bonaparte's strange, abnormal, morose, timid and uncommunicative character in pre-adolescence, as well as the solitariness which made him unpopular with his schoolmates. This Napoleon himself admitted when he said: "My schoolmates did not like me much". Chuquet, also, in his description of Napoleon at this time, mentions his "nervously compressed lips" and his "fits of rage and fury", while Jung, surely his most intuitive biographer, says: "The child turned in on himself, living a wholly imaginative existence of memories and day-dreams". After which he goes on to attribute Napoleon's strange character at fourteen as due to the "impetuous thoughts that boiled in this adolescent's head". A year later, while still at the military school in Paris, Chuquet notes his introversion, when he says: "He is always in his thoughts". And Jung, with great perspicacity, diagnoses him as "incipiently neurotic", when relating how, during his first leave at home, he alarmed his family by the tirades he uttered; tirades borrowed from Voltaire and Rousseau, of which only his old uncle approved, he being still a Corsican at heart. Meanwhile his mother sat placidly, impassively listening, under the impression that "her son was ill. And so he morally was, sapped by his mental fever".

Similarly, when dealing with his treatise *Sur le Suicide*, Jung writes:

"Everything is strange in this cry of a seventeen-year-old Werther, officer of the King. Hatred of France, ruthless desire for pleasures he cannot afford, erotic pictures, thirst for fame, the need to pose to his co-citizens, hatred of his surroundings, all may be found in this work by a sick, impulsive person, whose every act will be determined by a strange, a truly hallucinatory fever, until he has brought his maddest dreams to pass!"

But though we may find many a neurotic feature here and there in Napoleon's later life, we shall confine ourselves, nevertheless, to the material already presented, which confirms our contention that such a degree of psychic tension might equally well have engendered a neurosis.

Despite the immense significance we have attached to Napoleon's doubtlessly unusually strong libido, we, however, believe it was the reality conditions of his times which dammed back and prevented the development, in him, of an inhibiting and destructive neurosis. Indeed, it was the reality of his epoch which, from this same psychic material, created a far grander, more diverse, more fruitful destiny for him than any that we know in history; a destiny which even the wildest imagination could hardly conceive.

True, this fashion of seeing his career is opposed by the very testimony of the fallen Emperor who later, in an excess of exaggerated modesty, and forgetting the part his own personality had played, said on St. Helena: "Nothing is simpler than my rise . . . it lay in the special nature of the times . . . I am the product of circumstances". Nevertheless, our findings agree with those of certain other biographers, among whom is F. Kircheisen, when he says: "The epoch in which Napoleon lived encouraged his genius", and "his extraordinary capacities could only have developed in an atmosphere such as that of the Revolution". We, however, not content with merely noting this influence, must seek to explain, to understand, how this came about and was given its special direction.

*   *   *

To those familiar with the dynamic principles which govern the functioning of our psychic mechanism, it will be clear that, where ambivalent feelings exist, opposing trends will only be able to focus on the same love object so long as love can continue to neutralise the negative trend. Where this ceases to happen, a doubling of the love object will occur, and the two libidinal currents, unequally mingled, will create a number of love-objects, now positively, now negatively, tinged.

This mechanism may easily be observed in Napoleon, whose powerful libido would doubtless oppose the concentration of these opposing currents on one object and it is from this basic psychic position that we shall try to understand our problem.

In his life, also, we see a number of fathers and, not to mention his own, let us begin by citing merely Marbeuf and Paoli, while noting how his attitude towards these father-derivatives, as might be expected, was as ambivalent as towards his actual father.

We shall deal separately, later, with his relation to Paoli. For the moment, let us note merely that not only did he feel that hatred for Marbeuf which we have analytically determined, but also that indications of a certain attachment to him exist. We have already noted a manifestation of this in his life and now wish to point out, quoting Chuquet, that though in his many youthful writings Napoleon so pitilessly attacked the French generals, such as Narbonne, Fritzlar and Sionville who governed Corsica before it was granted autonomy, never at any time does he include Marbeuf among them, even though a commemorative tablet describes the latter as "Expiring Corsica's Tyrant".

Nevertheless, those we have already cited do not complete the tale of Napoleon's substitute fathers for, as was shown by that most revealing act of his Brienne schooldays, the King is also included among them: that father whose stamp, through the evolutionary process, is engraved so deeply on the human heart.

To all his biographers, Napoleon, at this time, was a convinced, fanatical republican, as is testified by Charlotte Robespierre who termed him the "Montagnard', and his conversations, well before this, at Valence, with Sucy and Montalivet. But, above all, it is his youthful writings which reveal this officer of the King as the deadly enemy of the royalty he served, and which leave no slightest doubt as to his real sentiments. Thus, he begins his *Dissertation sur l'Autorité Royale* as follows: "This work will begin with general ideas about the origin and growth in men's minds of the name of King . . . it will then deal in detail with the usurped authority which the Kings enjoy to-day in the twelve monarchies of Europe". "There are but very few Kings who have not deserved dethronement". And, in the *Discours de Lyon* we read: "We well know how egotistical kings have always been. They imagine they contain in themselves their people, their nation, etc".

For the analyst, in *Sur l'Amour de la Patrie*, there is a significant indication of the nature and source of this hate of royalty; it is the passage in which he cites Dion of Syracuse as the exemplar of true, pure love of the fatherland. It reads: "Dion is of great wealth, noble birth and deservedly, much respected. What lacks he to be happy? Pusillanimous souls, you cannot guess, yet you dare speak! His fatherland is enslaved to a tyrant who is his ally, a tyrant he loves and respects yet, nevertheless, a tyrant".

What justifies my conclusion that this passage would reflect Napoleon's psychic relation to his father, is the fact that here the analogy evidently became too transparent even for him, his unconscious trends having risen too near the surface. Thus we see that, quite unnecessarily, he deletes this passage, correct though it is in form and content, and substitutes another which makes no mention of relationship, love or Dion's esteem for Dionysos. Indeed, this is the second longest deletion in Masson's edition.

Having thus discovered a solid foundation for our supposition that, in Napoleon, the image of the King took the place of the father's, we would point out that it is precisely here that one may observe what was postulated above; namely, the auspicious congruence in his life of phantasy and reality, a congruence so close, of these two determining factors, as to occur but rarely in human destiny.

Napoleon passed his youth against the background of the great Revolution, an upheaval unique of its kind and one in which the phylogenetic hatred of the father was unleashed as never before, to bow the human soul beneath its yoke. F. Mueller-Lyer,[1] from the purely sociological viewpoint, demonstrates what an immense breach the Revolution made in the father's hitherto solidly entrenched position.

The effect of this general hatred of the father, in Napoleon's case, was to arouse and kindle his father-complex and cause it to oscillate between love and hate. To him, this mass-libido directed on the father, endowed its symbol, the King, with a flesh-and-blood reality upon which he could now direct his own libido, which had been so sterile and even, destructive, till then, in its fixation on the father.

What proves our preceding argument is that Napoleon became as ambivalent towards the King as towards the father (and Marbeuf); only half of his soul was revolutionary and the enemy of kings, while the other half remained hostile to the revolution and in favour of the King. Apart from the passage cited above, dealing with Dion's love for Dionysos, we find in his biographers ample evidence of this ambivalence in his youth. At Seurre, for instance, where in 1780, he had to repress some "twopenny ha'penny" revolts, Coston says he outspokenly criticised revolutions in general. When a few weeks later, similar revolts broke out at Auxonne, where he was garrisoned, the raging populace filled him with disgust and, according to Kircheisen, he expressed distaste at the curses hurled against the royal family. Coston, again, tells us that Napoleon, after swearing fidelity to the new Constituent Assembly on 14th July, 1791, expressed himself thus: "Until now, had I been ordered to turn my cannon on the people, I do not doubt that habit, prejudice, education, the name of the King, would have led me to obey". But, when the King's attempted flight on 20th June, 1791, failed, a flight which irrevocably decided Louis XVI's fate, we see from the speech Napoleon subsequently made to the Club de Valence,

[1] F. Müller-Lyer: Die Familie, Munich, 1912.

that he felt nothing but goodwill for the King; he speaks of him as "pursued by fate", and adds: "The blame for all this rests on the counsellors of the King who have hurled him into the abyss". This sympathy finds clear expression in the comments inspired by the events of 20th June and 10th August, 1792. For, on the first date, after the King had been hooted and reviled by a mob from the suburbs, which forced its way into the Tuileries and crowned him with a Jacobin bonnet, Napoleon said to Bourienne, his friend: "Coglione! How could they let that riff-raff get in. They should have mown down four or five hundred with cannon and the rest would still be running". This sympathy was still more clearly revealed on 10th August when Jacobin mobs attacked the Tuileries, massacred the Swiss Guard and, in their fury, forced the King to take refuge in the National Assembly, where he was held and placed under arrest. Whereupon Napoleon said: "I feel that, had I been called, I would have defended the King".

Considering, however, how much his attitudes reflected the emotions of the masses, it need not surprise us that the general exasperation and hatred against Louis XVI, which mounted ever higher as the drama drew to its close, should have switched his libido on to the same tracks and intensified, to the utmost, the inherently negative trends of his ambivalence to the father. For we now reach the time, beginning November 1792, when the Convention, in those moving debates, argued the fate of Louis XVI, imprisoned in the Temple. Those debates re-echoed through France and, like Robespierre's speech on 3rd December, were stamped "with the profoundest loathing of royalty": a loathing equal to that for the King.

But also, for Napoleon, in this shape of the King, there was one characteristic well fitted to arouse all his hate of the father and drive it to extremes; namely, the suspicion, during these Revolutionary years, that the King was appealing to foreign powers for aid with which to attack the fatherland. Was he not accused, in the debates before the Convention, of calling his co-sovereigns, "those foreign tyrants" to arms, in order to punish his own people? And, at his trial, was not the main accusation against him that of "plotting against the general security of the State"?

Thus, in the phantasies of the young Napoleon, Louis XVI,

like his own father, Carlo Buonaparte, wished to deliver the mother to strangers. Small wonder then that this should awaken so mighty an echo and that, thus stirred, the smouldering ashes of his old hate for the father should first glow, then flame, into an all-consuming blaze.

This is the reason why Louis XVI's fate, strictly speaking, also fashioned Napoleon's fate.

It was this fate of Louis XVI which, as we shall see, also determined and established Napoleon's attitude towards the two basic viewpoints which form the subject of this study.

First and foremost, it is not difficult to show that his attitude to France, in its oscillations, followed the vicissitudes of the royal tragedy.

Thus, after the fiasco of the King's flight (30th June, 1791) he who, as a diehard Corsican, had never actively interested himself in French politics, thenceforth ignored national differences and made them subordinate to the Constitutional question. Indeed, at Valence, before the Club of the Friends of the Constitution, though still serving the King, the royal officer roused his audience to great enthusiasm with a speech stamped with the most ardent love for liberty.

And when, on 14th July, 1791, the troops and citizens swore loyalty, no longer to the King, but to the National Assembly as the highest authority, he breathed a sigh of relief and said: It was only the Nation he recognised now.

A few days after, 27th July, 1791, while still deeply moved by the humiliations and restrictions imposed on the King, Napoleon, "his brain full of these great public events", and spurred by "the meridional blood that courses through my veins as fast as the Rhône", sent the Commissioner of War, Naudin, a letter which has seemed strange to his biographers; a letter in which, for the first time, he expresses the need for solidarity with France: "Tranquil as to my country's fate, (Corsica) and the glory of my friend (Paoli), my one care now is for the motherland".

In our opinion, it was Napoleon's strongly ambivalent feelings to his father which explains why his impulse towards the French proved so transitory. Soon we see him a Corsican again and, two months later, when back in Ajaccio, he manifests all that drive whose object is to cast out the French but which ends with his abortive attack on the citadel.

This same ambivalence towards the father also surely accounts for the fact that the events of 20th June and 10th August, 1792, already cited by us, did not cause him to turn to France although, on each occasion, his sympathies were for the King. Yet at St. Helena, speaking of the events of 10th August, Napoleon said: "Never has any of my battlefields given me the impression of so many corpses as did those masses of slaughtered Swiss". According to Chuquet: "His one thought is his island and he incessantly reverts to it". When he wrote to his kin on the state of France, it seemed cold and almost indifferent: indeed "your first thought would be that he is one of those foreigners which seem to him to swarm in Paris, and that he only looks on as a mere observer". It was then, too, that he wrote to Joseph: "It is more likely than ever that all this will end with our independence"; after which, despite a sharp reprimand from the Minister, he reappears in Corsica on 15th October, instead of going to join his regiment.

Three or four months later, however, we see him rallying to France once more under the impact of the debates before the Convention—debates which so powerfully reactivated his negative feelings towards the father—as well as of the King's trial which the Convention instituted in December. According to Chuquet, Napoleon is said to have exhorted his countrymen to declare for France at the municipal elections which were then being held in Corsica.

But it was only after 18th January, 1793, when sentence of death had been passed on the King, that Napoleon attached himself to France in a decisive, unambiguous and irrevocable manner.

Chancellor Pasquier relates it thus in his *Memoirs:* "Bonaparte, who, like Pozzo, had originally adhered to Paoli, lost no time in leaving him to defend the rights of the French Government. It was on the news of Louis XVI's condemnation that he reached this decision. I have this fact from M. de Sémonville who was then in Corsica as Commissary of the French Government. Bonaparte came and woke him up in the night. *"M. le Commissaire", he said, "I have carefully considered our position: the people here are ready for any folly. The Convention, no doubt, has committed a great crime and I deplore it more than anyone; but Corsica, whatever happens, must always be joined to France: it can only exist on that one condition: I and my kin, I declare, will defend the cause of union".*

E

Thus, it was only after the father, the detested author of so many ills, who had prevented Napoleon possessing the mother and yet had shared her with strangers, it was only after he had paid for his crimes with his head, that Napoleon finally rallied to France.

The King's execution, therefore, gave reality value to the essential part of his Oedipus phantasy, from which it naturally follows that, by rallying to France, he was able, symbolically, to possess the liberated mother.

Moreover, this acceptance of a situation which the father had created, also implies identification with that father and thus expresses love.

Identification also resulted from the intense guilt feelings aroused by the satisfaction of his hatred, as witness his saying to Sémonville that it was "a great crime" which he "more than anyone" deplored, but which becomes, by that fact, both a redemption and an expiation.

Finally, Napoleon's identification with Marbeuf might also, too, have determined this need to atone.

With the casualness of the unconscious we know so well from dreams and neurotic symptoms, that unconscious which only considers present needs, France which, till then, had signified Marbeuf and surrendering the mother to him, now became, for Napoleon, the symbol of the mother herself; that motherland to which his passionate love would thenceforth turn, which he would ardently covet, which he would call his "polar star" and defend to the last.

*   *   *

Of the four men vested in Napoleon's mind with the father's attributes, that is Marbeuf, Louis XVI and Paoli in addition to Carlo, it is Paoli who occupies a specially significant place as representing the ideal, good and model father.

Not only did the Corsicans know him as "il babbo" (the father), and the Bonapartes as "compère", but he was admirably fitted to personify this ideal through the prestige of his past and his heroism during the wars of independence. In terms of the unconscious, he represented the father who protects the mother from the strangers he drives off and, thus, the opposite of the real father who had helped to join the mother to the foreigner Marbeuf. It was therefore natural that all the sublimated manifestations of Napoleon's ardent feelings should turn in admiration and respect to Paoli.

Thus we see that glorified father-figure dominate all his youthful existence and, at this time, hold first place in his heart.

Even during his stay in Paris, in the summer of 1792, there was no diminution in his unwavering admiration for this ideal father. And when he day-dreamed that France, weak as she was, would peacefully relinquish Corsica, being unable to hold it, and that Corsica would then have a national government of its own, it seemed to him that Paoli would again be its General and Regent as before it was occupied by France, and he says: "He is all, he will be all".

Nevertheless, in proportion as the fate of the imprisoned King became darker and more tragic during the debates before the Convention, the progress of his trial, and the increasing public hatred against him, raised similar echoes in Napoleon's heart and animated his ancient hatred for the father. Discouraged also by the constraint with which Paoli now treated him, he moved ever further from his youthful ideal.

Although we have no authentic testimony for this, it nevertheless seems to me clear, for psychological reasons, that Napoleon's final and open animosity to Paoli can only date from the time the King was beheaded. For, given his need— a need which so sharply distinguishes him from the neuropath —to find support and contact in the masses and reality; a reality which, in this crucial matter, as in so many others, accorded with his psychic constellation; he was compelled, once and for all, to assume the extremest negative attitude to the father.

Every father, however good, however ideal he be, must be overturned, merely by the fact of being the father, and exactly as expressed by Oncken,[1] when he speaks of Louis XVI's fate: "The murder of a King merely for being a King".

Thus it was that Napoleon's last father imago, Paoli, was fated to fall. He no longer hestitated, openly, to declare himself the latter's enemy, or to ally himself closely and definitively with Paoli's bitterest enemy, Saliceti.

[1] Wilhelm Oncken, Das Zeitalter der Revolution, des Kaiserreiches und der Befreiungskriege: Grote, Berlin, 1884.

Our deduction that the King's execution proved a determining factor in Napoleon's development, is corroborated by the fact that, at a time when no question of political or nationalist feeling was at stake, Paoli then being as faithful to the Republic as was Saliceti, Napoleon, having to choose between them, opted for Saliceti and attached himself to the latter.

Paoli, we may say, had not hesitated to censure the King's execution, for though Corsicans were indeed enemies to kings, they were not their executioners, whereas Saliceti, alone among the Corsican deputies, had cast his vote for the King's death.

Yet there were other unconscious motives likely to inspire the change in Napoleon's attitude to Paoli, for, as we have said, once the father (the King) had disappeared, he himself became the father through identification with him and, which corroborates our interpretation, adopted his father's political views (i.e. the joining of the mother to Marbeuf). It need not astonish us therefore that he should now wish to remove Paoli, that last of his father-figures.

In any case, this identification with his father would make him repeat Carlo's behaviour to Paoli for, had not the former, after long and faithful service to the latter, in the same way deserted him for the French; thus Naploeon, in so acting, was but imitating his father.

It is suggestive that all these motives found copious nourishment and support in the evermore openly expressed Paolism of many of the delegates to the Convention, a Paolism which Napoleon, with his trends now exacerbated, could interpret not only as self-defence but, rather, as the wish in Paoli to arrogate sovereign power and renew the struggle against France. Now, however, that he had fully identified himself with his father, so keeping faith with the new situation Carlo had helped to create, Napoleon began to oppose the stirrings of revolt among the Corsicans, the sole motive for which was protest at the King's execution, as his words to Sémonville well show: "The people here are ready for any folly".

We should, however, misjudge the essence and power of Napoleon's ambivalence to imagine that, thenceforth, his conduct towards Paoli would follow a single path, with hate alone to guide it. For even during this struggle, the positive pole, his love for Paoli, still revealed itself clearly, as witness his efforts to establish relations with Paoli after the decree of 2nd April which ordered his arrest, as well as by his moves to mend their conflict and, in particular, by the warm and generous defence of him which he wrote. True, the form of this address, "strewn with question marks", as Chuquet says, implies a certain lack of conviction in the author and, to us, seems to question the very motives behind his political choice, and its degree of sincerity.

In addition to the causes his biographers give for the rupture between them, causes to which we have given due weight as, for instance, Paoli's manifest hostility to him after the publication of Lucien's attack and the consequent persecution of his kindred, we would add yet another strong emotive factor, a factor of unconscious origin, whose effect was also to silence his love for Paoli. This negative attitude became ever stronger until it finally predominated, as is clearly testified by the crushing indictment which he later wrote of Paoli.

The deeper I have gone into Napoleon's life and, especially, into the period now dealt with, the surer I become that what decided his irrevocable break with Paoli was his suspicions as to the latter's attitude to England; which attitude according to recent research, though fluctuant, became ever more favourable towards that country.

At the beginning of his conflict with the government, Paoli, in fact, was loyally French and had no thought of betraying France. At that time his enemies' accusations were merely calumnies which, it is true, derived some plausibility from his earlier connections, and his unconcealed affection for England. It was only later that Paoli, annoyed both by the Government's distrust, and by the numerous cabals and intrigues woven against him, as well as by the premature enmity of the Convention, reconciled himself by degrees to those thoughts of reaching an understanding with the English which, soon after, led to his surrendering Corsica to them.

Napoleon, as he said on St. Helena, was himself, at this time, strongly affected by these rumours, which added fuel to his hostility to Paoli; this then would explain the flagrant contradictions in his two addresses, written barely a month from each other. In the first, he does not yet suspect Paoli or, if the interrogative form implies a lack of conviction and the ensuing arguments are meant to combat his own doubts, he refuses to admit his suspicions. Later however, his suspicions become strengthened, partly because of Paoli's unyielding stand, despite the good-will of the Convention, and partly because he may already have been in negotiation with England. These suspicions soon became that certainty which found undisguised expression in his indictment of Paoli, which, as we know, drew inspiration from other motives.

The following reflections well prove that it was just Paoli's anglophile policy which so profoundly affected Napoleon's fate. We know for certain that, as a youth, Napoleon had so much liking and affection for England and the English, that he was considered an "Anglomane" in Ajaccio, as were also Joseph, his brother, and his friend Masseria. Chuquet, after seeking the origins for this predilection in his study of Rousseau, Reynal and Boswell, ends by tracing it, mainly, to the welcome once received there by Paoli, which attribution we consider just. This love of England appears very clearly in his *Nouvelle Corse*, already quoted, where one of the characters saves his life by pretending to be English, whereas all the French are mercilessly killed.

After his flight from Corsica, however, we see him developing in a quite opposite direction; one that is radically anglophobe. Early in September, 1793, according to Coston, he suddenly hastens to Paris, while pacifying the rebellious south, having heard that Toulon has been treacherously surrendered to the English, and begs to command the artillery besieging the fortress. This statement, it is true, is ignored by modern historians who claim, on the contrary, that Saliceti would have offered him this command, left vacant by the death of the previous commander. Indeed, ten years later, in the First Consul's reply to the English newspapers (13th October, 1803) we read: "In Europe you enjoy the reputation of a prudent nation, but you have greatly degenerated since your forefathers' time. On the Continent all your speeches inspire scorn and pity". And in his letter to the English of 15th August, 1805, he says: "Do not imagine you have allies on the Continent. You are the enemy of all nations and all are glad to see you humbled". We are all familiar with his subsequent attitude towards England and the English, an attitude he sought to motivate by political arguments which, to speak as a psycho-analyst, he "rationalised". By then, however, both had become his pet aversion. Everywhere he detected their corrupting influence (see his letters from Italy to the Directory). He strove to banish them from Mme Rémusat's *salon* and always considered them his sworn enemies; he would have liked to raise all Europe against them, and it was against them that he decreed his continental blockade, which lasted for years and closed every continental port from Hanover to Taranto. And during his relegation to the Isle of Elba, in his *Considerations sur l'Etat de l'Europe* he wrote: "As to the English, I will only say that history does not cite a single fact which would prove that a trading nation has ever worked for the good of humanity". Finally, it was hate for England that shaped the course of this unique Corsican star, until its light faded at Waterloo.

Thus, his attitude towards England also impresses us as having a similar affective origin, showing all the strength of a complex, as his hatred for Paoli, and this confirms our earlier contention that it was Paoli's attitude to England which played so decisive a part in inspiring Napoleon with such bitter enmity and making him break with Paoli.

It is not difficult to interpret this reaction of his—despite the few months of his new love for France—if we consider his unconscious phantasies. For Paoli intended nothing less than the repetition of that great crime originally committed by Carlo Buonaparte, with whom his son had but so recently sided and who can say at what heavy cost? Thus, this excellent father Paoli had himself been ready to surrender the mother to strangers, exactly as those wicked fathers Carlo and the King had done and for which crime the latter had paid with his head.

Now that this mightiest pillar of his soul had crashed, he gave himself up to defending the mother from the father's perfidious designs and, so doing, forever demolished the temple he had formerly set up to that father-ideal. *For the fate of the King had taught him how perfidious fathers should be treated: indeed, he went so far as to demand Paoli's head* by accusing him of high treason to the bloodthirsty Convention.

It was therefore due to the final and utter collapse of his love for the father, caused by his conflict with Paoli, which made that rupture so tremendously significant not only to his own development, but to the history of the World.

How catastrophic its effects were for his own development, and how destructive to his ethics, we know from what the Emperor said to Talleyrand, when the latter, thinking to please him, handed him the manuscript of the *Discours* which a special courier had been sent to seek at Lyons. The Emperor tore it from his hands and threw it into the fire, "because it was cram-full of principles he would not be flattered to have nourished in youth, had anyone happened to reproach him for them".

For world-history, this rupture was to prove immeasurably important, since Napoleon's unconscious, once and for all, now established a wholly negative attitude to the father. Thenceforth we would embark on an incessant and ruthless struggle against him.

IV

From this time, Napoleon's insatiable desire to win the mother never gave him a moment's respite and his subsequent ardent struggle to tear her from the father constitutes, indeed, one of the greatest epics in human history. It was the guiding principle of his unique existence, a principle to which he would subordinate everything; one he would pursue always and everywhere and by every means in his power. "For I am not a man like others, and laws of morality and convention cannot be made for me".

Primarily, we see his relation to Corsica change completely. For however the small boy may have explained his busy father's abandonment of his mother to Marbeuf, it nevertheless remains that, thenceforth, Corsica no longer had the slightest affective significance for him. In 1795, as Inspector of Artillery, he was to accompany an expedition which, however, did not take place, intended to seize the island from the English and, the year after, as Commander-in-Chief of the Army of Italy, he himself planned an operation to reconquer Corsica; but no emotional affect, now, accompanied either occurrence. Fournier was right when he said: "His Fatherland no longer had the strength to inspire an interest greater than that inspired in him, say, by Corfu or Malta".

Moreover, it was clearly as a result of the same complex that Napoleon, as Masson relates, once he became the omnipotent First Consul, turned his back on his fatherland and compatriots, as his own mother testified, (she who, in spite of the surprising change in her fortunes, had remained as faithful to her past as to Corsica), when saying: "But since Toulon, that is how he is: he would not even let one talk to him in Corsican".

And indeed, it was only after much effort that Mme Mère succeeded in getting the Emperor to provide for his Corsican kindred. Of all the huge Corsican clan of the past, only two (Arrighi and Ornano) did he appoint to his suite, and then only after proving them in Italy, Egypt, San Domingo, and from Cadiz to Moscow. "Enough of Corsicans now!" He had no intention of delivering France to them, but he did assign them Corsica and even divided all his own Corsican possessions among them, solely to prevent them over-running France!

Thanks to this indifference, this aversion, Buttafuoco could now return upon the Emperor the blame which, in his time, Lieutenant Bonaparte had cast (page 5). In his posthumous works, we find Buttafuoco apostrophising him thus: "How many reasons has not Corsica to say to you: What, my son, is there no feeling in your heart for the isle where your eyes first opened to the light? When you reached the age of reason, I augured well of you. When I saw you on a vast stage, my heart throbbed with joy; I hoped then that your fatherland, that your brothers, would be dear to you. It is frightful that one of their brothers should neglect them so much".

But now that Corsica was lost to Napoleon and had become worthless in his eyes, we see him begin his tireless, insatiable hunt to find a substitute for that first love of his. His tormented, famished imagination greedily coveted country after country in a seemingly endless succession of substitutes which, however, being such, could never remotely satisfy his avidity. Throughout this frantic search, he plunged country after country into seas of blood, spread terror through the world, transformed the face of Europe, and all in vain, since nothing could assuage that hunger!

As the first link in the long chain of substitutes, perhaps the most tenaciously coveted was Italy. In the *Mémorial de Sainte-Hélène* we read: "In January 1795, Napoleon passed a night on the Col di Tenda, whence at dawn he perceived the lovely Italian plains which were already the object of his thoughts. Italiam, Italiam!"

We know what torrents of blood he shed to possess that country, supported by Austrian, Sardinian, Neapolitan and even Papal help and, to appreciate the significance of this exclamation, "Italiam, Italiam", it is worthy of note that, according to Chuquet, Mme Laetizia, *née* Ramolino, was as much Italian as Corsican. A small detail will confirm this deduction; namely, that Napoleon used the Italian form, Napolione Buonaparte, for the last time, when signing the register after his marriage to Josephine de Beauharnais. The letter to Mossi, written a week later, already bears the French form Bonaparte, from which he never thereafter departed. We may also, perhaps, attach some importance to the fact that his love letters to Josephine often employ Italian terms of endearment.

Hardly had the peace of Campo Formio been concluded when, evidently moved by the powerful chords of Corsica, he was already eager to capture the islands of Malta, Corfu and Xante, as "far more important to us than Italy", he wrote to the Directory.

Thence we see him hasten to Egypt, Palestine, Damascus, Aleppo and Constantinople for, "I overthrow Turkey, I establish a great empire in the East, and return to Vienna via Adrianople": not to mention India, which his unparalleled avidity had already devoured in imagination. Nor was the Emperor any more content with the "Mistress", as he called France, but went on coveting other countries just as hungrily as when he was Commander-in-Chief and First Consul. We see him overthrow and re-smelt empires, scatter nations like chaff to "place Europe at his feet", as he put it, and become "Lord of the universe"; and all under the urge of his incestuous desire for the mother, and of a boundless challenge to the father, unparalleled in history.

We should have to recapitulate the whole history of the Napoleonic age to demonstrate in detail all the hatred and defiance he felt towards those father-figures, the diverse Kings of Europe, in his endless pursuit of the mother. Let us briefly recall the way he treated the Emperor Francis of Austria; King Frederick William III of Prussia; the Kings of Spain, Portugal, Naples; the German Kings and confederate princes, and even Pope Pius VII, once they were defeated: how he provoked, humiliated, degraded and humbled them and emphasised their dependence on him. I give some examples from his biographers:

Fournier says: "The princes of the Confederation of the Rhine assembled in Dresden to pay homage to Napoleon, who dominated them more absolutely than any Roman Emperor of the German nation had done for a long age past. Francis of Austria, the last of these, was present. Was it Napoleon who had sought this interview with his father-in-law, to use his relationship to the world's oldest dynasty in order to increase his own importance? At that same time he had invited Francis I to accompany him on his war-like expedition. Nothing came of it, however. In any case, the Austrian Emperor, despite his familiar footing with his son-in-law, was just like the King of Prussia and other petty kings: the humble lackey of this all-powerful upstart".

G. Kircheisen, writing of the meeting at Tilsit, which immediately followed the decisive Prussian defeat at Friedland, says: "Actually, a meeting between the two emperors took place next day, 25th June, 1807, on a raft on the Niemen. The King of Prussia, Napoleon not having invited him, remained on the bank. Later, the kings met at Tilsit . . . Napoleon avoided discussing outstanding matters with Frederick William and treated him as of no importance. He confined his conversation to the most trivial subjects, such as uniform buttons, shakos and the like, and made a mock of him at every opportunity".

From the same source we quote a letter written by the Duchess Louise of Saxe-Weimar: ". . . You cannot conceive the off-hand way in which Napoleon treats the four kings who have come to Erfurt. I assure you, it would be well worth seeing. Yesterday, for instance, he kept them waiting a whole hour in the vestibule, before the dinner . . ."

Nevertheless, there was no dynasty he hated so much as that of the Bourbons, whose fine offers he had curtly rejected even while Commander-in-Chief. Speaking of them, he said that "were they restored, he would well have found means to dispossess them again". After Austerlitz, in a simple communiqué, he proclaimed "that the rule of this dynasty has ended in Naples" and later, to the horror of Europe, had the innocent and last representative of that dynasty, the Duc d'Enghien, shot.

Finally, a proclamation, dated 1804, shows that he would tolerate no father, and intended to replace them all, for, as he said, "peace will never return to Europe, so long as it is not united under one head, one Emperor . . ." These words reveal the true, the deepest motive underlying his acts.

Thus, in this apparently solitary soul, which we might present as the paradigm of ambition, the libidinal drives that created the most astounding destiny of the world are finally revealed as determined by sublimated sexual motives.

To my mind, this reduction to general, human and typical instincts found in all human beings, in no wise diminishes the significance, the grandeur, of this man, or his incomparable importance as a cultural factor. Despite our findings, Wolseley's dictum that "he was the greatest of the great", still remains true.

Nor will we gainsay Victor Hugo, when he says: "He had everything, he was perfect. In his brain, the cube of human faculties was magnified to the sixth power. He made legal codes like Justinian, dictated like Caesar, his conversation mingled Pascal's lightning with the thunderbolts of Tacitus, he made history and he wrote it, his communiqués are Iliads . . . In the East, he left words behind him huge as the pyramids, at Tilsit he taught majesty to emperors, at the Academy of Sciences he controverted Laplace . . ."

As our analytic conclusion we shall add that, all said and done, humanity's admiration for, and its constant interest in, this great figure, derives from the immense reverberations which this mighty, yet transparent Oedipus complex awakes in our hearts, prey as we are to the same, more or less, repressed conflicts.

Perhaps it was less through calculation, as Fournier thinks, than to the influence of a similar feeling that, when Voltaire's "Oedipe" was acted at Erfurt before "an audience of Kings", Alexander of Russia rose and embraced Napoleon, to the applause of all present.

BIBLIOGRAPHY

I. A. Chuquet.—La Jeunesse de Napoléon. Paris, 1897.

II. Coston.—Biographie des premières années de Napoléon Bonaparte. Paris, 1840.

III. A. Fournier.—Napoleon I. Eine Bibliographie. Wien-Leipzig, 1913.

IV. Jung.—Bonaparte et son temps d'aprés les documents inédits. Paris.

V. G. Kircheisen.—Die Frauen um Napoleon. München, 1912.

VI. F. M. Kircheisen.—Napoleon, sein Leben und seine Zeit. München, 1911.

VII. Hans Landsberg.—Napoleon's Briefe. "Das Museum". Berlin, 1906.

VIII. Lucien Bonaparte.—Mémoires, édités par Jung.

IX. Tancrede Martel.—Napoléon Bonaparte. Œuvres littéraires. Paris, 1888.

X. F. Masson.—Napoléon dans sa jeunesse. Paris.

XI. F. Masson.—Napoléon et sa famille.

XII. F. Masson.—Napoléon intime.

XIII. Masson et Biagi.—Napoléon, Manuscrits inédits.

THE SENSE OF GUILT*

How appropriate it is that the present series of lectures on the problem of guilt should be given at the Akademische Verein für medizinische Psychologie, you may see from a rather neglected remark made by Nietzsche in his *Genealogy of Morals:* "On the other hand it is, of course, just as necessary to gain the participation of medical men in these problems (regarding the value of all previous valuations)", and again: "All tables of values . . . are waiting for a critique on the part of medical science".

The man from the medical profession, for whom Nietzsche was calling, has now providentially appeared and, quite un-influenced by Nietzsche, has revived the problem of the sense of guilt—which since Nietzsche's days had lain practically dormant—thereby making a wide clearing in the almost im-penetrable jungle of ethical theories.

The consequences are already apparent. Thus Schlick, a well-known philosopher, in his *Problems of Ethics*, states that only an empirical science of the laws of physical life is entitled, and able, to provide us with a casual explanation of ethical behaviour—the central problem of ethics. And a physician, Dr. Kant of Tübingen, in his recently published *Biology of Ethics* has made the sense of guilt his central problem.

It would seem, therefore, that, through the genetic and structural explanation of the sense of guilt given by Freud, a firm starting-point has been gained for an empirical or natural ethics—in spite of the deviations and errors of many writers on the subject.

Even at a time when it restricted itself to research into the libido, psycho-analysis never lost sight of the problem pre-sented by the sense of guilt. With continuing progress and the broaching of the subject of ego-psychology, this problem moved to the fore to such an extent that Ibsen's dictum about

* Translated by I. Jarosy. First published in *Psychoanalytische Bewegung*, IV, 4, 1932. This lecture was first delivered on the 14th of January, 1932, as introduction to a series of lectures òn the problem of guilt given at the Akademischer Verein für medizinische Psychologie, Vienna. The other, non psycho-analytical, lectures in the series, were given by Dr. Oswald Schwartz, Dr. Friedrich Schneck, and Dr. Rudolf Allers.

the writing of plays—that it meant sitting in judgment on oneself—may well be applied to the psycho-analytic concept of neurosis.

Psychical facts and phenomena cannot easily be confined within the narrow bounds of a definition: something will always be left unresolved. I shall therefore demonstrate the phenomenon of the sense of guilt in two clinical examples, and deduce its nature from these, instead of first giving a definition of the concept—in the manner of a thesis—and then trying to substantiate it.

A colleague of mine, who was seriously ill, once handed over to me the case of a woman patient of about thirty-nine; he was unable, owing to his state of health, to carry on the treatment, which had already lasted several months. After the first interview with me, the patient declared herself fully satisfied with this arrangement. During treatment, however, she behaved in a manner that soon aroused my attention. She acted as if no change of doctor had taken place, and provided me with hardly any information regarding the outward circumstances of her life; she did, however, tell me a large number of dreams, bubbled over with ideas and free associations, and surpassed herself in the discovery of hidden meanings and apparently sensible interpretations.

Then, during the fifth or sixth session, a strange incident occurred. After only forty minutes, the patient suddenly jumped up and said good-bye to me. I took out my watch, and pointed out that the session was not yet over. The patient thereupon remarked: "But you said: that's enough now!" I asked her whether she was sure she was not mistaken, and this she denied. She had fallen a prey to hallucinatory delusion, which I felt inclined to link up with her general behaviour. From the very beginning I had never doubted that the patient had only been so liberal with her dreams and their interpretations, because she wished to escape, for as long as possible, from recounting some embarrassing episode in her life. As you will hear, I found this suspicion confirmed a few weeks later. Meanwhile, however, I was able to gain a deeper insight into her colourful and varied psychic life. She was of southern origin, and her temperamental, impulsive character had, until late in her youth, been enchained in a pious and narrowly conventional environment. No wonder that the ageing woman was frigid when she finally married. And frigid she remained, even when her very unstable, strongly perverted husband practically assisted her to a series of bacchantic experiences.

During this period of her life, characterised by a desperate search for erotic sensations, the following event occurred: one morning, while she was asleep, her husband being away for two days, a burglar surprised her in her bedroom on the ground-floor of her house. She thereupon made this man, who did not seem in the least aggressive, return her property, but gave no alarm, nor did she ask him to leave; instead, she invited him into her sitting-room, asked him to sit down beside her, and then handed him a sum of money—and all this with the supposed intention of reforming him. A few minutes after he had left through the door, he returned by way of the window, and leapt upon her as she was sitting on the bed. She abandoned herself to him twice, without any attempt at resistance, apparently (according to her own account) because she was frightened of being strangled—even though there were several occasions on which she could have given an alarm. After the man left, she hurriedly dressed and hastened to her sister-in-law, to whom she recounted the incident in a state of utmost excitement, followed by a long screaming-fit. When her husband returned she also told him the whole story, without keeping anything back, and he accepted it calmly and kindly. On his and their relatives' advice, the incident was reported to the police, and the criminal was eventually caught. Twice she had to give evidence as a witness—the first time before the public prosecutor. The suspicion evinced by the questions of this experienced judge of human nature considerably undermined the defences behind which she had hidden her true realisation that she herself had desired and even brought about the adventure. She ended the description she gave me of her second interrogation, before the examining magistrate, with the words: "I can't try to explain to you what an annihilating look he gave me, when he broke off the interrogation with the words: That's enough now!" And before I could bring up the small incident of the session that had taken place several weeks ago, the patient herself referred to it, and to the fact that she had put the magistrate's words in my mouth, thus putting me in the magistrate's place.

Here are some further details regarding this case. Until she was nearly thirty, her entire world consisted of her parents and her mother's unmarried sister; she herself, as the only child, constituted the centre of this puritan environment, which exerted a strong formative influence upon her. They all treated her with great love and care. Then the two women died, within a short time of each other. A few months later a change seems to have occurred in her widowed father's way of life. Until then a devoted family-man, he apparently began to seek after success with women, and seems to have attained it, too. In fact, worried friends advised that the ageing man be sent to an insitution.

You will remember how, after her experience with the burglar, the patient showed no scruple whatever about telling the story to all her close and more distant relatives; remember, too, that her only affective reaction was a mere screaming-fit, which made up for what she had omitted to do during the assault. There is no doubt that she tried hard to regard the incident as a purely external misfortune, to which she had contributed nothing and for which she could not therefore be held responsible. The similar, very naive and un-psychological views of her relatives confirmed her in this attitude—an attitude which ultimately had the effect of not allowing her to confess the truth, nor to listen to her inner voice, the voice of her conscience. She went in mortal dread of this moral part of her personality and its damning verdict. It is this that makes her behaviour in the analytic situation comprehensible. For, from the very beginning, she projected upon me not only the real judge, but also—in him—her own inner judge and, thus, at the same time, the great dread which rested upon her conscience.

It was this dread which forced her to occupy herself with dreams and their interpretations, in order to hide from me the incident that gave rise to her conflict. This, of course, was in complete contrast to her volubility immediately after the event.

I now come to the second case, which I regard as considerably more informative.

I was visited one day by a man of about forty-five, who occupied a high official position in a Central European state. He was broad-shouldered and of slightly more than medium

F

height; his face was not especially striking, except for the uncertain, restless, shifty eyes and he spoke in a low voice. Altogether he gave the impression of a man not just depressed, but seriously frightened, who was controlling his anxiety with great effort. Hesitatingly he told me why he had come. He had been living for weeks in terrible dread. For many months he had carried on an intimate affair with the wife of one of his friends; everything seemed to indicate that the latter had known all about it and had tolerated it. A few weeks ago, however, this friend, who was young and healthy was found one morning dead in bed. The cause of death had not yet been established; no one knew whether he had committed suicide or died a natural death. Since that day the patient had been nearly out of his mind with dread of becoming entangled in this affair—of being found guilty of his friend's death, or, at least, of being regarded as an accessory. He had even conceived the strange and completely unfounded idea that the friend had been murdered by his wife, since the latter had once threatened to shoot him, the patient, should he ever leave her. Through this tragic event he became still further estranged from the woman in his feelings, and would have liked to get away from her altogether but, apart from the dread already mentioned, he was afraid of being murdered by her: as a result his whole life was now flooded by these dreads.

His state of mind showed up physically as it were in the analytic situation, and in his relation to his doctor. First, in his bodily behaviour, he lay curled-up on the divan, as though trying to make himself small; his legs were convulsively drawn up, and his hands, characteristically, were always clasped behind him, as though he were trying to shield himself from being beaten. It was, by the way, not I but the patient who remarked upon this. At the same time he was hardly able to tell me anything in a coherent manner and frequently stammered—apparently in desperate dread of revealing anything that might incriminate him.

It would not surprise me if you were to object, after hearing my account of this case, that it possessed no visible connection with the sense of guilt; the patient was not, like the woman previously mentioned, engaged in a genuine conflict with his conscience; he even felt completely free, inwardly, of any guilt in regard to his friend's death, and should therefore be regarded as an anxiety-neurotic. I can, however, effectively disprove this argument by pointing out that there was a situation in the patient's life which showed a far-reaching similarity to, if not a complete analogy with, the situation which precipitated his neurosis. For in his late youth, too, the patient had been in love with another man's wife, and with all the ardour of his impetuous temperament. And here, too, there was a husband of whose death the patient felt guilty.

His own father was a drunkard, who brutally maltreated his family and particularly the patient, and who sank lower and lower in the social scale. As a fourteen-year-old boy, the patient had one night seen his father engaged in preparations to commit suicide, as a result of which he died next morning. The boy noticed his father writing a letter to his mother, who was asleep in a room on the first floor. He even read the beginning of the letter, "Dear Riecke", and accepted the father's admonition to do all in his power to be a support to his mother and sisters; finally he saw his father prepare and drink some liquid—and all this "apparently" without understanding. Under the influence of the treatment a very remarkable development of his ego took place; as in the first case, the analyst was raised from the rank of an almost materially experienced father to that of representative of the conscience. Only then, after many months of treatment, was the primitive and infantile dread of punishment transformed into a genuine sense of guilt which, until then, had been carefully kept from attaining consciousness, and whose place had been usurped by the dread of being punished.

This case is thus particularly illustrative of the genesis and development of a part of the human personality which may justly be called its focal point. According to psycho-analysis, it is not only completely autonomous, but is set far above the rest of the ego, and has therefore been given the name of super-ego. Its development may be briefly recapitulated as follows: this "inner" man (to use St. Paul's phrase) owes his genesis and development to a process of internalisation. Though discovered completely independently by Freud, this process was brilliantly and intuitively foreseen by Nietzsche. He regarded it as a consequence of individuals coming together to form a community, and therefore as an inevitable concomitant of cultural development. He very nearly bound up with this process the beginning of the formation of the soul, which he regarded as a consequence of the community's preventing the free discharge of instincts.

One is first subjected to this process of internalisation as a child; it represents the child's only way out from the Oedipus-situation—that psychic burdening with contradictory instinctual tendencies, which finally becomes insupportable. And that which is internalised—the parents and protectors, who are at the same time the first representatives of society, with its "thou shalt" and "thou shalt not"—represents, as it were, the germ of the super-ego.

From these beginnings the range of internalisation continually increases and embraces ever wider circles. It leads to a gradual unfolding of the personality and, at the same time, binds it with indissoluble ties to its environment and its surroundings. It will therefore hardly appear surprising that the super-ego represents, at one and the same time, the precipitate of, as well as the response to, all norms regulating the relation between the individual and the community. Its function, in our view, is to safeguard all those achievements which secure and guarantee the existence of the community.

And here I should like to hazard the opinion that it should be a particularly tempting task for the psychology of religion to investigate the possibility of an historical correlation, similar to that just demonstrated in regard to the super-ego, between the form in which guilt finds expression and the developmental stage of the idea of God. For I imagine that the degree of anthropomorphism attaching to the idea of the deity—from almost physical conception to complete divorce from matter and abstraction into an idea—could somehow be co-ordinated with the three forms of expression in which we encounter the religious experience, i.e. dread, sinfulness, and the sense of guilt. One need only recall the relation, based purely upon fear, which obtained in classical antiquity between men and their completely anthropomorphoid deities, or think of the close relation between sinfulness and anxiety brought to light in Kierkegaard's investigations. Sins, furthermore, were originally infringements of materially conceived taboos, and expiations were for that reason purifications, so that the concept of a mental sin and its atonement by prayer represents an enormous advance; finally we may recall the purely abstract idea of God put forward by many philosophers. If one keeps all this in mind, one will hardly dismiss the possibility of such a correlation out of hand. For complete, or even partial proofs, I have, however, neither the time nor the necessary qualifications.

One thing more I should, however, like to stress: that, according to statements made by psychologists of religion, the gods were orginally demons, who inspired dread and horror in human beings—as Volz, for instance, has convincingly demonstrated in the case of Jahve ("The Demonic in Jahve"). But even the converse may be claimed to be true: that to every dread belongs some demon. This idea leads us directly to a consideration of the relation between the ego and the super-ego—a relation which clearly confronts us in the two above-mentioned cases. One can, after all, hardly overlook the anxiety which characterises them both.

And this is hardly surprising. Just as during the infancy of mankind it was the aggression attributed to the deity which turned the latter into a demon, so the infantile ego experiences its budding super-ego, the introjected parents, in an aggressive and terrifying form. This account gains in plausibility by the fact that demons are regarded as the returning souls of the dead ancestors.

Now psychology claims that it is the child's own aggression—a reaction against the instinctual renunciation enforced by its upbringing—which, its outlets being blocked, flows into the super-ego and makes the latter appear so threatening to the ego. The analogous happening, the projection of one's own hostility against them, upon the dead, who are thereby transformed into demons, can certainly serve to support the psychoanalytical theory of the development of the super-ego.

What does the ego dread from the super-ego? We know that the contents of the dread change in accordance with the stage of ego-development. But all these special contents possess one common denominator: the threatening danger of a loss of love. For the germ of the super-ego is found in the relation of the child to its bodily parents; the withdrawal of love would here mean annihilation. This imperative desire for love remains the basic trait of the relation between ego and super-ego, up to the latter's most highly developed and entirely spiritualised manifestations. That at this level the desire for love will manifest itself in a correlative rather than in its original form, probably goes without saying.

It is certain that one of the very frequent shapes taken by this dread of loss of love is the dread of loneliness. Especially prevalent among small children, it is also fairly common among older ones, and even among adult neurotics; agoraphobia, too—the fear of open spaces, that inspires a feeling of loneliness—should be classed among the shapes taken by the dread of loss of love. The nature of this dread can also be characterised as the ego's dread of losing contact with, or being deserted by, its protector, the super-ego.

Here is what my female patient told me—streaming with tears—during the session following her confession: "Yesterday evening I felt that I no longer had you with me, I didn't know where you were, I was too bad for you".

Still more clearly was this dread manifested in an episode with my male patient. After an interruption of several days he appeared in my consulting-room on Monday at the usual hour, but without having previously notified me, as agreed. He was therefore not received by me. During the next session this patient—a married man and father of an adolescent girl— said to me: "On Monday I felt as lonely as an orphan".

This feeling of having been deserted or even rejected by one's super-ego explains the severe agitation, the frequently desolate state of mind, to which—all rational motives to the contrary—patients succumb, if the analyst is for some reason forced to interrupt their treatment for even a short period. The analyst should always bear in mind that with such psychopathically disordered patients, and still more in the case of depressive ones, particular care must be taken in this respect.

The way in which neurotics deal with this situation should increase our psychological understanding. Let us recall that the sufferer from phobias clutches at his companions in order to overcome his inhibitions in walking. The male patient referred to above, who had had neither sexual relations nor any other intimate contacts with his wife for many years and completely rejected her, did not hesitate to sleep with her, that day, even though he felt still more estranged from her than usual. He had to feel close to some person, whoever it was. Sent away by me, and therefore rejected by his super-ego, he searched—in accordance with the immaturity of his personality—for a substitute in such love as he was able to obtain at the moment.

Both the sufferer from agoraphobia and my patient attempt to escape from their psychological distress by turning towards another person; by establishing a relation, no matter how impermanent, loose and worthless. Let us, however, remember that the analytic situation contains nothing that would absolutely differentiate it from the way human beings habitually behave towards one another. It is only the analyst's purposive de-personalisation that allows the true nature of the patient's relations to his fellow men to manifest themselves in a clearer, more illustrative form. This confirms the view I have already repeatedly expressed that our relation to other persons is, to a large extent, modelled after the relation between our ego and our super-ego.

For one of the most important of social relations, that of pity, I was able to provide in a separate study what I believe to be convincing proof of this thesis, based on clinical analyses. I stressed there that my empirical research-work had led me to results identical with the speculative conclusions of Nietzsche and Eduard von Hartmann. I shall publish further relevant observations on this subject in the near future.

After all that has been said, we may conceive of countless egos which, not from a free desire for love but out of an anxious tension, hunt after innumerable love-objects which represent the super-ego as they would like it to be, or offer themselves as phantasied super-egos of this kind. That is true, and represents an essential part of the libidinal aspect of society, the part the libido takes in the formation of communities. Here is the mainspring, and at the same time the explanation, of the phenomenon, which even Freud found mysterious, that Eros strives incessantly to gather men into larger units. How right that great metaphysician Schopenhauer was, with his *principium individuationis*, when he says that we see the world through the veil of Maya, and that *individuatio*, variety, is only a semblance, a delusion, the thing in itself being one and identical essence.

If we place the outline given above in a wider framework, we shall obtain an idea of how collectivity can provide a substitute for a lack of harmony with the super-ego through the attempt to substitute a new tie for one that has been lost.

It is no doubt logical to try to replace the collective principle in the individual soul, the super-ego which one believes one has lost, by the real collective.

This brief investitation has led to a rather surprising conclusion, whose importance should not be underestimated, in my opinion. For we suddenly recognise in the sense of guilt—which until now has appeared to us only a source of pain, or at most of masochistic gratification—the carrier of a highly important social function. Its task is the establishment, by the most intensive efforts, of bonds between human beings, cementing those already existing and safeguarding the institutions that serve this purpose.

If it were not so tragic one would have to be ashamed at the slow progress of the human intellect, which was unable to perceive what the prophets of mankind, the great poets, already knew thousands of years ago. The results of the present investigation were clearly expressed by Aeschylus in his "Eumenides". There Orestes, the matricide, is furiously pursued by the demons, the Furies; Pallas Athene saves him from his avengers and, in order to pacify them, raises them up to be "Furies no longer, but holy Eumenides". And so these "children of old Night" become

> "Assigners true to all that be,
> To every house its ill and good,
> To every hour its potency;
> Righteous participants through all,
> Of Gods the most majestical".[1]

But the heavy sacrifice which the individual must make to the community, i.e. the increase in the sense of guilt which was demonstrated by Freud, was no less well known to the poet.

For the Furies become holy and turn into Eumenides for society alone; for the individual, the "children of old Night" remain demons difficult to assuage—the super-ego rendered cruel and tyrannic by one's own repressed aggression—whose duty it is to

> "Seek out all man's guilt".

[1] (tr. Gilbert Murray.)

* * *

The conclusion to be drawn from all this appears to be that the sense of guilt not only represents a consequence of, but also provides the impetus for renewed efforts of Eros in its struggle with the death-instinct, and that Eros is not only able to tame aggression but to put it to use for its own purposes. That is how the victory of Eros, and therewith the continuation of the human species, appears to be safeguarded—though, as already stressed, at the very high price of a continual decline in the chances of individual happiness. ("Here exactly the same laws hold good in the psychic sphere as in that of biology, where the individual is unhesitatingly sacrificed for the sake of the species.")

Are we, then, confronted by a vicious circle, with no way of escape?

I do not really think so. For the cultural oscillations of this age, which we are now witnessing—some anxiously, some fascinatedly—seem to admit at least of the possibility of a solution to this problem. I am not trying to put forward any new revelation; I only want to point briefly to a road which mankind has followed since its earliest days, and which has recently been repeatedly touched upon by psycho-analysts.

I am referring to the problem of work which has become, as perhaps never before, the focal point of the present cultural epoch. This is shown by the stress laid upon the right to work, and also by the categorically demanded, almost forcibly exacted, duty to work, which applies to every individual in the community (and I am not overlooking the fact that the motive is one of the most imperative of all drives, the need for food). As I believe the problem of work to be of the utmost importance for the theme of the present investigation, I should like to devote the remainder of this lecture to it, though without claiming to give it more than superficial treatment. It is a problem which is not only exceedingly complex, from the point of view of the psychology of instincts, but which manifests itself in an immense variety of forms.

We must first of all distinguish between the concept of work and that of occupation. There are many occupations which hardly deserve the name of work; the word "occupation" makes one think of something episodic, something conditioned by a special situation, rather than of something that occupies the personality completely and intensively. Psycho-analysis claims that it is the instinct of mastery or aggression which is active in work; this is plainly so in the case of manual work, but also, though on another level, in intellectual, and partly, in artistic work. The important, though variable, contribution made by the libido we shall leave out of account in the discussion of our particular problem.

Work provides not only the most important, but the sole socially permissible opportunity for the discharge of aggression; it protects one's neighbour, renders repression unnecessary, and thus prevents an increase in the sense of guilt. Here is a small example from my own practice. A young sculptor was in a state of intense dread of the imaginary danger of being castrated by me. His fury was considerable, but its outlet was blocked by anxiety. He then produced a dream: he was cutting Einstein's hair. "Ein Stein" (lit. "a stone")—that is how hard I am. The same day, the young artist, who until then had worked only in clay, began—most significantly—to sculpt a male figure in stone. A day later he told me another dream, which had the same meaning as the first one: he was cutting away one of the statue's edges—i.e. he was castrating me in revenge.

The relation between work and aggression was clearly shown in one of the episodes of the Russian film "The Road to Life", which recently met with such a sensational reception. (The effect which this film produced was, by the way, mainly due—beyond all aesthetic motivations—to the gratification which the fulfilment of a cultural ideal afforded the spectators.) I refer to the episode where the boys, who are eagerly at work in their settlement, suddenly run out of material, because no further supplies have been sent. Without a second thought they begin to demolish the machines and the furnishings of their house.

But work can also provide narcissistic gratification for those engaged in it—whether through the social need for the product, or the appreciation of their achievement; this is especially true where it is a question of shaping something, when the worker is, as it were, confirmed in his omnipotence.

At the same time, however, work seems to possess the character of punishment, an expiation. That would explain Freud's complaint that human beings are not particularly eager to work, except when the work is forced upon them. I received the same impression from one of my cases which, however, has not been nearly far enough analysed to allow convincing conclusions to be drawn from it. But sayings like "In the sweat of thy brow . . ." and the coupling of work and prayer in "ora et labora" all point in the direction of atonement.

Another small, though not decisive indication of the psychic significance of work is furnished by the fact that it is so often accompanied by a song: the ego no longer needs to cringe, it can let itself be heard and is singing the song of its liberation.

*　　*　　*

There is a saying, I don't know by whom, which runs: "The gods turn to pleasure the work of the man they love".

It is full of good sense as it stands. But if we invert it, as we do in the case of even the most apparently logical dreams, we shall discover its hidden meaning:

He who works is loved by the gods, is loved by his super-ego —and has no sense of guilt.

THE PSYCHOLOGY OF PITY *

THE problem of pity has for many centuries been the subject of controversy among the most outstanding thinkers. The controversy has dealt especially with the question—of merely historical interest to a psycho-analyst—whether pity is primarily an egoistic or an altruistic emotion. The supporters of the former theory have reasoned that pity, being an emotion with a strong relation to the ego (of the one who pities) must be "egoistic". The father of this theory is Aristotle. He conceives of pity as displeasure at a threatened evil or pain which might befall oneself or a member of one's family. Among the scholastics and through the age of enlightenment up to modern times this theory has been adopted by many thinkers, e.g. Hobbes, Helvetius, Lessing, Feuerbach, E. v. Hartmann and Nietzsche.

But no less notable thinkers have opposed to this the altruistic theory. They have contended that pity is determined not by the relation to the ego but primarily by relation to the Thou. So pity is considered to originate in love, sympathy, affection, social instincts and the like. Apparently the earliest proponent of this theory was the "philosopher of love", the pre-Socratic Empedocles.

Among the post-scholastics the altruistic theory was argued by Cumberland, who made pity spring from benevolence, the motive of all social life. So Shaftesbury, Hume, Smith, Ferguson, Home, Herbert Spencer and, especially of course, J. J. Rousseau, Moses Mendelssohn, etc. Mendelssohn thought of pity as an emotion which was "nothing but love of an object connected with a concept of a misfortune".

Among the moderns the outstanding representative of the altruistic theory is Schopenhauer, who considered pity to be the only exception to man's boundless, all-pervasive egoism.

Such a brief survey shows the profound interest of the philosophical world in the phenomenon of pity. This is understandable if we realise that pity has been considered a primary means of social cohesion and, by some thinkers, the funda-

* Translated by Gertrud M. Kurth and Paul Goodman. First published in *Imago*, XVI, 1, 1930. First published in English in *Complex*, Vol. I, 2, 1950.

mental element of morals. Another reason for the great
attraction of this problem is the difficulty it offers for psychological explanation. E. v. Hartmann, for instance, thinks of
it as enigmatic; and before him Schopenhauer called it,
"baffling and mysterious, the great mystery of ethics, its arch-
phenomenon and the boundary stone beyond which only
metaphysical speculation would dare to step . . ."

The trouble is that all traditional theories lack secure
support even where they seem to approach the real crux of
the matter; they make use of fundamental concepts which
themselves remain unexplained. In this respect we believe
that an attempt at clarification by means of psycho-analysis
offers better prospects.

*   *   *

Among psycho-analysts it has been only Freud, to the best
of my knowledge, who has interested himself in the phenomenon of pity. He mentions it in only a few casual remarks,
but they are meaningful. Above all, he says that pity originates
in identification with the sufferer, the object of pity. Further,
he hints at an intimate connection with the partial drive of
sadism; however, pity is not taken to be a transformation of
sadism into its opposite, but rather a reaction-formation
against it.

Let us start by discussing the first part of Freud's contention,
the connection between pity and identification. Historically,
this opinion has had numerous outstanding forerunners. But
here again there is a diametrical opposition. On the one hand
Ubaldo Cassina said in 1788, "Pity originates in a momentary
deception of phantasy by which we ourselves take the place
of the sufferer and then imagine ourselves to experience his
pain". But both Rousseau and Schopenhauer, among others,
explain pity by identification in a sense opposite to that of
Cassina. Rousseau says: "Pity transports us out of ourselves
. . . We leave our self in order to enter the other person's self
. . . We suffer in the other one". Schopenhauer contradicts
Cassina even more emphatically: "It is clear that it is the
other one who suffers, not we; we experience suffering in his
person, not in ours . . . we feel his pain as *his* and do not
imagine that it is ours".

Analytically, the difference between the two conceptions

could be defined as follows: Cassina's identification is genuinely introjective and narcissistic, whereas Rousseau's and Schopenhauer's is the type of identification we find in hysteria, where the object remains intact and its existence is emphasised.

Freud's derivation of pity from identification is further corroborated by the close connection between pity and the urge to help. According to Freud, "It is a consequence of identification that aggression against the person with whom one identifies is curtailed, that one spares him and helps him".

I am inclined to find further support of Freud's position in the fact that pity has frequently and by very noteworthy thinkers been considered decidedly irrational. According to the Stoa it is a "disease" and as such "a contraction of the mind contrary to reason". Similarly, for Spinoza it is "evil in itself and useless". Kant, Nietzsche, and Paulsen hold similar positions. I believe that the irrationality indicates an unconscious process underlying the identification.

Let us turn then to an investigation of the content of this identification and attempt to gain deeper insight into the nature of pity.

We believe that the infantile root of pity is the beating phantasy [the phantasy that a child is being beaten and oneself looking on, analysed by Freud in "A Child is Being Beaten", *Coll. Papers*, Vol. II]. This phantasy is almost ubiquitous. Further, it is closely related in time with the development of pity. According to Freud, the phantasy occurs toward the end, or even after the termination of the Oedipus situation; that is, near the beginning of the latency period, at which time there develops in the child, among other reaction-formations, pity. Further, the discomfort with which those who phantasy the beating react to actual mistreatment of a child bears resemblance to the initial discomfort that we experience when confronted with another person's suffering. Above all, both phenomena, pity as well as the beating phantasy, have as their common premise an obvious sadistic component. As the reader may remember, the masochistic beating phantasy has a sadistic preliminary stage; and in pity, the great mercy shown by obsessional neurotics constitutes ample evidence.

There is a striking conformity in content. The phantasy of being beaten by the father develops, by regression to the pre-genital, sadistic-anal phase, from another, genital, phantasy, the desire "to be loved by the father". The phantasy develops through feelings of guilt which, in Freud's words, "can discover no punishment more severe than the reversal of this triumph: 'No, he does not love you, for he is beating you'. Accordingly, it is not only the punishment for the forbidden genital relation, but also the regressive substitute for it". Thus it represents a condensation of the desire both for love and for punishment, and is invested to a high degree with not only erotic but also aggressive meaning.

Psycho-analytic observation leaves no doubt that our unconscious conceives of and evaluates every kind of suffering as a tragic guilt, inevitably punished. It is not by accident, but meaningfully, that we speak of suffering as the "blows of fate", or that we say, "The sufferer has been struck by fate".

Now, however, we suddenly find ourselves in contradiction with an essential part of Freud's interpretation of pity. We have traced pity to the beating phantasy as evidence for his proposition that pity is an identification. But whereas he emphatically states that pity is not a transformation of sadism into its contrary, our investigation has brought us to the opposite conclusion that pity, like the beating phantasy, is nothing but a clear-cut manifestation of masochism.

*   *   *

This ambiguous conclusion will appear less puzzling when I point out that the genesis of pity developed so far refers to only one type of the emotion of pity; there exists another type that originates in a considerably more complicated mechanism. This second type is completely opposite to the first, and the essential element in it is not identification but object-relation.

Let us consider the case described in Freud's "History of an Infantile Neurosis". Freud's patient had been seduced by his sister at the age of three years and four months, an event that altered his character; from his fourth birthday on he suffered from a wolf-phobia in consequence of, and as a defence against, a homosexual wish-dream; half a year later he succumbed to an obsessional neurosis that lasted until he was ten years old. The chief symptoms, "naughtiness" and the phobia, revolved around an intense castration anxiety. The anxiety was consequent on threats and scoldings that the child had encountered from three women who took care of him, whom he sexually "attacked"; and it was reinforced by his observations of his parents' sexual intercourse *a tergo*, that he had made at the age of one and a half years. The anxiety dream that caused the outbreak of the phobia immediately before his fourth birthday was interpreted in its entirety; it not only uncovered the existence of the memory of the parental intercourse, but proved that at that time, at the age of four, the situation had been fully understood.

A striking symptom of the subsequent obsessional neurosis was that the child had to exhale strongly at the sight of cripples, beggars and old, ugly and wretched-looking people. The boy interpreted the compulsion to mean that he did so in order not to become like them. In the analysis the symptom was first traced to a time when the father was ill in a sanatorium; he looked ill and the little boy felt very sorry for him. As the analysis continued, there appeared memories of a much earlier time, of people whom the child had pitied, the sight of whom forced him to exhale; an old day-labourer, probably a deaf mute, of whom it was said that his tongue had been cut out; servants who were either sickly or Jews. "Then suddenly", writes Freud, ". . . the analysis plunged into the prehistoric period and led him to assert that during the coitus in the primal scene he had observed the penis disappear, and he had felt sympathy with his father on that account . . ." In still another context it became clear that he conceived of his father as being castrated and therefore felt pity for him.

The psychological conclusion to be drawn from this case, for our purposes, is above all the imperative tendency to abolish the existent identification, to effect a separation by eliminating the introjected object; in the case of Freud's patient by exhaling it. (In a somewhat similar case of my own, by excreting it through the bowels.) We see pity replacing the former cohesion and acting as it were as a substitute for the identification that has been undone. What happens here could be described in a popular joke: a banker to whom a beggar comes for help, says to his butler, "Throw him out, he's breaking my heart".

We must now discuss in more detail the liquidation of the

identification, in order to understand why and how pity develops in such cases. We wish to point out emphatically that the basic motive is castration anxiety.

The close connection between fear and pity and the motivating significance of fear in the genesis of pity has through the ages been stressed by philosophers. (E.g. among the moderns, Charron, Hobbes, Helvetius and Rousseau.) Aristotle most pertinently discusses this connection in the *Poetics* and more explicitly in the *Rhetoric*, where we read that what rouses pity in us when happening to another is precisely what, happening to us, would fill us with dread. This passage in the *Rhetoric* is the basis of Lessing's interpretation of the Aristotelian concept of catharsis. (*Hamburgische Dramaturgie*.) "This fear . . . that our fate might parallel his . . . is what brings pity to fruition". And further, "Nothing can arouse our pity that would not at the same time arouse our fear". According to Lessing, interpreting Aristotle, "Fear constitutes an indispensable ingredient of pity".

In its essence and function, the castration anxiety is the antagonist of the beating phantasy that underlies identification; it is a force fully opposing it. The castration anxiety is a manifestation of tenacious clinging to the genital stage. Effectually, in the tendency to alienate the sufferer it is demonstrated that the one who pities refuses to participate in the object's regression, and that he decisively rejects both the concomitant feelings of guilt and the punishment. Thus, the temporary regression of libido provoked by the initial identification is reversed by a progression to the genital stage and here definitely fixated.

The meaning of the alienation lies in the restoration of the original contents of the phantasy, in Freud's formula: "No, I do not want my father to beat me as he beats the other child, I want him to love me". Or to transpose this into the nuclear formula of pity: I do not want the dark powers of fate, the mighty super-ego, to chastise my ego, I want love and support.

Let me cite a case of self-pity in corroboration of this conception. There was a patient of mine, an obsessional neurotic whom fate had indeed chastised frequently and heavily. At the peak of his emotional distress, he would stand before a mirror, tenderly caress his own face, and say, "You poor, poor thing".

G

The ego's wish to be loved and treated kindly by the super-ego, roused by the suffering of another, is now projected upon the sufferer. In this way the wish is, as it were, realised: the sufferer is treated as an object and in the same way as the pitier would like his super-ego to treat his ego. In addition, this projection, the substitution of the ego by the Thou, is greatly facilitated by the fact that the tension between ego and super-ego can effect such a far-reaching alienation as to create for the ego a relation of the non-ego, the Thou, to the ego-ideal.

Possibly the inmost core of the ego's desire is the elimination of this tension and a stage of total unity with the super-ego. Perhaps Schopenhauer's metaphysical interpretation of pity is nothing but a disguise of the ego's desire for the restoration of this unity which had been disrupted by the feelings of guilt.

From what has been said so far, we may conclude that the enigmatic phenomenon of pity is nothing but our own conflict resolved according to our desire and projected upon another person. This idea is well expressed by Nietzsche: "Pity is always our own suffering, of which the sufferer himself is free; it is our own as his is his own. It is only our own suffering of which we want to get rid through active pity".

* * *

Our investigation has resulted in two psychologically clearly differentiated types of pity of which the one is an identification pure and simple, the other a real object-cathexis. In the latter, subject and object do not merge; on the contrary—in conformity with the ideas of Rousseau, Schopenhauer, and the phenomenologist Scheler, who sees a "phenomenological ego-distance" as a premise of pity—we find here a clear-cut separation of subject and object, the ego confronted by a well-defined Thou.

A number of thinkers have recognised the existence of two varieties of pity. Charron, for instance, says: "There are two kinds of pity", which he differentiates in their origin either as a secret agreement with, or our own fear of, what happens to the other person. The former, he says, is stupid, feminine, passionate, and originates in weakness; the latter stems from will and energy, is courageous, good, virtuous, and helpful to the distressed. We find a similar distinction in Hegel.

We see that other investigators have ascribed to pity almost polar opposite qualifications. E. v. Hartmann calls it an entirely passive reaction and the one moral principle of an entirely passive nature. Pity is characterised as a "feminine quality" in antiquity, e.g. by Plato, the Stoics, Seneca; and among later thinkers by such as Spinoza, Mandeville, Hume and Montaigne. This view conceives of pity as a melting and resolving agent that paralyses, and thus constitutes an obstacle to active help; briefly it is a quietive.

However, we find a sharply opposed view represented as numerously and as energetically. Activity and the urge to help are considered inherent in pity, which thus has to be called a motive. This is the attitude of Fichte (in a polemical reference to Kant) and before him of Platner, and centuries earlier of Aquinas.

We are inclined to accept these contradictory views as significant evidence of the correctness of our own interpretation. The so-called feminine type of pity doubtless is the one that we discussed first as the pity of identification, whereas the other, the active type, corresponds to the type of pity that originates as a reaction-formation. We know that the beating phantasy, which is the basis of the identification, is at the same time a basic manifestation of feminine masochism. We know also that reactive pity develops through the threat to narcissistic masculinity, and owes its origin to the tenacious defence of this masculinity.

Therefore it seems justified to differentiate the two types as feminine and masculine pity. We found in our investigation that, in feminine pity, the masochistic ego in its need for punishment finds instinctual gratification to such a degree that we may consider this type of pity a sexual gratification. We may appropriately quote Nietzsche: "Schopenhauer's pity is perversion proper". Therefore the element of hedonism, of obvious pleasure, which has been emphasised by so many authors as a characteristic of pity has to be restricted to this feminine type, stemming from the pleasure in and search of suffering. In the descriptions of pity in the *Confessions* of St. Augustine, in the writings of Shaftesbury, Rousseau, Moses Mendelssohn, and Herbert Spencer, we cannot overlook the glaringly masochistic nature of pleasure in suffering.

It is this feminine type of pity that is referred to in Nietzsche's supremely intuitive words: "Look how cutely the bitch voluptuousness begs for a piece of spirit if a piece of meat is refused her. You love drama and all that breaks your heart? But I am suspicious of your bitch. Your eyes are cruel and you eye the sufferer lasciviously. Has not your voluptuousness donned a disguise, and calls itself pity?"

None of this applies to masculine pity. In masculine pity the ego does not strive for, does not lust in, suffering, but it rejects pain and is hostile to it. Here and only here the urge to help is inherent in, and peculiar to, the ego; through active help, pain must be resolved or even abolished. The ego wants to be free of feelings of guilt, free of desire for punishment. It defends itself strongly and variously against this instinctual demand of the id, especially by progression and object-cathexis with narcissistic, desexualised libido aiming at active help.

Finally, let us remember that pity has been exalted by numerous philosophers of ethics to be a paramount principle of morals. Our investigation and its result serve as convincing illustration of Freud's differentiation between moral masochism and genuine morals, the differentiation that aims at separating moral masochism as a sexualisation of morals from genuine morals originating in desexualisation. We may understand also what Freud considered to be pity, and accordingly morals. It is the masculine active type of pity, the genesis of which we have uncovered, and that Nietzsche anticipated when he said of "those who have pity":

"I offer myself up to my love, and I offer up my fellow men as I do myself; thus speak all creative men".

ON THE PSYCHOLOGY OF COMEDY*

WE are indebted to psycho-analysis for much valuable insight into the psychology of tragedy. Not only has psycho-analysis made us recognise that the "tragic guilt" of the hero, postulated by aesthetics, actually stems from the repressed Oedipus-wishes of the dramatist but it has also drawn our attention to the interrelation of dramatist and audience; that is, to the fact of a common guilt as the decisive psychological factor which, on the one hand, enables the dramatist to create his work and, on the other, produces the Aristotelian catharsis, or "purging of the passions". Freud,[1] in particular, established the psychological traces of the primal crime in classical tragedy and following in his tracks, Winterstein[2] has recently subjected the origins of tragedy to intensive study and radically clarified them.

By contrast, how little has psycho-analysis bothered about comedy! So far it has hardly attracted any interest worth mentioning: at most it was granted a modest domicile in that basement of research, the footnote, there to be dealt with in a cursory manner.

And yet it seems to me that comedy well deserves serious and detailed investigation, and not only because it contains the problem of the comic, which is admittedly one of the most difficult and complicated in psychology; a problem, in fact, which even Freud[3] approached "not without some trepidation", although he was able later to clarify it greatly. As this rough outline will help to show, the psycho-analytical investigation of comedy can bring to light much that may claim our fullest interest.

My analysis of several classical comedies led to the surprising result that I found them characterised by a mechanism of inversion: *the feeling of guilt which, in tragedy, rests upon the son, appears in comedy displaced on the father; it is the father who is guilty.*

* Translated by I. Jarosy.   First published in *Imago*, XII, 2/3, 1926.
[1] Freud, *Totem and Taboo*. Routledge & Kegan Paul.
[2] Alfred Winterstein: *Der Ursprung der Tragödie*. Imago Bücher VIII.
[3] Freud: *Wit and its Relation to the Unconscious*. Routledge & Kegan Paul.

This fact was probably already noticed by Diderot; at the same time it seems to have elicited an effective disagreement on his part, for in his *Discours sur la poésie dramatique* he writes: "It seems to me that Terence succumbed, on one occasion, to this fault. His 'Heautontimorumenos' ('The Self-Tormentor'), is a father who grieves over the violent decision to which he has driven his son by excessive strictness; he therefore punishes himself by miserably depriving himself of food and clothing, shunning all company, dismissing his servants and tilling the soil with his own hands. One may justly remark that such a father does not exist. The largest town would hardly be able to furnish an example of such strange sorrow in a hundred years".

We shall attempt to substantiate our thesis, though only in outline, with the help of other examples. The jumbling together of works belonging to very different cultures, and to epochs which are frequently millennia apart, may be explained by the fact that we are guided by, and seek to establish, one particular point of view and so, for the time being, consciously neglect all others.

The *Merchant of Venice*, until fairly recently, was regarded by Shakespearean scholars as one of the most debatable works of the poet—not only as concerns its basic theme, but as regards its dramatic genre. On the basis of our theory, which postulates that, in comedy, the father-figure must be represented as weighed down by guilt, we must regard this work as comedy, for the father's guilt is almost expressly indicated. Antonio, who is so dangerously threatened by Shylock, is certainly a father-figure. That this psycho-analytical assumption is well-founded, is shown by the fact that he derives from the Messer Ansaldo of the text which Shakespeare used as his source (Fiorentino's *Pecorone*); that Messer Ansaldo who appears as a "fatherly friend" in the story is a man full of love, of infinite patience and ready to make great sacrifices for his adopted son. The poet, however, allows Antonio to become "guilty" in the first act of the play:

> Therefore go forth ;
> Try what my credit can in Venice do :
> That shall be rack'd, even to the uttermost,"

and to give Shylock his bond.

It need hardly occasion surprise if we here regard a money-debt as a mere substitute for moral guilt. The extremely close connection between the two, which, so far as I know, Müller-Braunschweig[1] first demonstrated among psycho-analysts, Nietzsche had already emphasised in his *Genealogy of Morals*.[2] The intimate connection between these two groups of ideas, as well as their substitutive relation, is unquestionable. The very ancient provision of monetary fines in criminal law, and the fact that not only German, but also many other languages (among them French and Polish) use the same word to denote both a material debt and moral guilt, provides eloquent testimony to the truth of this view. And, last but not least, the substitution of the idea of a money debt for that of moral guilt is hardly surprising to the psycho-analyst, who frequently observes this substitutive relation in the dreams and resistances of his patients.

The same expression of this motif is also found in that finest of German comedies, Lessing's *Minna von Barnhelm*.

The complications of the plot, it will be recalled, are based on events which occur before the play opens: Major von Tellheim, entrusted to collect a levy from a hostile Diet, in order to avoid resorting to harsh measures, himself advances the money to the King against a note of credit issued by the said Diet. But when he requires its repayment once peace is concluded, his demand is rejected and, suspected of accepting enemy bribes, he is compelled to submit to a judicial enquiry. This he regards not only as a heavy blow to his honour, but as an insurmountable obstacle to his marriage with Minna, who loves him and whom he loves.

Again we can only reduce this coherent and richly elaborated story to the bald formula that it is the father (the King) who is guilty. This is comfirmed not only by the fact that the ensuing entanglements are resolved by the King's personal intervention and payment of his debt, but even the minor scenes of the comedy, as those in which the valet Just and Werner appear, are permeated with Tellheim's resistance: "I will not be your debtor". In spite of excellent rationalisations, one can hardly regard this constant resistance as indicating

[1] Dr. Karl Müller-Braunschweig: *Psychoanalytische Gesichtspunkte zur Psychogenese der Moral, insbesondere des moralischen Aktes.* Imago VII, 1921.
[2] Chapter 4: ". . . that the cardinal moral idea of 'guilt' originates from the very material idea of 'debt'."

anything but the son's complete rejection of all guilt, the more completely and demonstratively to stress the father's.

With this interpretation we have, however, penetrated straight to the root of that guilt which is levelled against the father: the King stands in the way of Tellheim's love and marriage!

That this, in fact, is the play's latent basic trend is shown by the following circumstance, as I have already pointed out in my study of *Macbeth*;[1] namely, that in dramatic works the basic motif is presented twice; in a way that is nearer consciousness, and then in a remoter manner; i.e. in a fairly direct as well as a veiled form. This phenomenon can be observed with such regularity that even the converse—every motif that occurs twice in a drama is its basic theme—now seems to me, after considerable re-examination, entirely valid.

Now *Minna von Barnhelm* does actually contain such a second, considerably less veiled hint of the father as obstacle between the lovers. It is the passage where, somewhat mysteriously, Minna informs the obdurate Tellheim that she is persecuted by her uncle and guardian Count Bruchsall, who has disinherited her for not wishing to accept a husband of his choosing. Hardly has the Count made Tellheim's acquaintance however, when the latter addresses him as "my father" and the Count, in turn, calls him "son".

The reproach "Father—disturber of love", which establishes the father's guilt, is the latent content of most comedies of the kind discussed.

This motif is brought out extremely clearly in Molière's *L'Avare*, where neither the father-son relationship nor their sexual rivalry is in any way masked. Here Harpagon steps between his son and the latter's bride, because he himself desires to marry her.

But the same motif also appears in *Tartuffe*, if one regards the hypocrite as a mere derivative of the father Orgon who, thereby, becomes the son's rival for the mother's affections.

In Terence's *Phormio*—one of the finest of classical comedies —the father, who is opposed to the love-choice of his son (Phaedria), is similarly made amenable to the son's will by the unmasking of his sexual misbehaviour. The play

---

[1] Cf.: "The Riddle of Shakespeare's *Macbeth*" and "The Problem of the Duplicated Expression of Psychic Themes..'

significantly closes with the father's words: "But where is Phaedria, who must be our judge?"[1]

The following comedies betray, in their manifest content, nothing of those "family" relationships which, in the plays just discussed, stood out so clearly; their basic psychological situation is, nevertheless, the same.

In Plautus's justly famed *Miles Gloriosus* for instance, the bombastic, vain fool, Pyrgopolinikes, is placed in a double relationship: as father towards the young Athenian Pleusikles, whose sweetheart he carries off, and as son towards the jovial Ephesian Periplekomenos, whose supposed wife, in the intrigues of the plot, he attempts to seduce away from him.

In conclusion we may cite Kleist's *Der zerbrochene Krug*, which is no less illustrative of our thesis. Its theme is an investigation into whether the father (Judge Adam) or the son (Ruprecht) is responsible for a nocturnal burglary, and the "breaking of Eve's pitcher!"

In complete accordance with our thesis, the verdict "guilty" is passed on the father.

* * *

The significance of these conclusions will be elucidated by a passage from Bergson's *Laughter*[2] He believes that the essence of the comic consists in the mechanisation of life, an effect which can be obtained by the process of *inversion* as well as by two other processes, *repetition* and *reciprocal interference of series*. He states: "Picture to yourself certain characters in a certain situation; if you reverse the situation and invert the rôles, you obtain a comic scene . . . There is no necessity, however, for both the identical scenes to be played before us. We may be shown only one, provided the other is really in our minds . . . The plot of the villain who is the victim of his own villainy, or the cheat cheated, forms the stock-in-trade of a good many plays. We find this even in primitive farce . . . In modern literature we meet with hundreds of variations on the theme of the robber robbed. In every case the root idea involves an inversion of rôles, and a situation which recoils on the head of its author".

---

[1] *The Plays of Terence*, Trans. William Ritchie, London, 1927.
[2] Henri Bergson: *Laughter. An Essay on the Meaning of the Comic.* Trans. C. Brereton and F. Rothwell. Macmillan & Co., London, 1911. pp. 94-96.

"Here we apparently find the confirmation of a law, some illustrations of which we have already pointed out. When a comic scene has been reproduced a number of times, it reaches the stage of being a classical type or model. It becomes amusing in itself, quite apart from the causes which render it amusing. Henceforth, new scenes, which are not comic *de jure*, may become amusing *de facto*, on account of their partial resemblance to this model. They call up in our mind a more or less confused image which we know to be comical. They range themselves in a category representing an officially recognised type of the comic. The scene of the 'robber robbed' belongs to this class. It casts over a host of other scenes a reflection of the comic element it contains. In the end it renders comic any mishàp that befalls one through one's own fault, no matter what the fault or mishap may be—nay, an allusion to this mishap, a single word that recalls it, is sufficient".

It is probably unnecessary to stress that we claim this central significance of the "model scene" for the element we have singled out.

*　　*　　*

In this passage a penetrating philosopher has approached remarkably near our own position and has even increased the area within which we assumed the factor we discovered in comedy, and its allied manifestations, to hold valid. As regards the riddle which comedy presents, little however has been gained towards solving it.

It can be taken for granted that the writer of comedies possesses the same creative impulses, and is subject to the same psychological laws, as those long known to be valid— especially through the excellent work of Sachs[1]—for the writer of tragedies; this applies especially to the imperative urge to effect the discharge of his repressed complexes, which the dramatist is able to satisfy by, as it were, distributing his feeling of guilt among the many.

On the other hand, the analyses of the comedies cited, summary though these be, leaves little doubt that the material employed is identical with that employed by the writer of tragedies: in both cases the Oedipus situation is involved.

[1] Hanns Sachs: *Gemeinsame Tagträume.* Imago Bücher, V.

It may be due to this identity that, in so many plays, their nature remains unclear long after the action begins to unfold, so that for a time the final result may equally be comedy as tragedy: it is only a delayed swift turning-point which finally decides us as to its genre.

But how does it happen that from such identical psychological pre-suppositions, such completely, even diametrically opposite effects, result; that from a similar foundation, tragic guilt and expiation arise in one case, and effervescent high spirits in the other?

We believe that we possess the key to this riddle in the factor we have isolated in our analyses: namely, displaced guilt.

In the last resort, this infantile phantasy of the father as the disturber of love is nothing but a projection of the son's own guilty wish to disturb the love of the parents. *By displacing this phantasy on the father, by endowing him with this specifically filial attitude, it becomes clear that the father is divested of his paternal attributes, and thus is removed as a father and degraded into a son.*

This displacement proceeds from the same psychological motives as the "unmasking" generally employed in so many comedies, of which we cited *Tartuffe*, *Der zerbrochene Krug*, and *Phormio*; which motives are summed up by Freud in the formula "You, too, are only a human being like myself". Like the unmasking, this phantasy is employed in comedy in order to degrade the father, to degrade him to a son, or to the level ordinarily appropriate to the son. This turning-the-father-into-a-son, this inverted world, *"le monde renversé"*, as Bergson puts it, represents the very core of his *"inversion"*, the innermost purpose of the displacement of guilt.

Only the fact that the father is given the status of a mere son explains why, in comedy (from classical comedy to the contemporary bedroom farce), it is generally the father who is beaten in the trial of strength. For the same reason, returning to our examples, Harpagon must lose the game and, thereby, the love-object, and the King in *Minna von Barnhelm* must not only clear obstacles away, but even far exceed the necessary meed of reparation.

Only this reduction of the father to a son can explain how writers of comedies can unleash so wide a range of aggression (scorn, derision, etc.) against the father, and allow, for instance, Antonio in the *Merchant of Venice*, and even more obviously Bramabras, taken by surprise in his love-suit, to stand in such open danger of being castrated. Only by such a reduction can we understand the call to the pardoned man: "'Twill soon be finished with your fatherhood!"

This doing away with the father and his dissolution in the son, this withdrawal of the super-ego and its merging in the ego, are all in complete psychological conformity with the phenomena of mania.

In each case we find the ego, which has liberated itself from the tyrant, uninhibitedly venting its humour, wit, and every sort of comic manifestation in a very ecstasy of freedom.

We shall resist the temptation to discuss the psychological relation, now very apparent, between tragedy and melancholic depression—a connection already hinted at in the words of the Byzantine Suidas: "ἤ χρὴ τραγῳδεῖν πάντας ἤ μελαγχολᾶν,"[1] and shall limit ourselves to the statement that comedy represents an aesthetic correlate of mania.

[1] I am indebted to Winterstein for drawing my attention to this passage.

THE RIDDLE OF SHAKESPEARE'S MACBETH*

THE problem of this paper is suggested in a remark of the distinguished Shakespearean scholar, Gervinus. In one of his studies, he urges that a bridge be thrown between Shakespeare's inner life and his poetry "with a few speaking touches, and a connection pointed out, which may show *that with Shakespeare*, as with every rich poetic nature, *no outer routine and poetic propriety, but inner experiences and emotions of the mind were the deep springs of his poetry*,—then for the first time we should have reached a point which would bring us near the poet; we should gain a complete idea of his personal existence, and obtain a full picture, a living view of his mental stature".[1]

Perhaps interpretations of *Macbeth* differ so widely because few scholars have adopted this plan, which seems to be the only correct one. Ulrici, for instance, while underestimating the ambition motif, interprets the drama as based on the relation between the external world and man's willpower and energy.[2] Other authors conceive the plot of the tragedy and the character development of its heroes as arising, for the most part, from the conflict between ambition and conscience. From none of these comments could we infer any of Shakespeare's "*inner experiences*".

This need not imply that the poet's emotional keyboard lacked ambition. On the contrary, a thorough analysis should also disclose this psychic element, which, by the way, is so obviously stressed by the words of Macbeth and his Lady. But we do deny that ambition has the central position generally assumed for it in the psychological structure of the plot. When he wrote *Macbeth*, Shakespeare was already at the peak of his successes. It seems unlikely, therefore, that his ambition should have had the tremendously high tension one would expect from the powerful impact of the play. To be sure, Macbeth's

---

* First published in English in *The Psychoanalytic Review*, Vol. XXX, No. 4, 1943.

[1] Georg Gottfried Gervinus, *Shakespeare Commentaries* (translated by F. E. Bunnètt), p. 22. New York: Scribner, Welford & Armstrong, 1875.

[2] Herman Ulrici, *Shakespeare's Dramatic Art* . . . (translated by L. D. Schmitz), Vol. 1, pp. 460-461. London: George Bell & Sons, 1876.

ambition might be sufficient reason for the murder of Duncan, and even for the persecution of Macduff (although the two deeds are only indirectly connected with each other). But it is wholly inadequate to explain the murder of Banquo, or to elucidate a number of important side issues and countless enigmatic details of the drama.

Small wonder, therefore, that Bodenstedt, Gervinus, Ulrici, Brandes, and others have reached such contradictory opinions concerning the heroes—although all of them consider ambition the motive causing the conflicts. Bodenstedt's admission that "Macbeth and his Lady are among those characters on whose interpretation scholars have not been able to agree",[1] exposes the utter inadequacy, if not incorrectness, of the stress on ambition.

A reconsideration of the problem of *Macbeth*, though it has been discussed so much already, would therefore seem perfectly justified. The reader will have to decide whether or not the author has obeyed Gervinus's admonition to avoid producing a poem of the historian instead of a history of the poet.

I

As with most of Shakespeare's plays, the date of the origin of *Macbeth* has not been established exactly. But we do know that it could not have been written before 1604, nor after 1610.[2] The later date is fixed by the first known performance of the tragedy. The earlier date, however, is derived from an important historical event: in 1604, the Scottish King, James, was crowned King of Great Britain and Ireland; the play contains an unmistakable allusion to this event.[3]

---

[1] Friedrich Bodenstedt, *Shakespeare's Frauencharaktere*, p. 303. Berlin: A. Hofmann & Co., 1874.

[2] Recent investigations, however, have restricted this period to three years, 1604, 1605 and 1606.

[3] . . . and some I see
That twofold balls and treble scepters carry.
(IV, i, 120-121.) (Kittredge edition.)

There are still other indications that the play was composed with the King in mind. For instance, the healing power of Edward the Confessor is mentioned. As Edward himself had prophesied, this power was supposedly passed on to his descendants, including, of course, King James. The allusion is unanimously characterised by scholars as "dragged in by the hair", and is definitely out of place.

Shakespeare, moreover, elaborated the witch motif in very great detail, devoting whole scenes to a factor which is made very little of in his source (Holinshed's *Chronicle*). This procedure is obviously connected with James's interest in witchery, a preoccupation which was exceptional even in a time submerged in the belief in witchcraft. James had only recently composed a *Demonology*, and had personally interrogated an alleged witch.

The most striking evidence of the poet's concern with the King is his choice of subject. At this time, all England was familiar with the Macbeth legend. In 1605, when the King had visited Oxford, students had greeted him with a rhapsody containing elements of the legend. It seemed to be particularly well suited as an ovation for the King. Having come to Scotland and its throne only by way of wedlock, the Stuarts were particularly eager to deny their Gallic origin, and to affirm their "Scottish" ancestry by referring it to Banquo and Fleance, although both are now considered purely legendary.

The dramatist's intention to pay homage to his King is further revealed by another modification of the original material. As already noted, Shakespeare took the plot of his play from Raphael Holinshed's *Chronicle of Scottish History*. There, Banquo is depicted as an accomplice to the murder of the King, while Shakespeare shows him to be completely outside it. He did this—according to general opinion—precisely because it would have been impossible to present the King's ancestor as a bloody assassin (all the more so since the play was probably performed in James's presence). In the face of this data, it is difficult to avoid the conclusion that *Macbeth* really represented an apotheosis of James upon his accession to the throne.

Our first problem, therefore, is why the dramatist offered this homage: from what inner urge did it arise?

This question may conceal a much deeper problem than

appears at first. In any case, we are fully justified in putting it, since such flattery is altogether incompatible with Shakespeare's usual habits. He had, on the contrary, been extremely chary of praise for James's predecessor, the great Elizabeth. Yet, in the course of more than ten years, she had frequently attended performances of his plays; Shakespeare had himself repeatedly appeared before her as an actor; and the playwright had achieved acknowledgment and wealth under her reign— even receiving a grant of arms. Still, as Brandes points out, "Shakespeare was the only poet of the period who absolutely refused to comply with this demand" of the Queen for "incessant homage".[1]

For this very reason we consider most unsatisfactory the analysis which some authors give of Shakespeare's attitude toward James. Wagner[2] and W. A. Schegel, for example, believe that in writing this play the dramatist had intended "to please the King particularly". And Brandes thinks that "if the unobtrusive, mildly flattering allusions to James . . . [had been] in the slightest degree deferential, [they] would have been gratuitously and indefensibly churlish, in view of the favour which James had made haste to extend to Shakespeare's company".[3]

Opposing all these explanations, stands the dramatist's entirely different behaviour toward Queen Elizabeth. Just why the poet was so anxious to ingratiate himself with the new king, or even to avoid any appearance of a demonstration against him, is still not clear when we recall that the Queen, who had done so much for him, had received no such consideration.

This contrast between James and Elizabeth, and its intimate relation to the plot of the tragedy, has already been emphasised by Freud in his essay on *Macbeth*.[4] Despite its cursoriness, this essay is of prime importance; careful study of it was indispensable for the present paper. Not only does it throw light on the particular question raised here, but it also clears the way for a general understanding of the play.

---

[1] Georg Brandes, *William Shakespeare* . . . (translated by William Archer, Mary Morison and Diana White), p. 41. London: William Heinemann, 1905.
[2] Wilhelm Wagner, *Macbeth von William Shakespeare*. Leipzig: Teubner, 1872.
[3] Brandes, *op. cit.*, p. 418.
[4] Sigmund Freud, "Some Character Types Met with in Psycho-analytic Work" (1915). *Collected Papers*, Vol. IV., pp. 318-344. London: The Hogarth Press, 1924-25.

According to Freud, the tragedy is basically concerned with the contrast between sterility and fecundity. This follows from the fact that the weird sisters assure Macbeth "that he shall indeed be king, but to Banquo they promise that *his* children shall obtain possession of the crown".[1] In Freud's opinion, the plot is developed in accordance with this prophecy.

Furthermore, Freud points out that the same contrast between sterility and fecundity is illustrated by the historical succession to the English throne which took place, as it were, before the very eyes of the dramatist, shortly before the play was written.

"The 'virginal Elizabeth', of whom it was rumoured that she had never been capable of childbearing and who had once described herself as 'a barren stock', in an anguished outcry at the news of James's birth, was obliged by this very childlessness of hers to let the Scottish king become her successor. And he was the son of that Mary Stuart whose execution she, though reluctantly, had decreed, and who, despite the clouding of their relations by political concerns, was yet of her blood and might be called her guest".[2]

In order to make more obvious this parallel to the historical situation which he discovered, Freud refers to Macbeth's words:

> Upon my head they plac'd a fruitless crown
> And put a barren sceptre in my gripe,
> Thence to be wrench'd with an unlineal hand,
> *No son of mine succeeding.* (III, i, 61-64).[3]

These words repeat Elizabeth's outcry almost literally.

* * *

The mythological content of the Scottish legend of Macbeth, which is the foundation of the play, seems also to corroborate Freud's conception of the basic motif. Although he dealt with the subject only in passing, he probably came very close to the psychological problem concealed in it. Even a superficial examination of the legend reveals the contrast between fertility and its opposite as the core.

---

[1] *Ibid.*, p. 329.   [2] *Ibid.*, p. 328.
[3] Except when within other quotations, the text of *Macbeth* is quoted from the edition of George Lyman Kittredge. Boston: Ginn & Company, 1939. (Italics have been added in the last line of the passage quoted above.)

H

According to Simrock's comments,[1] there can be hardly any doubt that the legend symbolises the processes of vegetation, that it is in reality a vegetation-myth. There are actually considerable analogies with the legend of the Hessian King Grunewald as well as with that of the Giant King of Saxo Grammaticus (VII, 132). From these parallels, Simrock concludes that Macbeth, like these legendary characters, is a hibernal giant, whose reign comes to an end when the May festival begins and the green wood comes marching.

What Simrock says about the meaning of the second prophecy (". . . none of woman born/Shall harm Macbeth", IV, i, 80-81), however, is less specific. He sees in Macduff an analogy to mythical characters like Rogdai, Rusten, Woelsung, and others, men or demigods, who have supposedly been "ripped" from their mothers' wombs, in token of their strength and power.

This explanation of the second prophecy need not conflict with that of the Birnam woods prophecy, if we recall Simrock's hint that being "ripped from one's mother's womb" is a sign of the demigod. It would be an expression of deep reverence for the fructifying power of nature that Spring—in contrast to Winter, which is personified as purely human—be endowed with divine attributes and thus implicitly represented as victorious.

Since, however, we expect to reach a thorough explanation of this special problem in the course of our investigation, let us conclude these preliminary remarks by merely repeating that the myth of *Macbeth* somehow contains the contrast between sterility and generative power.

*   *   *

Although this theme recurs in so many aspects of the drama, it is inadequate as a basic motif—as the readers of Freud's essay will remember. It does not explain in what sense the problem of fertility or its opposite may have been meant by Shakespeare; it cannot be related to the further development of the drama; above all, it cannot elucidate the crucial psychological problem.

[1] Karl Simrock, *Die Quellen des Shakespeare . . .*, pp. 255-260. Bonn: Marcus, 1872.

In the first place, this conception of the basic problem of the tragedy is remarkably weak historically. Its relation to the external historical situation, which Freud revealed in so promising a way, is only slight. It cannot establish any profound and revealing parallel.

On the other hand, Freud attempts to explain the transformation of Macbeth into a raving murderer and of his Lady into a distracted penitent by the couple's childlessness. They are understood to have conceived their disappointed hopes of children as a punishment for their crimes. This interpretation, however, failed—as will be remembered—because Shakespeare, by reducing to eight days the ten-year period which Holinshed had described between the murder of Duncan and the subsequent crimes of Macbeth (particularly the murder of Banquo), had left "no time for a long-drawn disappointment of their hopes of offspring to enervate the woman and drive the man to an insane defiance".[1] Freud is forced to conclude:

> What, however, these motives can have been which in so short a space of time could turn the hesitating, ambitious man into an unbridled tyrant, and his steely-hearted instigator into a sick woman gnawed by remorse, it is, in my view, impossible to divine. I think we must renounce the hope of penetrating the triple obscurity of the bad preservation of the text, the unknown intention of the dramatist, and the hidden purport of the legend.[2]

We shall therefore attempt to gain a deeper understanding of the problems discussed by a more detailed psychological analysis of the characters of the tragedy, of their grouping, and of their interrelations.

II

The psychological structure of the tragedy, which seems so bewildering at first, becomes clearer if we conceive the king as a father-symbol—a conception revealed and confirmed again and again by psycho-analysis.

[1] Freud, *op. cit.*, p. 331.   [2] *Ibid.*

We should then conclude that Macbeth's psychic function is twofold. First, like Banquo and Macduff, he is son to the father (King), Duncan. Secondly, however, when he himself has become King, he is father to Banquo and Macduff: these two come to be seen as his sons, just as they are originally conceived as Duncan's sons. Macbeth's first phase thus concerns the relationship of son to father; his second phase involves the opposite relationship, that of father to son.

In order to facilitate orientation, let us first investigate the son-father relationship. Needless to say, the murder of Duncan cannot be classified, analytically, as other than parricide.[1]

As a son, Macbeth is therefore parricidal, or—to put it less strongly—hostile, rebellious; Hecate calls him the "wayward son". (III, v, 11.)

The motive of the parricide, the reason for the hostility against the father, is personified in Lady Macbeth. She is the "demon-woman", who creates the abyss between father and son. We can prove the correctness of this interpretation by a

---

[1] There are lines of the text which corroborate the nature of Duncan's murder as we conceive it. Because of the basic importance of this conception for the content of the tragedy as we intend to develop it here, and because such psycho-analytic statements still meet with incredulity in many places, we quote Lennox's short speech in which parricide is mentioned repeatedly, though with ironic intent:

> *Who cannot want the thought* how monstrous
> It was for Malcolm and for Donalbain
> To kill their gracious father?   (III, vi, 8-10.)

This quotation actually contains two negations. One is in "want", which is of rather indefinite nature, and means basically: not-to-have, to miss, to feel the lack of; this passage should therefore read: "Who can want . . ."

Curiously enough, a second negation, "not", is appended to "want"—and this double negation leads to the affirmation and approval of the parricide.

Naturally, commentators have noticed the contradiction in this significant passage. I quote *Darmesteter* (*Macbeth*, Édition classique par James Darmesteter, Paris: 1881, Librairie Delagrave): "La negation est de trop dans *cannot* et ferais dire la phrase tout le contraire de ce qu'elle signifie—si le sens n'était trop claire de lui-même". (*The negation in "cannot" is superfluous and would make the phrase mean the opposite of what it should*—if the sense in itself were not perfectly clear.)

This speech of Lennox is very well known among the commentators on account of its ironic content. *Darmesteter* calls it "un modèle d' ironie voilée" (a model of veiled irony); the remark refers particularly to Lennox's words when he says Banquo was killed because he went out late. Actually, however, the irony here does not lie in this ambiguity of motivation, but rather in the fact that the poet is telling us the truth about Macbeth's crime—doing so, however, in such a way that we do not notice it. By proposing the ridiculous motive of Banquo's going out late, the poet creates an atmosphere of absolute incredibility, into which the information about the real fact is thrown. The essential irony is that the audience is duped by receiving the truth in such a way as to be further than ever from recognising it.

number of instances. To begin with, Lady Macbeth is accomplice only to the crime Macbeth commits as son, i.e. before he had become King (father). From the moment he obtains the throne, she has no part at all in his criminal deeds: apparently she is not privy to his murderous plans against either Banquo or Macduff.

Shakespearean scholars seem scarcely to have been startled by this fact. Supported by psycho-analytic insight, however, we gain the most important corroboration of our conception of Lady Macbeth from the following dialogue. (In the great seventh scene of the first act, in which she finally induces the still reluctant Macbeth to murder, the Lady refers to the past):

> What beast was't then
> That made you break this enterprise to me?
> . . . Nor time nor place
> Did then adhere, and yet you would make both. (I, vii, 47-48, 51-52.)

Since the discussion referred to in these words is not in the text as we have it, Brandes and others conclude that much has been omitted from that text. We, however, think that these lines nicely illustrate Darmesteter's judicious words: "Dans nombre de cas où le texte semble corrompu, il est probable qu'il n'est qu'obscur et que nous devons accuser notre maladresse de commentateur plutôt que l'incurie des premiers éditeurs". (in a number of places where the text seems to be corrupted, it is probably only obscure, and *we should rather hold our ineptitude as commentators responsible than the inaccuracy of the first publishers*.)[1] For the words quoted point to abysmal psychic depths. Lady Macbeth, the "demon-woman", refers Macbeth to the past—indeed, "woman", in the guise of the three witches, had already stepped between him and the father.

A good deal has been written and argued about the witches in *Macbeth;* the most select minds of Germany, such as Goethe, Schiller, Grillparzer, as well as Schlegel, Vischer, Ludwig and others, have been concerned with this question. However, Holinshed tells us plainly who these "weitches" (as he called them) are, and the dramatist himself has them name themselves the "weird sisters" (I, iii, 32). "Weird" means destiny, fate; Holinshed also speaks of the witches as "goddesses of destiny".[2]

Schiller is doubtless right in concluding that the three

---

[1] Darmesteter, *op. cit.*
[2] *Holinshed's Chronicles* . . ., Vol. V, p. 269. London: J. Johnson . . ., 1808.

witches represent the three Fatal Sisters, the Norns of the Edda, the Parcae of the Romans, the Moires of the Greeks. According to an essay by Freud, the same is true of Lear's three daughters, Cordelia, Regan, and Goneril, and of the three caskets in *The Merchant of Venice*.[1]

To the same engrossing essay by Freud, we owe the insight that the motif of the three sisters, which is customarily conceived as an allegory of the past, the present, and the future, also means "the three inevitable relations man has with woman", the three forms into which the image of the mother is cast for man in the course of his life: "the mother herself, the beloved who is chosen after her pattern, and finally the Mother Earth . . ."[2] Lady Macbeth's vague allusion to the past refers in reality to the mother as the origin and the deepest source of hostility against the father.

That is why the poet has the three witches meet the hero on a "blasted heath" with the prophecy that he will become Thane of Cawdor. The title of Thane of Cawdor does not mean an elevation in rank; it is rather a symbol of treason. For Ross calls the Thane, a "most disloyal traitor" (I, ii, 52), and Angus reports that "treasons capital, confess'd and prov'd,/Have overthrown him" (I, iii, 115-116). By this detail Shakespeare implies that, through his mother, the son turns traitor to his father: Lady Macbeth, through the image of the mother, symbolises the abyss separating father and son.

Finally, this conception of Lady Macbeth is corroborated by the character of Banquo. Having no part at all in the murder, he stands for the exact opposite of the bad son, Macbeth, and must represent the good son.[3]

---

[1] Freud, "The Theme of the Three Caskets" (1913) *op. cit.*, Vol. 4, pp. 244-256.

[2] Freud, *op. cit.*, p. 256.

[3] Our designation of Banquo as the "good son" is a summary one, bound to rouse certain doubts, since the character does not entirely tally with it. As characterised by Shakespeare, Banquo shows a certain incompleteness, at least some indistinctness. This has been noted by several of the more serious scholars. Gervinus, arguing that imprudence causes the downfall of the minor characters, adduces the character of Banquo as another example of such poetic justice: "The same want of foresight ruins Banquo. He had been initiated into the secret of the weird sisters; pledged to openness towards Macbeth, he had opportunity of convincing himself of his obduracy and secrecy; he guesses at, and strongly suspects, Macbeth's deed; yet he does nothing against him or in self-defence". (Gervinus, *op. cit.*, op. 605-606.) Ulrici also describes Banquo as one who, "in self-complacent conceit, believes in the promises for his future good fortune, and thus brings destruction upon his own head" (Ulrici, *op. cit.*, p. 474.) Bodenstedt objects to Banquo's kindness, which is commonly taken for granted: "Banquo has long discovered all about Macbeth but has done

In connection with the immediate subject, however, two peculiarities of Banquo are important contrasts with Macbeth: no wife is mentioned for him, and he appears to have no contact with Lady Macbeth. When the Lady exclaims:

> Had he not resembled
> My father as he slept, I had done it. (II, ii, 13-14.)

she is telling us that the genii of the sexes disarm each other. At the same time, she teaches that man is urged by woman to fight his own sex, and she thus embodies the "other" sex, victorious over one's "own" sex. She stands for heterosexuality, which overpowers homosexuality.

In short, the woman—Lady Macbeth—makes Macbeth turn into a bad son, and thus the woman is the son's doom.

*   *   *

In his second psychic phase, Macbeth is the "father". As such, he has one son, Banquo, murdered, and also seeks the life of his other son, Macduff; consequently, he is the bad father, hostile to his sons and ready to kill them.

The validity of this interpretation is established by the great emphasis with which Macbeth orders the hired assassins not to kill Banquo alone, but also to kill his son, Fleance. When the murderers talk, after Fleance's successful flight, their stress is obviously on "son":

> Third Murderer: There's but one down; the son is fled.
> Second Murderer: We have lost
> Best half of our affair. (III, iii, 19-21.)

---

nothing to warn or protect old King Duncan against him". (Bodenstedt, *op. cit.*, p. 315. We are inclined to take this vague and compromising characterisation of Banquo as simply another way of expressing psychological insight. The dramatist seems to mean that it was, after all, only the woman (the mother) who opened an unbridgeable abyss between father and son, and drove the latter into extreme hostility. All other reasons—e.g. unequal reward for equal merits (so often noticed by scholars)—could only result in vexation or indifference toward the father (Banquo confesses to "cursed thoughts" [II, i, 8] against Duncan) but they could never produce the sudden turn into explicit hostility.

Still, Banquo can hardly be considered a "good" son. In reply to the King's scanty words of gratitude, he assures him, "There if I grow, The harvest is your own" (I, iv, 33-34), and yet, in the next act, harbors "cursed thoughts" against him. Both suspecting and envying King Macbeth, he nevertheless submissively states, "Let your Highness command upon me, to the which my duties Are with a most indissoluble tie for ever knit" (III, i, 15-17). Considering that Banquo thus, though wrathful in his heart, always shows himself devoted to his father, we will find the conception of him as the "submissive son" to be much more conclusive than that of the "good son". At the same time, this analysis fully retains the contrast to the "wayward" Macbeth.

This problem of hostility against the son becomes even clearer when Macduff's little son is murdered; though we are repeatedly told that Macduff has lost *all his kith and kin*, yet the son is emphatically singled out; it is the fate of the son that Shakespeare puts into the foreground.

What is the motif of this hostility against the son?

Suffice it that we hint at the famous vision of Banquo's ghost—often interpreted and as often misunderstood—which Macbeth sees taking his, the father's, seat, just as formerly he himself had dislodged Duncan from his seat. And let us recall Macbeth's words at this moment:

> Ay, and a bold one, that dare look on that
> Which might appal the devil. (III, iv, 59-60.)

Here the poet dramatises, with wonderful clarity, the fear of the son, now a father, upon confronting, in his own son, the same hostility he had himself harboured against his father —a motif Rank has also disclosed in Hamlet.

This *fear of requital*, a fear nourished and maintained by consciousness of the wrong committed against the father, explains Macbeth's desperate outcry at the news that although Banquo is dead, his son, Fleance, has succeeded in escaping:

> Then comes my fit again. I had else been perfect;
> Whole as the marble, founded as the rock,
> As broad and general as the casing air.
> But now I am cabin'd, cribb'd, confin'd, bound in
> To saucy doubts and fears. (III, iv, 21-25.)

It is the father within Macbeth, the never-silenced memories of hatred against his father and of the injury inflicted on that father in his thoughts, that nourishes suspicions of the very same feelings in the son; it is the father surviving within him that demands the death of the son. Malcolm, the cautious son, therefore speaks of

>   . . . wisdom
> To offer up a weak, poor, innocent lamb
> T'appease an angry God. (IV, iii, 15-17.)

Obviously, the relation to one's son appears to the poet as strictly conditioned by the relation to one's father; one will be, as a father, as one was as a son. *Macbeth demonstrates the fact that a bad son will make a bad father.*

The same close connection of the psychical functions of son

and father, is revealed in other characters of the tragedy, especially in Macduff and Banquo.

We are not absolutely alone in this supposition of a repetition of motif; a few Shakespearean scholars seem to have observed something similar. Ulrici finds it "an undeniable defect of the tragedy that the fundamental motive of the action represented, is not fully carried out in the personal character, life and fate of the hero, but, in part, merely in his outward surroundings". He also asserts that "the fundamental idea of the drama . . . is not merely reflected in the character, the fortunes and fate of the chief bearers of the action, but is also reflected in various degrees of light and shade in all the other figures", and that "the effect of the tragic pathos . . . is not only found in the history of the hero and his consort, but appears, as it were, halved and assigned to two different sides".[1]

For Macduff must be called a bad, obstinate son, quite as much as Macbeth. Despite his love for his father (amply demonstrated for Duncan, and hinted at even for Macbeth[2]), Macduff rebels against Macbeth. He does not attend the coronation at Scone; he uses "broad words", according to Lennox (III, vi, 21); and, unlike the submissive son, Banquo, who accepts unhesitatingly, Macduff refuses the invitation to the banquet offhand.

Why does he act thus?—because Macbeth has murdered Duncan, committed parricide, shown the traditional hostility against the father.

It is Macduff's rebellion against the father, however, which destroys all his kin. Persecuted by the father, he is forced to abandon them to the murderous hand, especially his son, who is stabbed to death before our very eyes. That is why he wails:

> Sinful Macduff,
> They were all struck for thee! Naught that I am,
> Not for their own demerits, but for mine,
> Fell slaughter on their souls. (IV, iii, 224-207.)

Here is the same motif as in the story of Macbeth; Macduff, too, demonstrates the fact that a bad son is also a bad father.

This identical content is communicated to us, however, in two distinct dialects. Macduff's fate proclaims in an

---

[1] Ulrici, *op. cit.*, pp. 476, 475.
[2] Malcolm to Macduff: "You have lov'd him well . . ." (IV, iii, 13).

undisguised, direct manner what the character of Macbeth expresses in a veiled and therefore indirect form; the latter seems to be a symbolic presentation of the former. Analysis of Macbeth should, then, disclose a technique similar to that which is frequently used in dreams. Everyone familiar with Freud's *theory of dreams* knows that they discard nuances and tints and instead adopt a lapidary brevity and a violent imagery. Almost every negative emotional relation is expressed by death, for example. Macbeth's murder of the King thus corresponds to Macduff's mere unconcern about him.[1]

The same insight is even more accurate for the female characters.

Is not Lady Macduff, in her little scene (IV, ii) but reproducing Lady Macbeth's actions in the first two acts? Macduff's wife incites her little son against his father, calling her husband a traitor who swears and does not keep his word, a man who should be hanged. She deeply degrades the child's father before him by saying how easily he could be replaced by another father. Schiller, in his translation, thought this scene so irrelevant that he left it out. But can Lady Macduff's words be symbolised more adequately than by Lady Macbeth's daggers? Hamlet, reproaching his mother with her sins, says: "I will speak daggers to her but use none" (III, ii); even in colloquial language, "words like daggers" is a familiar figure.[2]

What could have led Shakespeare to the double presentation of this motif? We shall not answer this question fully at this stage of our investigation. We may, however, venture the surmise that the character of Macduff, so poorly outlined in the legend, has been endowed so richly by Shakespeare because he saw in it a more concrete, more cleanly cut, more specific formulation of the motif which Macbeth's character expresses in a much more general way. This may explain why he developed the Macduff nucleus of the legend, treated it separately and paralleled it to Macbeth, almost pointing out that in this case Macbeth should be understood as practically identical with Macduff.

[1] It is beyond the framework of this investigation to decide whether, or to what extent, such simultaneous use of the veiled and the direct manners of presenting a leading motif can be considered a basic phenomenon of dramatic composition. This problem will be examined more thoroughly elsewhere.

[2] The common external fate of the two Ladies seems to confirm the correspondence stated here: although the poet does not usually refrain from having murders acted out, both Ladies die off stage.

Combining these elements, we reach a conclusion essential for the understanding of the tragedy: that *not Macbeth, but Macduff, is the true hero*. Similarly, the further development of the basic idea of the drama—the concatenation of the father function with that of the son—proceeds, not in Macbeth, but in Macduff, who becomes, as it were, the continuation of Macbeth.

*　　*　　*

Banquo is, so to speak, the positive of the picture of which Macduff is the negative. In saving himself from Macbeth's persecutions, Macduff disregards his son and sacrifices him; when Banquo is attacked by murderers, however, he gives his last thought to his son. "Fly, good Fleance, fly!" are his dying words (III, iii, 17). His fate therefore symbolises the idea treated in the play, that one's conduct as father is conditioned by one's attitude as son; here, the meaning is reversed, however, and the implication is that only a good son can become a good father.

Our original interpretation of Banquo as, notwithstanding his inner contradictions, a tractable son, is borne out if we interpret the allegory as meaning that while such a son may fall victim to his father, he will safeguard his own son. Furthermore, the apparition of the infinitely long line of Stuart kings (IV, i) shows that by saving his child a good son may expect further reward, since this action guarantees the undisturbed succession of generations: the House of Stuart originates from that same Fleance.

Applying this insight to Macbeth, *the basic idea is* discovered to be *that a bad son not only sacrifices his son, but, in so doing, also forfeits the blessing of continuous descent*.

*　　*　　*

This complex, we believe, this worry about the preservation of the clan, bears the main emphasis of the drama. The son is regarded primarily as a means to this end, that is, as the first-born male descendant. Although Banquo is represented in the procession of kings, therefore, Fleance is missing.

The historical incident to which the drama can be traced also supports the supposition that the author aims principally at the problem of preservation of the line of descent. When Elizabeth died, and the Tudor dynasty was ended, the transference of the crown to the Stuarts offered an analogy with the contrasting fates of Banquo and Macduff in the tragedy. The same disappointment at the disruption of the line of descent can also be inferred from Macduff's reaction to Ross's report of the murder of

> Wife, children, servants, all
> That could be found. (IV, iii, 212-213.)

In his desperate outcry, what he bemoans is the loss of *all* his children:

> He has no children. All my pretty ones?
> Did you say all? O hell-kite! All?
> What, all my pretty chickens ... (IV, iii, 216-218.)

This grief is not directed to the children as such, but to their function as links in the chain of generations. Macduff's exclamation, "He has no children", which has so often been re-interpreted, may favour this interpretation. It refers to Macbeth, and, keeping the congruity of the two figures, could be replaced by a resigned, "And so I have no children". That these words, in so general a form, and in the specific situation, can only reflect on the lost prospect of continuous descent, can hardly be denied. What else, moreover, could Macbeth mean when he tells his wife:

> Bring forth men-children only;
> For thy undaunted mettle should compose
> Nothing but males. (I, vii, 72-74.)

Some doubt may be aroused, however, by the unexplained distinction with which Macduff's son, among all his kin, has been treated. The individual treatment of this character's fate has proved very useful for our understanding of the drama: perhaps this son, even more than his counterpart, Fleance, has shown how the tragedy is built around the son problem. The question is why Shakespeare so fully displayed this part of the problem, "the Son", when he wrapped the other part, "the Father", in so foggy a symbolic darkness? What was his purpose, what did he want to express? Holinshed cannot answer; he does not mention Macduff's son. Could the character be elucidated from another viewpoint, from reality? Shakespeare's biographers may answer that question.

III

Among their meagre data, his biographers include the fact
that when he was twenty-one, Shakespeare left his hometown,
Stratford, his wife and his children, and moved to London.
The biographers agree that this serious step, this separation
from all that should be dearest to him, was mainly and almost
exclusively due to his conflict with the wealthy squire, Sir
Thomas Lucy. Caught while poaching, William Shakespeare
was punished somewhat severely by Lucy. His revenge was a
satiric ballad on the latter. The effect of this, however, was
that the squire now "redoubled the persecution against him
to that degree that he was obliged to leave his business and
family . . . and shelter himself in London".[1]

The biographers, however, have no more to offer than a
mere "probability"—despite the preserved first stanza of the
ballad, and despite the reference to the incident in the *Merry
Wives of Windsor* and the consistency of both. With rare conformity, they conclude their discussions with some such remark
as Kellner's: ". . . even without this conflict with Lucy,
Shakespeare would have been driven out into the world by
an inner spirit".[2]

And what if we suggested that Shakespeare's relationship to
his father might also have been one of the motives prompting
his departure? This conjecture gains considerable support
from a hint that the conflict between father and son became
more marked at this time. Shortly before Shakespeare's departure, the woman, Lady Macbeth, had stepped between
father and son. Not quite three years earlier, William, then
eighteen, had married a farmer's daughter, much older than
himself. She was of socially inferior parentage, and the
marriage was contracted under unusual circumstances, without
the father's consent, though this, for minors, was indispensable.
"It is absolutely understandable that the clever John Shakespeare was not asked for his consent—he would never have
given it",[3] Kellner remarks. With these facts before us, do
not Lady Macduff's words sound almost like a spontaneous

---

[1] Brandes, *op. cit.*, p. 10 (quoting from another source).
[2] Leon Kellner, *Skakespeare*, p. 7. Leipzig . . .: E. A. Seemann . . ., 1900.
(The quotation given has been reworded in translation.)
[3] *Ibid.*, p. 6.

confession of the dramatist's? (She reproaches her husband, who has fled before the king's wrath:)

> ... to leave his wife, to leave his babes,
> His mansion and his titles, in a place
> From whence himself does fly? He loves us not,
> He wants the natural touch. (IV, ii, 6-9.)

The certainty of this supposition is particularly strengthened by another fact. It is not easy to discover why Shakespeare has Macduff's son stabbed *after* the escape of the father instead of *before*. If the stabbing took place first, not only would there be sufficient motivation for that base deed (especially when compared with the causes of Banquo's fate), but there would be much better reasons for Macduff's flight—which otherwise lacks the added incentive of retaliation. As it is, the irrationality of Macduff's action leads his wife to exclaim, "What had he done to make him fly the land?" and "His flight was madness" (IV, ii, 1, 3). Some commentators seem to agree with her. Gervinus actually slights the fact that the sequence of events is reversed in this way, and says that Macduff was not prepared to oppose Macbeth until after the murder of his family.[1] And Ulrici calls the flight of Macduff unmanly and unfatherly.[2]

This incongruity, however, also disappears once we understand the allegory, and realise that a personal experience of Shakespeare's has been transposed into the drama. Exactly as in the tragedy, Shakespeare, while living far from his family and unconcerned about them for several years, lost his eleven-year old son, Hamnet. Surely Macduff embodies this intimate personal experience of the dramatist.

*   *   *

In 1601, Shakespeare is said to have entered a period of great depression, which darkened a long span of his life, but to which an admiring world apparently owes such master works as *Julius Caesar*, *Hamlet*, *Othello*, *King Lear*, and *Macbeth*. For this depression, various reasons have been given: the doom of Lords Essex and Southampton, with both of whom the

---

[1] Gervinus, *op. cit.*, p. 606.
[2] Ulrici, *op. cit.*, p. 474.

dramatist had close contact; the crisis in his and Lord Pembroke's relations with the "Dark Lady" of the sonnets; and finally the fact that the year 1601 was the year his father died. Freud aligned these motives in order of importance; he correctly placed one factor which was neglected before him, the death of Shakespeare's father, and he showed its significance for the striking metamorphosis in the author—who had previously been so very sunny and merry. How right he was is proved by Macbeth when, after the murder of the king is discovered, he exclaims, with ostensible hypocrisy:

> Had I but died an hour before this chance,
> I had liv'd a blessed time; for from this instant
> There's nothing serious in mortality;
> All is but toys; renown and grace is dead;
> The wine of life is drawn, and the mere lees
> Is left this vault to brag of. (II, iii, 96-101.)

What Freud has disclosed in *Hamlet*, consequently, is also true for *Macbeth;* this tragedy, as well as *Hamlet*, was created by Shakespeare under the impression of his father's death and "during a revival . . . of his own childish feelings in respect of his father".[1] Since *Macbeth* was written several years after *Hamlet*, however, the reaction-formations against those infantile emotions were much more advanced; by this time, the psychic situation of the poet had gone through a definite change.

Rank, in his instructive essay on *Hamlet*, stresses this attitude of love toward the father, which is present latently, and is fed by feelings of guilt and repentance.[2] In *Macbeth*, this positive feeling of fatherhood appears by far to outbalance the negative feelings of the son in the poet.

Father feelings predominate in the heart of the dramatist, because his repressions have now reached a deeper level. Earlier works of this period had shown a feeling of guilt toward his father as the reaction to infantile hatred for him; now, this reaction has become a feeling in the author that his own attitude toward his son is menaced. It is when the self-reproaches and feelings of guilt derived from this menace are

---

[1] Sigmund Freud, *The Interpretation of Dreams* (translated by A. A. Brill, p.p. 258-9. London: Geo. Allen & Unwin, Ltd.
[2] Otto Rank, *Das Inzest-Motiv in Dichtung und Sage* . . ., pp. 44-45 *et passim*. Leipzig und Wien: Franz Deuticke, 1912.

bound up with the fate of the neglected and (supposedly) sacrificed son, that they appear most intensely:

> Sinful Macduff,
> They were all struck for thee! Naught that I am,
> Not for their own demerits, but for mine
> Fell slaughter on their souls. (IV, iii, 224-227.)

IV

Similarly, through Macduff's stirring lament on the shattering of his hope for the preservation of his clan, Shakespeare's own pain can be sensed. During the years following the death of his father, two historical events occurred which harmonised with the despondency of his psychic disposition: the death of Queen Elizabeth and the accession of King James.

It seems psychologically consistent that the fate of the old, unmarried, "virginal" Elizabeth should start a powerful echo in the heart of the dramatist. Dying without offspring, the last of her line, Elizabeth was forced to bequeath her crown to an alien family. The demonstration that even such grandeur was transitory could not help turning the poet's mourning for his son into grief about his endangered descent. Biographers agree that he had little in common with the two daughters who were left, if he was not actually estranged from them. Suzanne, the elder, moreover, was either married or engaged, and Judith, the younger, was also eligible. Not a loved one was left to receive his inheritance, and there was nobody at all to continue his name and fame. No wonder Macbeth despairs!

> Upon my head they plac'd a fruitless crown
> And put a barren sceptre in my gripe,
> Thence to be wrench'd with an unlineal hand,
> No son of mine succeeding. (III, i, 61-64.)

It really does credit to Brandes' intuition that he so accurately estimated the significance of Hamnet's death for the dramatist's psyche. "We cannot doubt that this loss was a grievous one to a man of Shakespeare's deep feeling; doubly grievous, it would seem, because it was his constant ambition to restore the fallen fortunes of his family, and he was now left without an heir to his name".[1] The sensitive critic felt what we could only laboriously decipher.

*   *   *

Granting Elizabeth so prominent a rôle in the conception of the tragedy may seem arbitrary and high-handed. Nevertheless, we are prepared to suggest that the Queen's influence on the composition was even greater than we have yet intimated. With the royal life which had just ended, Shakespeare may have had a sympathy of unsuspected depth. Had not Elizabeth, like himself, been a bad child?

The relation of the young princess to her fostermother, Katherine Parr, the last wife of Henry VIII, was a troubled one, especially after Katherine remarried. Yet Elizabeth herself wrote that Katherine had bestowed "manifold kindnesses"[2] upon her.

Shakespeare's imagination must indeed have been active to recognise Elizabeth's attitude toward Mary Tudor—the half-sister who preceded her on the throne—as mother-hatred. Elizabeth had been able to attract not only the Earl of Devonshire, whom Mary had loved deeply, but also Mary's husband, Philip II.[3] She had actually played the part of a rebellious daughter toward Mary, being intimately implicated in the conspiracy of Wyatt and his confederates against the Queen in 1554. Elizabeth's very life was then imperilled, and it was thanks only to extremely cautious manoeuvring that she received no more severe punishment than detention in the Tower, followed by banishment to Hatfield.

And surely Shakespeare unconsciously sensed Elizabeth's hostility towards her mother in her treatment of Mary Stuart, Queen of Scots. How else can the many irrational details of

[1] Brandes, *op. cit.*, p. 140.
[2] Agnes Strickland, *The Life of Queen Elizabeth*, p. 22. London: J. M. Dent (Everyman's Library), 1910.
[3] J. E. Neale, *Queen Elizabeth*, pp. 45-52. New York: Harcourt, Brace. 1934.

I

that behaviour be explained? Elizabeth brought no charge
against Mary Stuart, and failed to have her sentenced, though
she imprisoned her for eighteen years; nor was she ever
unaware of Mary's political conspiracies and intrigues.
Besides that, she confirmed the death sentence of the Scottish
queen and yet appeared alarmed and disconcerted at the news
of the execution. These inconsistencies lead one to suspect unconscious influences. Elizabeth was probably repeating the
girlhood situation already described, and thereby ridding herself of those affects which she had had to suppress toward Mary
Tudor.[1] She identified the Scottish queen with Mary Tudor—
an easy process, since both, unlike Protestant, "bastard"
Elizabeth, were legitimate, Catholic, and named "Mary".
Philip II, moreover, assisted Mary Stuart in her troubles, just
as he had once assisted Princess Elizabeth. With so many
correspondences, it is only natural to conclude that the
mother-daughter relationship was also carried over in Elizabeth's attitude toward the Queen of Scots.

In addition to the "bad child" character, Elizabeth displays
a still closer accord with Shakespeare's experience. Like
himself, she had murdered her own son: as recently as 1601,
she had ordered the execution of her lover, Robert Devereux,
Earl of Essex, who had been very close to the dramatist. Nor
should Shakespeare have had any trouble in unconsciously
interpreting Elizabeth's relationship to Essex as a mother-son
relationship, since the Earl was thirty-one years younger than
the queen, and was the step-son of Leicester, her lover of
many years' standing.

*   *   *

Although Elizabeth was, therefore, Shakespeare's model
when he wrote this tragedy, we do not find her in one character
of the play, but in two. Analysis of the *Merchant of Venice* led
me to understand that Shakespeare—and perhaps other play-
wrights—often use, as a means of disguising an event, the
technique of splitting a psychic personality, distributing it to
two or more characters of the drama. Each of these is, of

---

[1] When she was told that Mary Stuart had been beheaded, Elizabeth
behaved like "a guilty child . . . self-convicted and terrified at the prospect of
disgrace and punishment . . ." (Strickland, *op. cit.*, pp. 500-501.)

course, only fragmentary, and therefore not easily interpreted: they must be pieced together in order to form a psychic whole. Freud accepts this opinion, and continues:

> "It might be thus with Macbeth and the Lady; and then it would of course be futile to regard her as an independent personage and seek to discover her motivation without considering the Macbeth who completes her. I shall not follow this hint any further, but I would add, nevertheless, a remark which strikingly confirms the idea—namely, that the stirrings of fear which arise in Macbeth on the night of the murder, do not develop further in him, but in the Lady. It is he who has the hallucination of the dagger before the deed, but it is she who later succumbs to mental disorder; he, after the murder, hears the cry from the house: "Sleep no more! Macbeth does murder sleep . . .", and so "Macbeth shall sleep no more", but we never hear that King Macbeth could not sleep, while we see that the Queen rises from her bed and betrays her guilt in somnambulistic wanderings. He stands helpless with bloody hands, lamenting that not great Neptune's ocean can wash them clean again, while she comforts him: "a little water clears us of this deed"; but later it is she who washes her hands for a quarter of an hour and cannot get rid of the bloodstains. "All the perfumes of Arabia will not sweeten this little hand". Thus is fulfilled in her what his pangs of conscience had apprehended; she is incarnate remorse after the deed, he incarnate defiance—together they exhaust the possibilities of reaction to the crime, like two disunited parts of the mind of a single individuality, and perhaps they are the divided images of a single prototype."[1]

As the model of the two leading characters, however, hardly anybody could have been in Freud's mind but Elizabeth—for we have seen how, with his unequalled intuition, he guessed from the beginning the part of the queen in the conception of the drama.

Thus it was Elizabeth whom Shakespeare moulded into the forms of Macbeth and his Lady. For his ability to do so, and in such eternal magnificance, we are indebted to that phantasy which made it possible for him to identify himself with the queen in his innermost experience. It was thus a kind of identification, almost an interchange of personalities, which permitted him to use the Macbeth saga in celebrating the succession of James to the English throne, since that story was so essentially in accordance with the historical event. The sterile queen seemed to him to be the murderer of her son, just as he felt himself, having murdered his son, to be sterile.

---

[1] Freud, Coll. Papers, Vol. IV., pp. 332-333.

To quote a sociologist, "Indeed, both queen and poet stand inseparable on the peak of their world".[1]

But was it not also on account of this identification that Shakespeare's feelings for the queen were, as Brandes says, so cool that he did not even write a few lines of praise at her death—despite Chettle's request.?[2]

V

It should be no surprise to find, therefore, that James and his accession to the throne are also merged with the dramatist's own fate. While the queen's death, however, wrought only despair and remorse in the author because of his self-inflicted grief, he drew expiation and wish-fulfillment from the character of James. James is the cue for the effervescent wish-symphony now surrounding the sadness in his heart: it is merely an expression of wish fulfillment that Macduff is "none of woman born".

This unnatural birth is, first of all, a contrast to the impotence and inadequacy of "mortal" man, especially since Macbeth is incited, by the prophecy, to "laugh to scorn/The pow'r of man" (IV, i, 79-80) thereby pointing, as it were, to a god as his successor. As this sharp contrast between god and man does not appear in Holinshed,[3] it would seem to have originated in Shakespeare. We may therefore conclude that he conceives Macduff as a deity with the attribute, "none of woman born".

However, have we not already met with almost the same contention? Does not Simrock, referring to Macduff's other

---

[1] Erich Marcks, *Konigen Elisabeth von England* . . . (Monographien Velhagen & Klasing, zur Weltgeschichte, II), p. 114. Bielefeld und Leipzig, 1897.

[2] Brandes, *op. cit.*, p. 250.

[3] Holinshed reduces the whole scene (IV, i) to a sentence: . . . "A certeine weitche, whome hee had in great trust, had told him he should never be slaine with man borne of anie woman . . ." (*op.cit.*, p. 274).

attribute, his being "ripped from his mother's womb", say this usually betokens the demi-god?[1]

We can even guess which god the author meant. This dark "none of woman born" has two possible contents: first, the stress may lie on "born", and imply "ripped from the womb"; secondly, it may lie on "woman", and imply the opposite, i.e. "one born of a man". The god would then be one who had been both "ripped from his mother's womb" and born of his father. There is only one such figure in the ancient pantheon: the Greek god Dionysus.

According to the best known so-called Theban saga, this god is the son of Semele, daughter of Cadmus, king of Thebes. She conceived him from Zeus, with whom she had secret intercourse in her palace in Thebes. Betrayed by treacherous advice from jealous Hera, Semele urges Zeus to visit her in his full celestial majesty, after she has wheedled the oath from him that he will fulfil any wish. As Zeus then appears in his true character with thunder and lightning, Semele dies, struck by the lightning. By order of Zeus, Hermes opens Semele's body, which is enveloped in flames, and wrests her child from the fire. Zeus takes the unripe fruit, sews it into his thigh, and in due time gives birth to the child.

Of course, Dionysus is par excellence the god of nature's blessings, of "the growth of nature, god of all fecundity and procreation',[2]

This is truly a magnificent achievement of Shakespearean phantasy: transforming the "barrenness" of which he had despaired into its immense antinomy!

As we know, the time the play was written is uncertain. Yet we dare set the year 1606 as the precise date:[3] ten years

---

[1] Simrock, *op. cit.*, p. 259.

[2] Dionysus also represents "the symbol of elementary creation in nature, a half-chthonic character, since, according to the creative power of nature symbolised by him in wood and field, he is submerged in sleep and death by the rough storms of winter, and later awakens to life again". All this harmonises perfectly with the myth of vegetation—as does no other mythological character (a fact, curiously enough, which has received little attention).

[3] Other signs, too, point to this date: the porter's reference to "plenty," (II, 3) the equivocator, and the change of men's fashions. It is further supported by the fact that Shakespeare's *Macbeth* is alluded to only in such works as we know had not come into existence before 1607. (Since the time this note was originally written, we have learned *that* 1606 *is* now the accepted date for the composition of *Macbeth*. See Kittredge, *op. cit.*, p. ix, or Lilian Winstanley, *Macbeth, King Lear & Contemporary History*, p. 37. Cambridge: The University Press, 1922.)

after he has become father (king), Holinshed's Macbeth murders his son (Banquo); and ten years after he has murdered his son, Shakespeare revives him—in Malcolm. While it is James who entices this magic tune from the poet's lyre, the author's love encompasses both sons equally, both the living king and his reflection in the play. James was the son of a murdered mother, as Malcolm was the son of a murdered father. And James is more than son; he is also a distant offspring of the clan. Banquo finds his continuation, even after many centuries, in James; Malcolm, for the dramatist, likewise represents a desired future descendant. For now the son is, like Banquo, a good son. Malcolm has

> Great Birnam Wood to high Dunsinane Hill
> . . . come against him [i.e. Macbeth]. (IV, i, 93-94.)

What is more, however, Macduff stamps out Macbeth—the hatred against the father. As the "motherless" Dionysus, Macduff does not even know the mother, Lady Macbeth, who is the doom of the son: only the father is his procreator, and that is God, nay, the King of the Gods.

*   *   *

But in his trouble the poet also seeks refuge in self-assertion. Since the early birth of Dionysus from Semele took place at Thebes, this was taken as the god's original home and became the most famous sanctuary for his worship. As, however, the second birth, from the thigh of Zeus, took place at Nysa in Thrace, Dionysus was generally considered the victorious god who, coming from abroad, had enforced his worship there. Had not the poet also to fight hard for acknowledgment and fame in his native Stratford? Had he not left it, years before, poor and humiliated, with the determination that "the little town which had witnessed this disgrace should also witness the rehabilitation?"[1]

At the risk of pressing the analogy too far, may we close, at last, with a figurative tribute, by suggesting that William Shakespeare in his own lifetime and ever since, has been the god of comedy and tragedy, of which Dionysus was the father.[2]

[1] Brandes, op. cit., p. 152.
[2] Thus Francis Meres wrote in "Palladis Tamia", in 1598: "As Plautus and Seneca are accounted the best for Comedy and Tragedy among the Latines: so Shakespeare among the English . . ." (C. Gregory Smith, Elizabethan Critical Essays, Vol. 2, pp. 317-318. Oxford: Clarendon Press, 1904.)

THE PROBLEM OF THE DUPLICATED EXPRESSION OF PSYCHIC THEMES*

FIRST of all I must draw your attention to one blemish in this paper; its other shortcomings you will no doubt discover for yourselves. For reasons which you will presently gather, I have been obliged to incorporate in this essay an earlier study, supplementing it, to be sure, with such fresh conclusions as I have been able to reach. However, if you do happen to have read the former paper, you will certainly have forgotten it long ago and I must therefore repeat its outcome here.[1] You will at least account it to me for righteousness that I have tried to spare you as far as possible, i.e. to present my results as concisely and clearly as I can.

Now to our subject. What I mean by a duplicated expression of a psychic theme is this: that both in the familiar field of dreams, neurosis and repeated parapraxes, and also in that of dramatic creation (so much further removed from our usual interests) there prevails a tendency to give a twofold expression to any important, or, as we may say, central psychic constellation, so that it appears in consciousness in two guises, which are generally quite different from one another.

In the first three compromise-formations named above the regularity and the stress of this twofold elaboration vary considerably, so that it can be observed only occasionally or fragmentarily. In drama, on the other hand, it is, I believe, a universal rule, to which there is no exception and which shows itself in an unmistakable way.

This characteristic of the drama first attracted my attention a good many years ago, when I was engaged on a psycho-analytical study of *Macbeth*. Here the twofold expression of the same theme struck me so forcibly that, even at that stage, I ventured to suggest that "this juxtaposition of both a disguised and a more direct presentation of the leading theme may be a fundamental phenomenon in dramatic production".

* Read before the Twelfth International Psycho-Analytical Congress, Wiesbaden, 4th September, 1932. First published in English in *The International Journal of Psycho-analysis* 14, 3 (1933).
[1] *Imago*, Bd. V, S.170 ff. Cf. Freud, Coll. Papers, Vol. IV, p. 323.

Some years later, after continuing my researches in this field, I stated: "This phenomenon occurs so regularly that, after further careful tests, I feel that I am quite safe in asserting the converse, namely, that anything which appears in a twofold guise in a drama is its fundamental theme".

You see that, apart from the very cogent reason that a phenomenon is always most usefully examined in that field in which it appears most clearly and regularly, I also have, so to speak, an "historical" motive for conducting you first into the realm of the drama and then proceeding, by such light as may be acquired there, to follow up the phenomenon of duplicated expression of a theme in the other spheres.

Once more I have chosen as the object of our inquiry Shakespeare's *Macbeth*, the contents of which, so far as it is necessary for our purpose, I will recall to your minds in half-a-dozen words. After the prophecy of the witches that he, Macbeth, will become king, while Banquo will be the father of kings, Macbeth murders King Duncan who is staying with him as his guest. Macbeth is then crowned king and becomes a ruthless tyrant who orders Banquo and his son, Fleance, to be assassinated; the latter, however, escapes the hand of the murderer. The plot against Macduff's life also miscarries, but his little son falls a victim to the tyrant. Macduff instigates a revolt against him and slays him, whereupon Malcolm, King Duncan's son, who has also escaped Macbeth's plots, is made king.

In my study I was able to demonstrate, as I think, convincingly, that the fundamental idea underlying this drama is the tragic realisation that a bad son is a bad father, so that he thus forfeits the blessings of posterity.

For you will recollect from my recapitulation that Macbeth appears in a twofold rôle. In the first place he is the murderer of King Duncan—a bad son who commits parricide. But, secondly, he is himself the king, the father, and in this rôle he is the bloodthirsty persecutor of every son-figure. "There's but one down; the son is fled", says the first of the murderers hired to assassinate Banquo and his son. "We have lost best half of our affair", rejoins the second murderer.

Now precisely the same psychological situation—the closest possible connection between the two rôles of father and of son —is elaborated a second time in the play, namely, in the figure of Macduff. He too is a bad and rebellious son. Not only does he ostentatiously stay away from Macbeth's coronation, but he utters "broad words" against him, abruptly rejects the king's invitation to the coronation-banquet and finally raises an armed insurrection against him and kills him. But, as I have already said, Macduff's little son falls a victim to the father-hatred of his own father, who abandons him and takes to flight, thus leaving him to fall into the hands of the murderers.

I think you will agree with me when I repeat that here we have a perfectly clear instance of the twofold elaboration of a single theme. But the mode of expression employed in the two elaborations differs greatly. The figure of Macbeth with its sheer force, its absence of *nuances* and half-tones, is far more like something in a vision or a dream, whereas that of Macduff approaches more closely to the preconscious mode of conception and seems more like an ordinary man, more comprehensible to us.

Now in my former study I showed that there is a very special reason for this difference, as well as for the significant fact that, while in Holinshed's story (the source of the plot) the figure of Macduff is very meagrely portrayed, the poet took up this figure, singled it out and developed it into something far richer, placing it by the side of Macbeth—as if it were a concrete, special instance of the far more general theme embodied in the latter. I believe that the reason is this: that, just as Macduff seems compelled by the conflict with Macbeth to flee and abandon his family, Shakespeare too in his youth, after a grave quarrel with his father, left his wife and children as in flight, betaking himself to London. Accordingly, Lady Macduff's bitter accusation against her husband:

> ". . . To leave his wife, to leave his babes,
> . . . . . . in a place
> From whence himself does fly? He loves us not;
> He wants the natural touch".

is the poet's own bitter self-accusation.

Similarly, in the murder of Macduff's little son, which follows directly on this scene, we have the portrayal of the terrible self-reproach of Shakespeare who, while living his own life in London after his flight, in entire unconcern about his family, lost his only son, Hamnet, and with him the hope of the continuance of his line and the handing-on of his glorious name. Hence the cry:

"Sinful Macduff,
They were all struck for thee! naught that I am,
Not for their own demerits, but for mine,
Fell slaughter on their souls".

The significance of this second version now begins to dawn on us. It serves as an expression of the sense of guilt, any trace of which in the figure of Macbeth we seek for in vain and find entirely lacking.

We can easily discover, moreover, not merely the meaning but also the purpose of this second representation, the psychological significance of this special emphasis on the sense of guilt. For the history of the origin of this play, as well as our knowledge of the accompanying circumstances, give us the key.

We know for certain that it was written as an act of homage to King James on his accession to the throne—a very strange circumstance in the case of Shakespeare, who was so sparing of homage to the great Elizabeth, though he owed her so much.

When he wrote *Macbeth*, Shakespeare was profoundly affected by the death of the Queen, with whom, as I pointed out some years ago, he had many a bond of common feeling—above all, the shared punishment, as it were, of "barrenness", and their forfeiture of posterity.

Was it not inevitable that the strange dispensation by which the throne of Elizabeth passed to the son of Mary Stuart, a mother whom she had murdered, should be felt by the poet to be a liberating, nay, redeeming act of justice?

Hence the homage of the play; hence, too, the solution it contains of the conflict: in faithful imitation of the actual development of events before Shakespeare's eyes he makes the son of the murdered Duncan ascend the throne.

It now seems clear that this high relief here given to the sense of guilt by the second transcription of the author's thoughts in the figure of Macduff, this process of having set it perfectly plainly before oneself, is the necessary condition by which the ego can come frankly to terms with it and be able to transmute it into the socially productive form of a sense of justice. Now let us apply what we have just learnt from the structure of drama to the investigation of kindred situations in *neurosis* and let us ask whether, there too, the tendency to a twofold elaboration, which is so plain in drama, exists and can be demonstrated? I believe that I can answer this question with an unequivocal "Yes", pointing out that the tendency expresses itself clearly in the process of *reproduction* in the analyses of patients. By this I mean recollection and translation into behaviour. I am really not sure whether we are not being too schematic in our treatment of the subject if, as is generally done, we conceive of this reproducing process, as being *either* remembering *or* "acting out". My own experience is such that I cannot but feel that it would be very much more accurate to say that, in general, the repressed theme is both psychically reproduced, i.e. remembered, and also receives motor resuscitation, i.e. is translated into behaviour. Reik seems to be of the same opinion when he says that "there are various transitions from reproduction by description to reproduction in behaviour". In order to illustrate my meaning by an example, I will borrow from Sachs, since at the moment my own experience does not supply me with so clear-cut a case. In a short communication, published in the *Zeitschrift*, he describes an episode in the analysis of a young married woman suffering from a strongly developed castration complex, which in her childhood had been aroused and maintained by her penis-envy directed to a brother two-and-a-half years younger than herself. Gradually and after strong and protracted resistance the theme of enuresis was opened up; recollections thereupon followed of how, when she was about four years old, she and her brother shared a bed, how he wetted it and she complained to their mother, who took off the soiled bedclothes. On returning home after this particular session the patient made a most unpleasant scene with her husband on account of what she called his "messy way of gobbling his food and spilling stuff on the tablecloth". At the end of his communication Sachs draws the just conclusion that the patient's tendency to belittle the male caused her to apply to her husband, by a process of oral displacement, the reproach which really had reference to the brother of her childhood days: he (the brother) was a dirty, inferior creature who, in spite of the advantage of a penis which he had as against her, could not even control his urination.

This seems to me a particularly good illustration of the

twofold expression of a theme, its psychic and its motor reproduction.

Now, however, we must proceed here also to examine both modes of representation in the light of what we learnt from the drama, i.e. from the point of view of their relation to the sense of guilt.

It is obvious that both these processes are governed by the requirements of the super-ego. Now it may possibly be contended, as against this statement, that to conceive thus of the process of recollection involves a contradiction, seeing that, as we all know, it is on the contrary *repression* which takes place by order of the super-ego. I would reply to this objection by pointing out that this argument is based on a manifest misconception of the process of repression, an inadmissible confusion between repression and forgetting. For the latter is quite distinct from repression in its essential nature; it is merely *one* of the means of which repression makes use.

At the same time, I do not believe that the requirements of the super-ego constitute the sole factor by which the character of the process of reproduction is determined; in my view it is also a question of the very variable degree of the ego's anxiety-reaction, and possibly this does not depend solely on the severity of the super-ego. If this reaction is excessive, the reproduction will take the form of a repetition of the act in question, i.e. of translation into behaviour. This, as we know, springs from the need for punishment and is thus essentially an expression of instinct striving after masochistic gratification. Hence, when repressed material is translated into behaviour, it seems that the ego, under the pressure of the super-ego, has passed completely under the domination of the id.

It is a very different matter when we come to remembering. It is, I believe, a prerequisite of recollection that the ego should be able somehow to master its anxiety and should feel itself free from the craving to suffer and the need for punishment, so that it is not obliged to evade its conscience (as it does in the case of "acting out") but can frankly face it and render account of itself.

You know that the ideal at which we aim in our therapeutic work is the formation of such a strong ego, and that this is why we try so hard to resolve the resistance which always underlies reproduction in action, so that, as far as possible, it may be prevented and remembering may take its place. Reflect now for a moment how closely the achievement of the analyst in such an ideal analysis corresponds to the creative work of dramatists.

Now let us turn to *dreams*. Here it seems as though the necessary conditions for the duplication of a theme were fulfilled in quite a special way, for we know that in any case two modes of expression are used in dreams: mental images and thoughts. And yet it is relatively seldom that dreams occur in which there is a double version of the theme. Why this is so we may learn from the following analysis of a dream in which it happens that such a duplication is very obvious:

A woman patient of about forty years old, whose castration complex had never been overcome and caused considerable disturbance of her sexual sensibility, and who had a number of masculine characteristics, related the following dream: *She saw Joseph lying on the table; the skin on his legs was "bad" (a rash); her friend Minna was there.* Continuing: *She took two thousand schillings from Willi; he noticed that the money was gone, she was afraid of being found out and she tore up the notes into little bits and threw them away.*

It is not difficult in any case to understand this dream, but the following occurrences, which preceded the dream and its interpretation, are important:—

(1) The patient, who was carrying on her analysis with me during the summer holidays, was greatly disappointed that, even when we were away, her contact with me was purely professional, whilst, in her childhood, the relation between her father and herself used to be specially intimate just when they were staying in the country during the summer.

(2) A day or two before the dream she was reading Wassermann's *Christian Wahnschaffe* and broke off abruptly and with a feeling of great disgust when she unexpectedly came to the place where a girl was found murdered—as a headless corpse.

(3) At the time when the dream occurred, the patient, who was generally very regular in her menstruation, had a period which began late, lasted for an unusually short time and was marked by a very scanty flow.

(4) The patient poured out a very detailed description of the character of her father, an old business man, in which she dwelt exclusively on his hardness and close-fisted character in

money matters, not only to his employees but to her, his daughter.

Willi, who had already often stood for the analyst in her dreams, was a young medical man who, to the patient's unbounded indignation, brutally deprived his rich wife of the free control of her own money. Joseph, his brother, was a gynæcological surgeon, with a great reputation in the town. In short, there was no doubt that this dream represented the condensation of a whole series of instinctual trends, aggressive, narcissistic, etc., and that in both scenes there was primarily a representation of the same theme, namely, the wish to castrate the father from motives of revenge. For, in the first scene, the surgeon was lying on the (operating) table; his figure underwent distortion and became that of Minna, who in real life had a bad complexion, i.e. he was turned into a woman. The purport of the second scene was the same; she deprived Willi of his money, just as he had deprived his wife and her own father had deprived her.

But what of the rest of the dream? Why does the patient then give up the father's penis which she has stolen? We find the answer in the text of the dream: out of dread of the father, because of the opposition of the super-ego, that is to say, from a sense of guilt. In this anxiety-situation there were only two sources open to the ego—either to give up its pursuit of the coveted object or to renounce sleep, for otherwise anxiety would certainly wake it in terror. It decided for the first, thus banishing the anxiety and making continued sleep possible.

Now what exactly strikes us is that here again—in the case of a dream as in the drama of *Macbeth*—it is in the second version of the theme that the sense of guilt finds expression. The reaction of the ego, however, its attitude to the super-ego, is quite different, in fact diametrically opposite, in the two instances. In drama and in memory, as we have already seen, the ego frankly admits its guilt, whereas in dreams it refuses to have anything to do with it and flees in terror. For our patient's abandonment of the father's penis, after she had stolen it, and her obliteration of the traces of her deed are essentially a retreat, the avoidance of an explanation with the super-ego, i.e. a flight from the latter. In dreams this desire to escape from the super-ego—the ultimate source of anxiety—

is tremendously strong, and the device to which it most frequently has recourse is that of waking the dreamer up, though it also has very many other ways of expressing itself. By way of illustration I may refer to certain dreams of one of the patients of O. Isakower, who has kindly allowed me to make use of them and to whom I am further indebted for a number of valuable suggestions. Each of these dreams consisted of a main scene, in most cases with an orgiastic content, and a kind of short epilogue. The peculiarity of these epilogues was that the patient was never certain whether they still belonged to the dream or to waking life. This uncertainty becomes intelligible when we learn that all these epilogues contained elements which can only be construed as menaces or warnings on the part of the super-ego: in most of them the analyst actually appeared in person. For example, the patient, in one such epilogue following upon an orgiastic dream, heard a voice calling to him: "You may be sure the filthy things you do in your love-affairs will be found out". In fact all these epilogues are in my view dreamt and the patient's uncertainty whether to place them still in the dream or already in the waking state is simply a betrayal of the vehemence of his desire not to hear the voice of the super-ego in his dreams but to escape from it.

I am unable to explain why we so much more rarely find in dreams that dread of the super-ego is converted into the wish which is its opposite and so allayed. The following dream, related to me by a lady who was undergoing a training analysis, is one in which such a transformation occurs with great distinctness: "Herr and Frau Dr. Bibring were talking to me and were very friendly"; this was accompanied by a feeling of great pleasure. The meaning of the dream will at once be plain to you when I tell you the analysand's association, which was that she and her friends had been joking about the name *Bibring* and turned it into *Biberich-Über-Ich*.

A word about those punishment-dreams which we regard as the expression of a wish of the super-ego: just because they represent a wish-fulfilment and also because they are incomparably less common than the dreams of which I have been speaking, they do not stand in contradiction to the view I have been putting before you—on the contrary, they are a standing proof of the hypothesis that in dreams the ego energetically resists the admission of its guilt, turns its back on it and flees from the super-ego.

What I have said about dreams is nothing new: rather it is a conclusion to which we are inevitably led by Freud's conception of the interplay of forces which determines the formation of dreams. The ego, when it succumbs to the narcissistic wish for sleep, refuses to grant any cathexis to the claims of the id, at most lending itself to them only with very considerable modifications; it is thus a mere matter of course that, except in very rare instances, its attitude towards the demands of the super-ego should be one of rigid repudiation.

If we now compare the results of our investigation of the three fields reviewed by us in this paper we find that the sense of guilt is variously dealt with as follows: (*a*) in drama it finds resigned recognition and this first enables it to be recast in a socially productive form; (*b*) in neurosis it is misused for purposes of instinctual gratification; (*c*) in dreams it is as far as possible ignored. Whilst in the last two the personality is cleft asunder, *drama, like an analysis which is correctly carried out, leads to its unification.*

That we have a very emphatic intuitive perception of this truth, obviously in an unconscious form, is reflected in the fact that in critiques of dramatic works stress is so often laid on *unity*, even though it is frequently displaced on to some detail or some more remote aspect of the whole. So, for instance, certain famous Shakespeare scholars like Gervinus and others (and, if I am not mistaken, Lessing before them) specially underline the poet's striving after moral unity in the creation of his characters. I even think it not altogether absurd to suggest that we might consider in this light the unity of time, place and action, which is held to be the criterion of a good drama. A strange fact, which certainly does not contradict my supposition, is that for centuries Aristotle was erroneously credited with the notion of this triad, whereas actually, as we are now told, all that he demanded was unity of action, whilst (according to recent researches) the other two unities were first demanded by French writers of tragedy and æstheticians in the eighteenth century.

This, however, is merely by the way. Returning to our real theme, we now see from what has been said that drama and a proper analysis appear as the successful solution of a conflict, while neurosis and dreams represent an unsuccessful solution.

You see to what results our discussion has led us. Having started from quite a different angle, i.e. the consideration of certain phenomena of *form*, we have reached conclusions which, drawn from the study of *material content*, have long been reckoned amongst the most securely established in psychoanalysis. This seems to me a powerful argument in favour of my view.

Supposing that I am correct in assuming the existence of this tendency to give twofold expression to a psychic theme and that I am not trying to find a problem where none exists (a point which it is now for you to determine), we must be prepared for a number of questions which may arise. However, not merely because of considerations of space but also because I myself am not as yet ready to formulate these questions, I will confine myself to the most general, though not the most important of them: namely, to what category among the phenomena known to us is this tendency to duplicated expression to be assigned?

You will have noticed that I have endeavoured to derive this phenomenon from the structure of the personality and the relations between certain of its parts. The same point of view also enables us to answer the above question.

Accordingly this twofold expression would have to be assigned to the category first observed by Silberer and named by him "auto-symbolism", and it may perhaps be placed side by side with the functional phenomenon (of which as yet we have so imperfect an understanding), though its scope is vastly wider than that of the latter. For, as you will remember, Silberer explained auto-symbolism also as the product of two antagonistic strivings within the personality: the wish for sleep and the inner constraint to think. Thus, in terms of structure, he derived it from the conflict between ego and super-ego.

THE PSYCHOLOGY
OF THE FESTIVAL OF CHRISTMAS*

I TRUST that you are not entertaining too high expectations of this present contribution, for I can assure you it is a quite unpretentious study.

In order that you may not be disappointed, I must preface what I have to say by explaining that, in the problem with which I have attempted to deal, there are, as it were, three possible cross-sections: psycho-analytical, historical and religious. In order to do justice to all three I should require at least as many months as I have had weeks of preparation. In the picture which I present to you there is therefore, if I may so put it, considerable foreshortening.

For this reason my treatment of the psycho-analytical section is subject to somewhat unusual restrictions: I have had to stop short in the middle stratum. For, in order to go deeper, it would be absolutely necessary to link up this theme with the whole body of Christlore, and this would carry us far outside the scope of the present paper.

Those of you who are psycho-analysts will, I fear, inevitably experience some disappointment at the outset.

When we come to the historical section I feel some doubt in my own mind whether the relations which I have tried to demonstrate really exist largely in my own phantasy. So far as I am aware, our material rests upon no firm historical basis and therefore it is extraordinarily difficult to ascertain with any certainty whether the course of events actually was as I have depicted it, or whether it merely might have been so. I am quite prepared for the historians amongst you to be

* Read at a meeting of the Finnish-Swedish Psycho-Analytical Society. 13th December, 1934. First published in English in *The International Journal of Psycho-analysis* **17**, 1 (1936).
Immediately after the reading of this paper, which was written for the Christmas season, I was informed of Erich Fromm's paper "Die Entwicklung des Christusdogmas" (*Imago*, Bd. XVI, 1930), of the existence of which I had hitherto been unaware. Many of the ideas which I here put forward as conjectures are shown by Fromm, on the evidence of history, to be facts, and he has explored their origin in social and depth-psychology far more exhaustively than I myself. It is therefore only right that I should refer those interested in the subject to Fromm's paper, while gladly conceding to him priority of publication.

indignant and to accuse me of amateurishness, incompetence and ignorance. But you will find no chink in my armour, for my reply is that it is all your fault! Why do you scold us amateurs? Why do you not do the job yourselves? If you would only appropriate our method and apply it to the material with which you are so vastly more familiar than we are! No doubt you would do it far better than we can—and certainly far better than you have hitherto done it yourselves!

Finally, as regards those of you whose standpoint is that of religion I think I may say that, relatively, you have the least grounds of all for dissatisfaction with my essay, for you must admit that it might have been worse!

With this preface let us turn to the subject of our discussion.

The problem which I present for your consideration is that of the psychological meaning of the festival of Christmas and is, I think, a perfectly legitimate subject of inquiry even for an orthodox Christian. In asserting this I am supported by the following passage taken from a work by Usener, a scholar of deep religious convictions who, at the end of last century, began an historical examination of the subject, so far as I know the first to be attempted. "From the time of the Apostles the death and resurrection of Christ—the pledges of our salvation—were celebrated with due solemnity, but nearly three centuries had passed before there was any general feeling that the Church should observe as a feast that day which was the starting-point of the work of redemption, 'the mother of all festivals' . . . the birthday of Jesus Christ. There is no word in the Gospels of the month or day, or even of the time of year, when the birth of the Saviour took place; unlike the founders of the Greek Schools of philosophy, unlike the testator who bequeaths to his heirs a rich inheritance, the Founder of our religion left no direction that His birthday should be kept in remembrance by a yearly or monthly festival".

Now this is not an isolated opinion, peculiar to Usener; it is a point upon which all who have studied the subject are agreed. For example, Meyer of Zürich expresses himself as follows: "The solemn celebration of special days in the life of Jesus was contrary to the temper and the opinions of the early Christians . . . It did not occur to men's minds that the birthday of Christ should be observed as a festival; Origen, deeply versed in the Scriptures, pointed out, three centuries later, that in the whole Bible there is no instance of a righteous man celebrating his birthday; we read of it only in the case of Pharaoh and Herod, the enemies of God. At the end of the fourth century A.D., Arnobius derided the pagan custom of celebrating the birthdays of the gods, as though gods could be born or draw breath for the first time". It can surely be but rarely that a student of history finds himself in such complete agreement with psycho-analysts as Usener is when he goes on to say in this connection: "The exact time of year at which this birth took place could not be discovered and promulgated as the result of any process of historical logic; those who arrived at it were influenced by religious emotion or conformed to the modes of *mythological* thinking. It is worth while to observe how in the origin of a festival so solemn, so deeply rooted in the hearts of us all, this mode of thought prevailed, unconscious and, for that very reason, proceeding with the inevitable logic of the laws of Nature".

In a list of Roman bishops, drawn up in A.D. 335, that year is reckoned as beginning on 25th December, so that this date is first of all marked out as the first day of the New Year. In a Calendar of Martyrs, however, for the year A.D. 354, the following note appears against New Year's Day, i.e. 25th December: "Christ was born in Bethlehem in Judæa". We know further that the Emperor Constantine allowed the festival to be observed at the Roman Court in the years 354 to 360. All this makes it practically certain that the festival was instituted by the Church. Hence our question as to the meaning of the celebration of Christmas should really be formulated thus: What motives had the Church in instituting this festival and by what tendencies was she probably influenced?

The psychological importance of the problem is, I think, in no way diminished when we state that we are dealing with an action by ecclesiastical authorities. If anyone questions this opinion, he evidently fails to understand the position of the Church in those days and her relation to the people: he is judging by present-day standards. It is sufficient for me to emphasise the fact that, at that period, although the early Church could record considerable success under the rule of Constantine the Great, Catholicism being actually declared to be the State religion, she was nevertheless in perpetual conflict with the old, pagan religion, the Neo-Platonists and, finally, with the Oriental religions which, thirty years later under Julian the Apostate, achieved a notable triumph. The state of militancy and constant insecurity probably kept the still young Church from throwing overboard those ideological contents which, as she developed, had found their way from the living heart of the people into her system. We have only to recall how the profound popular interest in ecclesiastical questions gave rise to intense excitement on almost every occasion when some important dogma was in dispute, in order to realise how close was the bond which then existed between Church and people, how the pulses of both beat, as it were, to the same rhythm. This vivid empathy into popular feeling is quite excellently illustrated by the very subject we are discussing, for within a single decade the festival of Christmas established itself throughout the whole gigantic Roman Empire, penetrating even to Egypt and Palestine! Can we doubt that the Church was thereby giving expression to a popular craving? But what was that craving?

The answer to this question is, I think, suggested by the choice of the date. The 25th of December is, as we know, the day of the winter solstice; the shortest day is past and the sun seems, as it were, to be new. So this day—this *natalis Solis invicti*—is the birthday of the Unconquered One. The Orient had a strong and splendid cult of the sun, and its gods bore the title "Invincible". This seems to have been taken over by the Romans: in the late-Roman, pagan Calendar, 25th December appears as the birthday of the *Invictus*. The cult of the Sun God was closely connected with that of the Emperor, who enjoyed the god's special protection and companionship. After a victory, Aurelian dignified him with the title of god of the Court and Empire—and it was common for coins to be stamped with his image. "Popular reverence for the sun", says Meyer, "and religious enthusiasm at the season when the days lengthened were still alive in the heart of the people . . . the leaders of the Church, too, shared at bottom in this feeling and this it was which influenced their thoughts and calculations so that they chose as the date of Christ's nativity the 25th of December, the time of the turn of the year. For Christ has actually conquered the Sun God and it is fitting that the Church in her triumph should do honour to Him on this day".

This is certainly a reasonable interpretation of an allegorical relation which, it must be admitted, is not very obscure. But, misled by its very transparency, these investigators have evidently overlooked the fact that this idea of the winter solstice may have a far deeper symbolical meaning. I personally have no doubt that this "turning" implies also a transformation.

This transformation may in the first place have had reference to the sun itself, in the sense that the old sun of the past year was changed into a new, young sun; in other words, the new, young sun took the place of the old sun. For, as Meyer tells us, "in ancient times it was very general for the sun, when the shortest day was passed, to be called in the vigorous popular phrase 'the new' or 'young' sun. Poets, astronomers and orators have made use of this idea".

Secondly, I think it is very natural to assume that the change thus indicated had reference also to the coming change in the seasons, the passing of the reign of winter and the approach of spring, especially when we remember that the countries originally concerned were of the East and South. And so we see the second deeper meaning in the symbolical reference to the displacement of aged winter, by youthful spring. I can quote evidence, though of an indirect nature, in support of this view. In yet earlier times, as far back as the second century, attempts had been made to select a certain day in the year as the date of Christ's nativity. This was done on the initiative of over-zealous individuals, and the dates suggested found no general acceptance, all of them being regarded as arbitrary and by no means certain. But the interesting point is this: in most cases such dates as 28th March, 19th-20th April, 20th-21st May were proposed, i.e. all of them days in the springtime. The author whom I have already quoted was struck by this fact, for he writes, "In spring, when new life burgeons", but his attention was focussed so exclusively upon the allegorical meaning that he never even thought of a deeper significance.

However, the strongest evidence of the correctness of this symbolical interpretation of the solstice is that, from quite a different angle, we arrive at the same conclusion, the same antithesis of old and new, the replacing of the old by the new.

It can hardly be questioned that the festival of Christmas is very closely connected with the idea of the turn of the year, i.e. the replacing of the old year by the new.

We have already observed this close connection when we noted that the Church dated the beginning of the year from 25th December. I believe that in selecting this date the Church was influenced by her unconscious perception of the symbolism in the situation, far more than by the motive usually ascribed to her, namely, that "every Christian system must begin with the nativity of Christ". And, on the other hand, almost all the scholars who have studied the subject are agreed that the festival of Christmas, as we know it, had its origin in the New Year's festival observed in the latter days of ancient Rome, the calends of January representing, as it were, the ancient stem upon which was grafted the Christmas feast. This view is held by Billinger and Tyle and also by Nielssen of Lund, who was the most distinguished Swedish historian of his time. Nielssen, however, held that there were also affinities between Christmas and the Nordic festival of Yule.

In ancient Rome the New Year was originally celebrated on 1st March. The principal ceremony—and this has a special bearing on the hypothesis I am submitting to you—was the entering of the new, annually elected consuls upon their office in place of the retiring consuls of the previous year. So important was this feature of the New Year's festival that when, subsequently, it was decreed that the term of office should date from 1st January, that date was adopted for New Year's Day also.

Now in Imperial times the calends of January had a twofold importance. In the first place they were marked by a solemn State festival, the principal feature of which was, as I have said, the conferring of office upon the new consuls, who, with a large escort, made their first appearance on the Capitol before the assembled Senate. But the calends of January were, besides, a popular festival of immense importance, which lasted five days. It is impossible in this paper to give even a brief account of the many traditional practices and customs which characterised this festival and which the untiring research of scholars has brought to our knowledge. I must, however, quote one or two passages from Nielssen's work so that you may see how strongly this Roman feast resembles our modern Christmas celebrations, both in spirit and in many of its principal features. "The festival of New Year", he says, ". . . had penetrated to the remotest corners of the Empire, and with one accord the people took part in it". "Throughout the Empire, to its farthest boundaries, the calends of January were celebrated. The people looked forward to them with the utmost eagerness. Festal robes were worn and a stream of presents poured forth on all sides, from the country to the town and from village to village. Trains of men and beasts, laden with gifts, crowded the high-roads and the footpaths. Scarcely had the day dawned when the people began to decorate their doors with branches of laurel and green garlands. Large quantities of valuable presents were carried through the streets of the town; people delighted in giving no less than in receiving".

This brief illustration must suffice to show that, on the testimony of those who have devoted their researches to this subject, there is a strong resemblance between the Roman celebrations and our own. It is high time that we turned our attention to the crux of the problem: what is the true meaning of this purpose, whose presence in the Christmas festival we have gone so far afield to demonstrate—the ousting of the old by the new? What, if I may so put it, is its ultimate real source? Now, if psycho-analysis is sure of anything, it is of the answer to this question.

For here we have arrived by way of symbolism at the very same fact that has been proved, a thousand times over and beyond all possibility of doubt, in our analytic experience with neurotics: the fact, namely, of the son's rivalry with his father.

It is a theme which is embodied in some of the greatest works of poets as well as in countless myths, fairy-tales and legends, now in one symbolic guise, now in another.

For instance, we read how old Macbeth,[1] with his blood-guilt, is conquered by the Forest of Dunsinane, i.e. by the soldiers concealed by green branches. Seventeen years ago, on the evidence of certain established facts in the life of Shakespeare, I suggested and, I think, proved conclusively that behind the nature-myth underlying the story of Macbeth there lies this theme of the son's rivalry with his father. In this

---

[1] If the play is interpreted as a Nature-myth, Macbeth, of course, stands for winter.

connection I quote the old Hessian legend of King Greenwood: "There was once a king who had an only daughter, endowed with wonderful gifts. One day there came an enemy, a king called Greenwood, who besieged the other king in his castle. Long they were beleaguered and always the daughter spoke words of encouragement to the king, her father, in his castle. At last came the month of May. Suddenly the daughter saw the enemy's army approaching, bearing green branches. Thereupon fear and trembling seized her, for she knew that all was lost, and she said to her father:

> Father, give yourself up as a captive,
> For here comes the green tree walking.[1]

Here we have the same symbolism as in *Macbeth*, but a much more important point is this: this story, as is transparently clear, embodies the son's wish-phantasy of occupying the first place in the woman's (i.e. the mother's) affections and here we have the root cause of his antagonistic attitude to his father. This is the primal source from which all his subsequent social relations derive their strength and colour, by which, in short, their qualities are determined. I feel that it is quite outside the scope of this paper to do justice to this mythological problem, perhaps the most important of them all. For the present it must suffice if I point out that a man's relation to his father is, as it were, the prototype upon which a whole series of social relations are modelled, e.g. that of subject and ruler, employee and employer, servant and master, and so on, and that on it are based and in it are centred in the minds of individuals not only the ideals of equality, liberty and independence, but also the opposite mental tendencies.

The relation of son to father will occupy us in the further course of this essay. For the moment we will leave the general proposition and go back to our specific problem: the meaning of the festival of Christmas. Now we find that the first question that suggests itself is this: what bearing upon this problem has the son-father relation, which we have just stripped of its symbolic disguise? How can it be said to play a part in the celebration of Christmas?

To answer this question we must review the circumstances

---

[1] "Vater, gebt Euch gefangen
Der grüne Baum kommt gegangen".

in which the Church decreed that Christmas should be observed.

The soil from which the festival sprang, the spiritual and mental atmosphere in which, *as I conjecture*, it originated, was the greatest doctrinal dispute which the Christian Church has ever known. I refer to the Arian controversy, which began about thirty years before Christmas was first observed and was terminated, about thirty years later, simply by a decree of the Emperor Theodosius the Great.

From the end of the second century onwards the controversy between the gnostics and their opponents gave rise to an extraordinary outburst of theological activity; numerous questions were propounded and discussed by theologians and the various schools of thought attacked one another violently, each striving to prevail in the Church.

The conflict of opinions, which lasted for a whole century, was above all concerned with the question of the nature of Jesus, the origin of His person and His twofold relation, i.e. to God and to man. Two explanations were put forward: the one led from the earthly plane to the heavenly while, according to the other, a heavenly being had come down to earth. The first problem gave rise to a second: were we to see in Jesus the revelation of a second Person in the Deity or did the Godhead remain one and undivided? This was the real point in dispute and this it was which in the subsequent course of the Arian controversy roused men's minds to fever-heat.

In this controversy the so-called *Logos-Christologists*, who derived their doctrine from Origen, were arrayed against the *Monarchians*, who claimed to uphold the monotheistic view, according to which there was in the Godhead but one Person Who alone was supreme. The exponents of this theory did not concede the Divinity of the Son, although in all other respects they held Him in the utmost reverence. The followers of Origen, on the other hand, conceived of the Logos as the divine reason manifested in the world, the being, the substance, the essence of the Godhead. The Logos, they held, existed from eternity in the Father and was of Him alone, but the Father Himself raised up the Logos to be a separate Person. Or, more concretely and precisely: the Father caused a second personal centre to come into being within that substance which hitherto He alone indwelt, so that a second Divine Person was "begotten", yet without division or cleavage of the substance, as in the procreation of human beings.

We see that both these doctrines are based on religious-metaphysical modes of thought which remind us forcibly of the mental processes in obsessional neurosis which, as we know, has a strong tendency towards transcendentalism. But there is another point to note:—

In the light of psycho-analysis these opposing schools of thought—in whose formulas and concepts there is, characteristically, far more mention of Father and Son than of God and Jesus—differ from one another by no means so widely as was supposed. The views of both parties in the controversy have far more points in common than points of divergence, for in both the fundamental psychic tendency is one and the same: the difference lies only in the emphasis placed on various conceptions. And their common platform is that to which I have already alluded: the attitude of the son to the father that is termed *ambivalent* by psycho-analysis, that inescapable psychological fate which decrees that, side by side with his love and respect for his father, there are in the son's mind powerful hostile tendencies which impel him to enter into rivalry with his father, to dispute his superiority, shake off his authority and, if not actually to supplant him, at least to rank himself as his father's equal.

And now I would ask this question. The strict Monarchian Arius did not, as I have pointed out, concede to Jesus a share in the Godhead but held that there was "at the centre of His personality a pre-existent, heavenly being, 'The Son', created by the Father out of nothingness before all time". Is there not in this conception, whereby Arius sought to enthrone the Son as near as possible to the Father, the same ambivalent tendency, only in a lesser degree, which in the Christologist Athanasius reached its climax in the assertion of the full divinity of the Son? Indeed, the two protagonists in the controversy differed not in their fundamental dogmas but in the degree of their ambivalence.

No wonder then, that with such a failure to recognise their own aims and such a lack of clarity as to their own intentions, the opposing parties in the Arian controversy could arrive at no decision, so that it continued for fifty-five years and was terminated only by an Imperial decree.

Nevertheless, even in the Logos-Christologists, ambivalence did not reach its zenith. For, they, no more than the Arians, could conceive of the Son as wholly independent of the Father, indebted to Him for nothing, as it were self-existent. Indeed, Origen's own doctrine of the Logos had laid stress on this very inequality between Father and Son: the Father made "of Himself", the Son "of the Father", begotten of Him from all eternity, without beginning, perfect God and unchangeable as the Father, *inferior to Him only in this—that He derived His existence from the Father.*

The same standpoint was taken by Athanasius, in whom the ambivalence was more pronounced in that he maintained even more uncompromisingly the Divinity of the Son. We read in Müller: "Athanasius, on the other hand, did not assert that the Father and the Son were perfectly co-equal. On the contrary he assigned to the Father the divine substance, from which the Son was begotten. Thus the Father is $\dot{\alpha}\rho\chi\dot{\eta}$ and the Son $\gamma\acute{\epsilon}\nu\nu\eta\mu\alpha$. His followers went on to declare that the Son was $\dot{\delta}\mu o\upsilon o\acute{\iota}o\varsigma$ and $\dot{\delta}\mu o\iota o\varsigma$, but never did they claim for Him complete equality with the Father".

In my view the introduction of the festival of Christ's nativity indicates a growing tendency to regard the Son as wholly co-equal with the Father, indicates, that is to say, a growing ambivalence. The Son, though born as man, yet already co-equal with God the Father: Himself God, not "of the Father" but as it were by virture of His own essential Divinity—this is the fundamental dogma implied in the inauguration of the Christmas feast.

In support of this theory let me cite the following well attested fact. Long before the birthday of Jesus was celebrated, the Early Church observed (right up to the fourth century) a Christmas festival on the 6th of January, the Feast of the Epiphany. There were two reasons which probably decided the choice of this particular date: (1) In Egypt the virgin-birth of the god, Aion, was celebrated on that day and (2) on the same day the Christian gnostics—the Basilideans—com-memorated the baptism of Christ. Now the fact that the Church chose this date shews very plainly that there was felt to be a connection between the baptism and the birth of Christ, and what this was we may learn from the doctrine of Basilides. He held that, originally, Jesus was merely man but that, at

His baptism, the spirit and mind of God, in the form of the dove, entered into Him. Thus, it was only at His baptism that Christ the Redeemer was born: in that moment God was made manifest upon earth.

About the middle of the fourth century the Feast of the Nativity was suddenly dissociated from that of the Epiphany and a special date—25th December—was assigned to it. That is to say, the Son was declared to be God, not merely through the indwelling of the Spirit of God, i.e. through the Father, but as co-equal with the Father through His own essential Divinity. This, I take it, is the meaning of Meyer's explanation of the fact of the separate celebration of Christmas: "If the nativity was held to be the beginning of the life of the God-Man, Jesus, there could no longer be any question of His deriving His significance as the Christ from His baptism, by which He assumed the office of the Messiah. Thus the prominence given to the Feast of the Nativity . . . was a protest against a less exalted view of the person of Christ".

This action on the part of the Church was, indeed, revolutionary and therefore significant, for behind the façade of mystical religion lay the assertion of the democratic principle of equality.

What, then, were the Church's reasons for taking such a step? What impelled her to venture upon it? Documentary evidence is entirely lacking, but I believe that it is at least probable that the Church at this point had the people behind her and that, with her genius for empathy, in this instance if in any she sought to respond to a deep-felt popular need— nay, to a popular demand. In my introductory remarks I reminded you that the tie between Church and people was in those days beyond all comparison closer than it is now: the Church was in actual fact the mouthpiece of the Christian congregations, who still were in the minority.

Thus the concerns of her people were then, to a far greater extent than now, those of the Church and, conversely, the Church could be sure of the keenest interest on the people's part in her problems and conflicts.

One way in which this interest shewed itself was that the whole Christian community participated with the utmost enthusiasm in the theological speculation of the age.

Thus it was while the Arian controversy continued to rage;

for it is to the period of that controversy that we must return if we would study the problem upon which the people, at any rate in the East, were concentrating most intently and which they made their most intimate concern, so that the words υἱός and λόγος echoed in the streets like battle-cries. The Church historian, Schubert, explains this eagerness by pointing out that in those days knowledge of God had an independent value of its own. For, he says, the ecclesiastical leaders of the people, and especially the great Alexandrians, completely altered the relation between faith and knowledge, fusing the two into one. According to their teaching, knowledge was faith and faith knowledge, but personal cognition, i.e. knowledge, ensured a more direct union with the divine Logos. He believes that this was why it was to the interest of every earnest Christian, even amongst the uneducated, personally to master these problems.

While not questioning the accuracy of Schubert's assertion I am not at all inclined to accept it as a complete and adequate explanation of the extraordinary degree of affect manifested by the people when participating in theological controversy. We read, for instance, that in the streets of Alexandria and Constantinople heads were broken over the formula of the homoousia.

I have much less hesitation in conjecturing that here, in the guise of mystical religion, an outlet was afforded for affects which had their source in the exigencies of a social situation in which tension was high and differences were sharp.

But why, you will ask, did the affects in question assume these mystical trappings?

The question is not merely a perfectly legitimate one but is of importance and that not for our problem alone: it touches on a more general problem which, as far as I know, has not yet been solved, namely, why no mass-movement is ever free from the element of mysticism. I need only instance the great French Revolution in which, after the old religious values had been overthrown, men yet reached out after a divinity, even though they did but deify reason.

The clue, as I believe, is to be found in the conception of *sin and guilt* with their inevitable penalties—a notion introduced by Christianity, i.e. if I am not mistaken, by the Apostle Paul.

Here, however, at the risk of repeating something with

which many of you are already familiar, I must interpolate a few remarks on the psycho-analytical conception of the sense of guilt. Our views is that it represents some sort of endopsychic perception of a state in which one part of the personality, the ego, is called to account—as it were, indicted—by another part, the super-ego.

Fundamentally the super-ego represents the extension of the early infantile relation of the individual to his parents but with this very important modification, that gradually the sensual-erotic tone of that earliest relation disappears and another aspect of it is stressed: the parents are felt and desired to be a protective, guardian institution.

As life goes on, the super-ego develops into a mental structure, the foundation-stone of which is the so-called parent-imagos and which is built up through the incorporation into the super-ego, as it were, of everything that represents authority. Here are embodied those who brought up the individual as a child and other governing forces of real life—civic authorities, rulers, communal feeling, scientific opinion and, besides these, metaphysical conceptions such as Fate and God—all these contribute their orders, instructions, rules and admonitions.

It can be no wonder that the super-ego, derived from such sources as these, is invariably felt by the ego to be a vastly superior institution whose authority and rule are absolute and which exercises over the ego itself a perpetual supervision, criticism and censorship.

Now a particularly important point for us to note is that the relation of the majority of people to their super-ego remains precisely the same as in their childhood, the period of their earliest development. As I have already remarked, their desire is that the super-ego should with unwearying vigilance protect and guard them and keep them secure in the vicissitudes of life. To make certain of this sheltering care the ego does its best to obey the demands of the super-ego, treating them as inviolable decrees, and it is the failure to observe these which gives rise to the sense of guilt.

The ego, dreading lest it should be abandoned and exposed to all manner of dangers by the super-ego, trembles at the thought of provoking its displeasure and resentment, while conversely every hardship and mischance in life is construed as a punishment and a chastisement inflicted by the super-ego.

Here we have the answer to our question why group-manifestations are associated with mysticism. The reason is that human beings inevitably translate their experiences, on whatever plane of life, into terms of the super-personal, i.e. the metaphysical, holding them to be the dispensation of God, of Destiny, etc. And this is why a knowledge of individual psychology is not only indispensable but supremely important for the understanding of group-phenomena.

So we arrive at the final survey of the main problem which we are considering. The members of the Christian congregations laboured under a sense of guilt which the zeal of the still relatively young Church had fostered till it was very highly developed. In their unconscious minds, where they were identified with the Son Jesus, they seized upon the true tendency of the theological controversy. Undeceived by all the formulas with their attempts at compromise and by all the half-statements of the protagonists they penetrated to the true heart of the matter. For what it really amounted to was nothing less than an attempt to dethrone God, the collective Super-Ego, with which the super-ego of the individual had such close relations. True, the attempt was not carried very far but there could be no doubt of its revolutionary character.

Thus, the passionate interest of the people in the theological controversy was but the expression of their revolt against God, and, moreover, a revolt arising out of despair.

For that same sense of guilt upon which Christianity had laid so strong an emphasis inevitably awoke in them the feeling that all the distress and deprivation they endured as the result of social inequality were inflicted upon them as a punishment by the super-ego—no matter whether it were collective or individual. And all this in spite of their prayers, repentance and expiation.

Their passionate feeling was, then, a flare-up of rebellion against a super-ego whose harshness, cruelty and implacability oppressed them so grievously. And how readily were they confirmed in this rebellious mood when they looked back only a short way into the past! Scarcely fifty years had elapsed since the persecution by Diocletian and scarcely a hundred since that under the Emperors Decius and Valerius: had not these persecutions, with all their martyrdoms and horrors, been inflicted upon them—or, if not inflicted, at least permitted

—by this same super-ego? And what of the hecatombs offered up by the early Christians? All this cruelty perpetrated upon the best of His sons! Had it not wrung from the most perfect of them all the reproach, "My God, my God, why hast Thou forsaken me?"

Away, then, with such a monstrous super-ego! And evidence was in fact not lacking to show that man can dethrone a God or overthrow his super-ego! Where were they now, all the deities of antiquity and of the Orient? Their worship, if it had not wholly disappeared, had at least suffered a severe reverse, its power broken and its credit gone.

And had not the Emperors been deprived of their divine attributes? Divus Augustus—god and emperor in one—enjoying his apotheosis for centuries in his own temples decorated with statues of his person, to which rich oblations were offered—now shorn of his divinity by the decree of Constantine, the temple rid of the imperial statue, a public place of honour without religious significance!

Away, then, with this super-ego!

Let them hear no more of a divine governance, against which, fifteen hundred years later, a great poet was to utter the reproach:

"You suffer us, miserable sinners, to fall
And then into torment deliver us all!"[1]

No, the God of their worship should be Christ, Who had redeemed mankind from all guilt and Whose gospel love should be their pledge of freedom from future guilt.

But in a deeper stratum of the mind there rose this wish, born of a grandiose identification with Jesus: If the Son be co-equal with the Father, be very God, then there is neither supremacy nor subordination: all is equality, i.e. unity and harmony, and therefore there is no more guilt.

Thus, when she ordained the celebration of Christ's Nativity, the Church fulfilled the wish of the people, yet only half fulfilled it, for God the Father still remained enthroned.

As you probably know, analysis sees in myths the age-long dreams of mankind and maintains that their purpose, like that of dreams, is wish-fulfilment. Thus, if we examine our myth, we find in the birth of Christ—the God-Man, in Whom

[1] "Ihr lasst den Armen schuldig werden
Dann überlasst Ihr ihn der Pein".

man is co-equal with God and God with man, so that all inequalities are done away with—the fulfilment of the unconquerable wish for equality.

Perhaps this is the unconscious basis of the title borne by the Messiah from of old: "The Sun of Righteousness".

And, if you have any lingering doubts, perhaps the following consideration will put an end to them. Some of you who are familiar with my material may have been struck by the fact that, when speaking of the antecedents of the Christian festival, I made no mention of the *Saturnalia*, the Roman feast of ecstatic revelry, which ended on 17th December. I said nothing about it until now because the Saturnalia gradually merged into the celebration of the Calends of January, which took over many of the rites of the older festival, amongst them (and here I am quoting) "the characteristic Saturnalian feature of the *libertas Decembris:* equality between masters and servants, in which the relation was sometimes actually reversed, so that slaves were served by their lords".

In conclusion, let me say that in this paper I have not related to you a fairy-tale such as it is customary to tell in the evenings at Yuletide, for I believe it to be based upon a profound psychological truth.

In collaboration with

EDMUND BERGLER, M.D.

INSTINCT DUALISM IN DREAMS*

I

WE are here presenting the second of a proposed series of investigations into the more important psychological phenomena considered from the point of view of the dualism of instinct, Eros and death.

In view of the energetic opposition which the hypothesis of a death instinct has met, particularly in Wilhelm Reich's book, *Character Analysis*, we ought perhaps to begin by determining whether or not this freudian concept can be upheld and whether, in the latter case, the basis for our investigation is still valid. We think, however, that this is neither the time nor the place for such a survey. Since we are of the opinion that a correct polemic consists of the support of a thesis rather than of the refutation of an attack upon it, we propose in the present case to limit ourselves to a presentation of a new piece of evidence for the existence of the death instinct which, as Freud complains, "is difficult to grasp, inarticulate, and hard to demonstrate". We believe that we can present evidence which is perhaps clearer than that heretofore presented. Our arguments against Reich will therefore refer only to those of his contentions which in some way cross the particular path which we have chosen for ourselves.

We believe that we have found this new evidence in a phenomenon which, unlike others that have been considered in this connection, does not belong to the field of pathology. It belongs rather to the realm of the normal and represents a biological state anchored basically in the periodicity which so widely dominates organic life. We refer, as you may already have guessed, to *sleep*.

While recognising the strictest limitation of his own field, Freud never lost sight of the intimate bond between the psychical and the biological and their basic determination by the organic. He illustrated the relationship between the two fields of knowledge with the following: "It is like the construction

* Translated by Polly Leeds Weil. First published in English in *The Psychoanalytic Quarterly*, IX, 3, 1940. Presented at the Thirteenth International Psycho-analytic Congress in Lucerne, 27th August, 1934.

of a tunnel, which is almost always started from both ends at once. The psychologists from one side, the biologists from the other, will one day break through the last section, and grasp each other's hands".

It does not seem necessary for the understanding of our argument to lay before you the whole rich and interesting field with which physiological investigations of the problems of sleep are continually occupied. For our purpose the following brief sketch should suffice.

In the literature dealing with the physiology of sleep we find two opposed views. One finds the cause and nature of sleep in certain states and processes in the brain. According to this view, sleep is ultimately a process in the nerve centres. These function as "so to speak, great blockades which occur in the general network of the excitatory paths, bringing to a halt the trains of excitation which run into or through the centres from all sides". This theory sees the mechanism of sleep in a "block-ade against excitation, which is ingeniously built into the life preserving nervous regulatory system".[1] The other theory, supported chiefly by Economo and Pötzl,[2] is incomparably more far-reaching than the so-called "brain-sleep" theory. According to this theory sleep is by no means a localised process in the brain but rather a generalised process in which a general body sleep is distinguished from the localised brain sleep.

We believe that we are correct in assuming that Economo—who himself has greatly enriched the study of sleep by the discovery of the important sleep centres—is of the opinion that the theory of sleep centres neither has been, nor will be able to answer the question of the *nature* of sleep. For sleep is to be conceived of as a more primary, biologically generalised, alternating state which has in the central nervous system not its ultimate cause but only its regulating mechanisms, and this only in part. Sleep is a complex biological state which alters the functions of most of the organs not only by rendering them quiescent but often by inducing *qualitative* changes. It represents a periodic fluctuation within the general functioning of the organism which is not primarily dependent for its polarity upon the functioning of the central nervous system.

As one can see, there are wide differences between the two

[1] Winterstein: *Sleep and Dreams.*
[2] Salomon: *Der Schlaf.*

theories. But brushing aside all that separates them, both theories are admittedly deeply influenced by Freud's views on sleep. The psycho-analytic characterisation of the state of sleep, as it is given for example in the Introductory Lectures to Psycho-analysis, is as follows: "Sleep is a condition in which I refuse to have anything to do with the outer world and have withdrawn my interest from it. I go to sleep by retreating from the outside world and warding off the stimuli proceeding from it. Again, when I am tired by that world, I go to sleep. I say to it as I fall asleep: 'Leave me in peace, for I want to sleep' . . . Thus the biological object of sleep seems to be recuperation, its psychological characteristic the suspension of interest in the outer world. Our relationship with the world which we entered so unwillingly seems to be endurable only with intermissions; hence we withdraw again periodically into the condition prior to our entrance into the world: that is to say, into intra-uterine existence".

Let us now listen to a proponent of the "brain-sleep" theory —Professor Winterstein. "We have noted above that the cessation of muscular activity *is not simply a purely passive occurrence* . . . Now we see that behaviour in the realm of sensation is apparently quite similar to that in the realm of motility. Sleep is not simply a blotting out of the functions. It seems much more like an active withdrawal. It is not an *inability* to hear or feel, it is the wish not to hear or feel, turning a deaf ear, pretending insensibility—the wish 'to be left in peace'."

Although Winterstein finds much in the freudian dream theory which is contestable, and argues vehemently against it, he does not hesitate to emphasise "how closely Freud's dream theory touches the modern theory of sleep, which explains the latter as an *active* process in the organism".

The proponents of the general sleep theory acknowledge their adherence far more readily. For example, Pötzl writes: ". . . Freud's conception of sleep . . . which has emerged from the purely psychic, is fully in accord with the results of the biological observation of the problem of sleep, and with those modern theories of sleep which emphasise the *active* quality in sleep, the *wish* to withdraw; and yet the freudian conception is older than these theories".

Thus in the modern investigations of sleep, whatever their

coloration, we find like a recurrent theme the assertion that sleep is not a passive or negative drying up of the springs of energy, a dying out of functions, but rather a positive, active process which brings about certain functional alterations.

Economo and Pötzl, the chief proponents of the general sleep theory, built their theory on a very broad basis. To solve the riddle of sleep they drew on the whole realm of living things, the totality of organic existence, plant life as well as animal. As a result of these researches in comparative biology the authors came to the conclusion that sleep in man and the higher animals is only a special case of a much more general principle to which all living matter conforms. Sleep they say is only a special form of a general tendency, an inner *necessity* of all protoplasm to enter into a state of rest from time to time and under certain circumstances, as well as the *ability* of protoplasm to put itself into (not fall into) such a state. "The necessity for protoplasm to enter into such a state from time to time", says Pötzl, "involves the same general question of energy which is also involved in the problem of energy in sleep. The activity by means of which the protoplasm proves itself equal to this necessity, includes those . . . processes, which . . . are usually described as *active* achievements in the transition into the state of sleep".

We do not feel that we are doing violence to the facts when we identify this tendency to rest which biologists consider immanent in protoplasm, a necessity for protoplasm, with the freudian death instinct, and when we further assume that sleep, as it becomes differentiated in man and the higher mammals from this primordial quality of protoplasm is an expression of the death instinct. How then, in the light of this biological view of an active, driving element in the state of rest, shall we approach Reich's arguments against the concept of the death instinct? He says, for example, "This assumption was superfluous in explaining the striving for a return to a state of rest. For this striving is completely explained by the libido's function of bringing about release from tension, and further by the libidinous longing for the womb". Or again, "The assumption of a biological striving for death becomes superfluous when one considers that the physiological disintegration of the organism, its gradual dying, begins as soon as the function of the sexual apparatus, the source of the libido, diminishes. Therefore no other cause for death need be sought than the gradual cessation of the functions of the vital mechanisms".

Where biology strongly emphasises the active factors in the processes to which we refer, Reich finds only an altogether passive slackening and cessation. One can hardly imagine a stronger contradiction and contrast than this. Fear of over-biologising in analytic psychology, of which Reich accuses the adherents of the Thanatos theory, does not justify the other extreme of neglecting the facts of biology. For then one arrives, as Reich does, at an anthropocentric point of view. We do not know how otherwise to describe this isolation of man from his cosmic relations and this reduction of his universal aspect to a given principle only because it is easily applicable to man, to the single pattern of tension and release.

Returning to our task of supporting the contention that sleep is a manifestation of the death instinct, we find that biology, which up to this point has given us so much information, fails now to furnish us with further material bearing on the similarities and relationships between sleep and death. This is not to be wondered at when we remember how little it has to tell us about the nature of death itself. One is tempted to assume that death is nothing other than the most extreme expression of that lower level of functioning found in sleep in the retardation and weakening of the heart beat and vascular tone, in the diminished sensitivity of the breathing centre, the loss of oxygen, lowering of temperature and decrease of glandular activity. Death would accordingly be the sinking to the zero point of this lowered rhythm of life already indicated in sleep, and at the same time its perpetuation, that is, the transformation of a periodic into a permanent state.

In support of this one might mention hibernation, a phenomenon which is looked upon as a *vita minima*. Also, clinicians have brought statistical evidence to show what folklore has always maintained, that death has a far more intimate connection with night than with day. Clever, intuitive doctors have always combatted excessive sleeping habits in certain diseases. We feel, however, that to attribute the difference between sleep and death to quantitative changes alone does not suffice, and that there is danger thus of becoming involved in a contradiction with the very theory which we have asserted. For this theory warns us against seeing in sleep merely the nadir of a rhythm. It is a fundamentally different state, brought about by *qualitative* changes of all bodily functions.

And so we stand confronted by the question we have raised, not knowing which way to turn, until a new path suddenly opens before us. Does it mean nothing that in the world of man's imagination sleep and death are inevitably paired, and that this connection is so ancient, and at the same time so current, that it is really embarrassing to focus attention upon such a platitude?[1] It is impossible that a deeper meaning does not attach to such commonplace comparisons as, "to sleep like the dead", "like a stone", "like a block of wood"; "sleep eternal", "the last sleep", as well as such sayings as, "death is eternal sleep", "death is a long sleep", "sleep is a little death". Poets too have dwelt on the relationship. Grabbe writes: "Fie! fie! on sleep. Time not spent in sleeping, I say, is won from death"; and "Sleep is half death, death the longest sleep; the more you sleep, the less you live". In Goethe we find:

> Slumber and Sleep, two brothers, in service to the Gods,
> Were brought to earth by Prometheus to solace his race.
> But that which the Gods took lightly was a burden to mankind;
> Their slumber became our sleep, their sleep our death.

This association is so common and so old that one stumbles on it everywhere in the present and in the past without looking for it. Says Cicero, in his *Tusculan Disputations: "habes somnum imaginem mortis"*. From the excellent research by Lessing, *How the Ancients Pictured Death*, we know that for the antique arts it was not only acceptable but obligatory to present sleep and death as twin brothers. After giving a masterful analysis of several antique works of art, Lessing summarises his polemic in the words "the ancients pictured death as sleep and sleep as death, sometimes singly, sometimes together". Beginning with the Iliad from which, moreover, antique sculpture is supposed to have taken the idea of sleep and death as twin brothers, down to the present day, this juxtaposition has been a favourite theme of poets.

All this seems to support the view of Schopenhauer that each night, so to speak, "we anticipate death", that is, succumb to death. Perhaps it is in this nightly quasi-experience of death

---

[1] Our colleague, G. Hans Graber, has drawn our attention to the fact that in his book *Procreation, Birth and Death*, he described the typical association of sleep with death in the human imagination.

in sleep that the cause is to be found of the astonishing fact that there is no concept of death in the unconscious, that "there is nothing in the unconscious which could substantiate our concept of the extinction of life". It would seem, accordingly, that there is no more mortally dangerous undertaking than to sink into sleep, and we might be considered to be exhibiting remarkable courage when we do so. The fact is, however, that this undertaking is quite without danger and has no doleful consequences, so that we must forego any pride in the accomplishment. In short, to borrow from Schopenhauer again, we pay death only the interest upon his loan. This, we now submit, is the work of Eros.

For the sake of clarity we have been neglecting Eros, but we must now reinstate it in its rightful place. For it is Eros which actually creates that which we understand as sleep. It is only when Eros has united with the original drive or instinct for rest, that the phenomenon of sleep is brought about.

The magnitude of this achievement of Eros in its fusion with the death instinct can be measured by the fact that the *destructive goal of the Thanatos component is not only neutralised, but actually transformed into its opposite—into the recuperative effect of sleep.* Eros transforms the instinct to rest into the pleasant wish to sleep primarily by offering the return to the womb as a pleasure premium. The understanding of this we owe to Freud. As a further measure, a heightened degree of defence, as it were, Eros invests the ego with all the libido at its disposal. For this it mobilises even the repressed libido itself—the infantile sexual wishes.

The great advantage of this point of view is obvious. Now we can fully understand those two characteristics of the dream which hitherto have been established only empirically. We refer to the wish fulfilling tendency of dreams, and to the fact that the wishes are sexual in character.

If then, appearances are not deceptive, we must add to the well-known function of the dream as the guardian of sleep a second function which towers above the first—the guarding of life. These tendencies largely coincide because of the use of the pleasure premium of wish fulfilment. But further, through the fact that Eros here contests the ground with the death instinct, thus replacing the peace and quiet of lifelessness with motion and the clamour of life, the original destruction and denial of life is replaced by its affirmation and construction. This struggle of both original urges in the dream, pulling the ego this way and that, now with the demands of the id, now with the commands of the super-ego, completes the analogy of dream with neurosis. To illustrate with examples is the task of the second part of this paper.

First, however, we wish to point out that the foregoing train of thought not only advances but notably enhances the rehabilitation of the dream started by Freud after it had been scorned for centuries. The dream is here exalted, as it were, to a regulatory mechanism of decisive, even vital significance.

At the same time we have the answer to the heretofore unanswered question of whether our dreams occur only occasionally, or whether they are compulsory phenomena occurring every night. From our argument it follows that sleep without dreams is as impossible as dreams without sleep, not counting daydreams which in any case differ vastly from nocturnal dreams. The dream is a constant because indispensable piece in the repertory of sleep; it is its most integral component, inseparable from sleep because indissolubly welded with it. This point of view can scarcely be contradicted even by physiologists, since recent investigation has produced very convincing evidence that experience is not interrupted even in the deepest sleep but continues undisturbed. We can now answer the question we have raised as to the common and differentiating traits of sleep and death with the following brief formula: *Sleep is death stirred by dreams; death is dreamless sleep.*

In spite of what we believe to be concise and conclusive proof, we should perhaps hardly venture to emphasise so startling a conclusion had we not come across a complete confirmation of our views after we had already written them down. Emanuel Kant, in paragraph 67 of *The Critique of Judgment* has this to say to our problem: ". . . now I would ask if dreams (without which we never sleep, though we seldom remember them) may not be a purposive ordinance of nature? For during the relaxation of all the moving powers of the body, they serve to excite internally the vital organs by the medium of the Imagination and its great activity (which in this state generally rises to the height of affection) . . . Consequently, then, without this internal power of motion and this fatiguing unrest, on account of which we complain about our dreams (though in fact they are rather remedial), sleep even in a sound state of health would be a complete extinction of life".

II

In our paper on *Transference and Love*,[1] we attempted to separate more sharply the component parts of the super-ego, frequently insufficiently differentiated, by applying the theory of the life and death instincts. We arrived at the conclusion that the two parts of the super-ego, the ego ideal ("Thou shalt") and the *dæmon* ("Thou shalt not"), differ psychologically, instinctually and genetically.[2] The ego ideal has two roots. One of these consists in the attempt of the ego to divert the course of the aggression of the death instinct from the ego as object to other objects which thereby become terrifying, a projected outer danger being substituted for an inner one. This attempt is unsuccessful. This achievement of the destructive instinct is parried by Eros which takes these fearsome objects into the ego where they become the object of its narcissism. The second root of the ego ideal is to be found in a compromise attempt of the ego to maintain its supposed omnipotence. This fictitious omnipotence is badly shaken by the demands of the outer world (weaning, training in cleanliness, etc.). In the face of these demands the child, because of its helplessness, must choose either to give up its infantile megalomania, or, although accepting the commands and bans of its parents, to preserve the fictitious omnipotence by pretending that the compulsory act is a voluntary one and clothing the introjected objects with its own narcissism. If, however, Eros were successful in its defence against Thanatos through the formation of the ego ideal by means of identification, the

---

[1] *Übertragung und Liebe.* See page 178 ff.
[2] The word "dæmon" has here not the prevailing English meaning of devil but is used in the sense of a malignant spirit akin to the *daimonion* of Socrates.

ego ideal would be exclusively the abode of love, which in fact
it is not. Thanatos parries this move of Eros with desexualisation by which, as we know, all identification is accompanied.
The erotic component of the ego ideal thus desexualised corresponds to that undifferentiated narcissistic energy which Freud
postulates in *The Ego and the Id*. This can unite with either of
the two basic instincts, Eros and Thanatos, to increase the
total cathexis of the one or the other. Thus the ego ideal,
like the neutral zone between warring armies, becomes the
actual prize in the struggle between the two forces, the shuttle-
cock particularly of the Thanatos portion of the super-ego
(*dæmon*). This owes its nature to the suggested unsuccessful
attempt of Eros to divert to outer objects by means of projection
the aggression which Thanatos originally directed against the
ego. The projection is unsuccessful in quantitively varying
degrees; first, because of the helplessness of the individual,
since the infant is powerless against its environment and can
scarcely handle any very great aggression; second, because the
objects against which the infantile aggression was directed,
the parents, have already been taken into the ego ideal. Both
lead to the damming up and flowing back of aggression against
the ego. The ego thus threatened takes fright and gives the
danger signal. The ego ideal, abode of the desexualised Eros,
is pressed by the *dæmon* into the service of its ego-destroying
tendencies. By constantly holding up the ego ideal as a
"silent model" and exposing the discrepancy between ego and
ego ideal, the *dæmon* produces feelings of guilt in the ego. In
this way the ego ideal, which originally was created as a prop
to the threatened narcissism, becomes a dangerous weapon of
Thanatos against Eros.

We are of the opinion that in the dream also the ego ideal
is constantly maintained as a model. Nor is this holding up
of the ego ideal as a silent model by the *dæmon* innocuous.
Every deviation from the self-established ego ideal appears in
the ego in the form of feelings of guilt. The strange thing
about this process is that the torments which the *dæmon*
inflicts on the ego always detour via the ego ideal. A discrepancy between ego and ego ideal must always exist before
feelings of guilt and need for punishment can arise in the ego.
By thus putting the desexualised Eros in service against Eros,
the destructive instinct conquers Eros with its own weapons.

If we try to apply this point of view which we derive from the Eros-Thanatos theory to the freudian theory of the wish fulfilling tendency of the dream, we reach the conclusion that this early concept still stands firm. In the light of the material which we presented in the first part of this paper bearing on the struggle between the two original instincts in sleep, we believe that in the freudian formula, "The dream is a wish fulfilment", only the erotic component of the instinct fusion appears to be considered. Unshakable as is the concept of wish fulfilment in the dream, if one seriously wishes to apply the Eros-Thanatos theory to the dream, which as far as we know no one has yet attempted, a supplement is required, which we shall now present and prove. It is this: besides the id wishes in every dream, there is to be found a second, equally important group of tendencies which centre around the super-ego. To our own astonishment we arrive at the startling conclusion that this second, most frequent and regular constituent of every dream is a more or less successful *defence against a reproach of the super-ego*.

In order to reduce misunderstandings to a minimum we should state immediately that we do not refer to the punishment dreams which have been described by Freud and Alexander and whose existence is to-day analytically recognised. We are speaking here of the typical wish fulfilment dream, and postulate that it has a double mechanism. That is, we deduce from our experience that the driving force of every dream derives from a repressed wish of the id and an unconscious reproach of the super-ego, from which the ego then creates the psychic structure which is known to us as a dream. Which of the two instincts becomes master of the situation following their collision depends on whether the unconscious id wish or the unconscious super-ego reproach succeeds in taking possession of the ego ideal and its undifferentiated narcissistic energy. Thus every dream must fulfil two functions: (1) to refute the unconscious reproach of the *dæmon*, and (2) to satisfy a repressed infantile id wish.

In proof of our thesis we select Freud's famous dream of 23rd—24th July, 1895. The Dream of Irma's Injection,[1] which has initiated whole generations of analysts into the understanding of dreams, and which may serve as a paradigm

[1] Freud: *The Interpretation of Dreams*: Geo. Allen & Unwin, Ltd. London. pp. 115-128. Also in *The Basic Writings of Sigmund Freud*. The Modern Library, N.Y. pp. 196-207.

for wish dreams. This choice has the advantage that the dream is known to all, whence the objection that is met with in analytic circles regarding nearly every dream interpretation, that the content of the dream has been misinterpreted, is in this instance not to be feared.

As we recall, the incident preceding the dream which is later used as the day's residue, is that an individual designated as "friend Otto" replies to a question of Professor Freud, somewhat hesitantly and ironically, that Freud's patient, Irma, is better but not entirely well. "I realise," says Freud, "that these words of my friend Otto's, or the tone of voice in which they were spoken, annoyed me. I thought I heard a reproach in the words, perhaps to the effect that I had promised the patient too much . . . This *disagreeable impression*, however, did not become clear to me, nor did I speak of it. That same evening I wrote the clinical history of Irma's case, in order to give it, as though to justify myself, to Dr. M., a mutual friend, who was at that time the leading personality in our circle".[1]

The dream consists of a complicated refutation of reproaches by the ego ideal, which had cast an aspersion of inadequate professional conscientiousness. The wish fulfilling refutation is known to you: not the dreamer, but Otto who had administered an injection with a dirty syringe, is to blame for Irma's illness. The young widow is incurable because of the damming up of sexuality through living in abstinence; her illness as a matter of fact is not psychogenic but organic; she rejects the analytic interpretation, etc. Thus we find a series of refutations of the accusation of inadequate professional conscientiousness linked with aggression against Otto and Dr. M., the representative of the ego ideal, and buttressed by the opposed authority of another, sympathetic friend. In short, the dreamer is exonerated.

The question remains: exonerated by whom? The answer is unequivocal: by his own conscience. Freud is justified in calling the argumentation in this dream "a defence in court". The plea is made before the inner tribunal of his conscience. What is a token of his amazing genius is that Freud, although he did not give it direct expression, sensed this as long as forty years ago. At a certain point in the interpretation of this

[1] Freud: *Ibid.*, London edn. p. 115: N.Y. edn. p. 196. Italics in this and further quotations are ours.

dream he says: "Curiously enough, there are also some painful memories in this material, which confirm the blame attached to Otto rather than my own exculpation. The material is apparently impartial . . ." And in another place, in reference to the use in the dream material of three cases in which his medical treatment had been followed by dire results, Freud says: "It seems as though I were looking for excuses for accusing myself of inadequate professional conscientiousness".

From the viewpoint which we have here advanced, we are able to understand these contradictions. The ego ideal makes use, or rather misuse, of the day's experiences to accuse the ego of the dreamer of inadequate professional conscientiousness. By means of a regular legal defence, turning the plaintiff's arguments against himself, making use of refutations, alibis, qualifications, derision of the ego ideal, citation of exonerating witnesses, the acquittal is achieved. The reproaches which seem so strange to Freud in a wish dream, belong to the bill of particulars of the district attorney, the *dæmon*, and this must be answered.

Yet the dream of Irma's injection admirably fulfils its second function, hallucinatory gratification of repressed infantile wishes. There are certain easily discernible erotic and aggressive wishes whose interpretation is merely hinted at and into which we need not go more fully.

We postulate for *every* dream this double mechanism— defence against the unconscious reproach of the ego ideal, dictated by the *dæmon*, plus fulfilment of repressed id wishes. In this dualism we see Thanatos and Eros at work, each attempting to gain possession of the ego ideal. In the typical wish fulfilment dreams it is Eros which succeeds. But in the "resignation dreams", which are to be discussed later, Thanatos is successful.

We now see the question of "the day's residue" in the dream in a new light. The "residue" up to now has been held to have the significance of an acceptable package wrapping in which contraband articles are smuggled across a border. "We . . . learn", says Freud, "that an unconscious idea, as such, is quite incapable of entering into the preconscious, and that it can exert an influence there only by establishing touch with a harmless idea already belonging to the preconscious, to which it transfers its intensity, and by which it allows itself to be screened".[1] Freud gives the example of a dentist practising in a foreign land who protects himself against the law by associating himself with a native doctor of medicine who then serves him as a signboard and legal "cover". "We thus see that the day-residues, among which we may now include the indifferent impressions, not only borrow something from the *Ucs.* when they secure a share in dream-formation—namely, the motive-power at the disposal of the repressed wish—but they also offer to the unconscious something that is indispensable to it, namely, the points of attachment necessary for transference".[2] On the other hand, the cathexis of the unpleasant residue is offset by the wish fulfilment of the dream, and so the dream is preserved as the protector of sleep. "We may succeed in provisionally disposing of the energetic cathexis of our waking thoughts by deciding to go to sleep . . . But we do not always succeed in doing it, or in doing it completely. Unsolved problems, harassing cares, overwhelming impressions, continue the activity of our thought even during sleep, maintaining psychic processes in the system which we have termed the preconscious. The thought-impulses continued into sleep may be divided into the following groups:

1. Those which have not been completed during the day owing to some accidental cause.

2. Those which have been left uncompleted because our mental powers have failed us, i.e. unsolved problems.

3. Those which have been turned back and suppressed during the day. This is reinforced by a powerful fourth group:—

4. Those which have been excited in our *Ucs.* during the day by the workings of the *Pcs.;* and finally we may add a fifth, consisting of:

5. The indifferent impressions of the day which have therefore been left unsettled . . . But what is the relation of the preconscious day-residues to the dream? There is no doubt that they penetrate abundantly into the dream; that they utilise the dream-content to obtrude themselves upon consciousness even during the night; indeed, they sometimes even dominate the dream-content, and impel it to continue the work of the day; it is also certain that the day residues may just as well have any other character as that of wishes".[3]

All these assertions of Freud about the day's residue are incontestable. We suggest, however, that the residues have a still wider meaning. *The residue is, among other things, the*

[1] *Ibid.*, London edn. p. 518.   N.Y. edn. p. 507.
[2] *Ibid.*, London edn. p. 519.   N.Y. edn. p. 508.
[3] *Ibid.*, London edn. pp. 511, 512.   N.Y. edn. pp. 500, 501.

M

reproach in direct or symbolic form, to the ego by the ego ideal, a reproach misused by the *dæmon* for its antilibidinal purposes by holding up the "silent model" of the ego ideal. At bottom we are dealing with ramifications of a chronic tendency to feel reproached, due to the domination of the *dæmon*.

The diametric opposite of the wish dream, in which Eros succeeds in appropriating the undifferentiated energy of the ego ideal, is found in the so-called dream of failure or resignation. Here the adversary of Eros, Thanatos, succeeds in annexing the desexualised psychic energy of the ego ideal, with the result that the hopelessness of all its erotic endeavours is demonstrated to the ego which then resignedly abandons them and even life itself. These dreams can be reduced to a common denominator, "give up all hope". An example of such a dream is:

> Because of the frost, the water supply and also the drain were shut off. I suffer from terrible thirst . . . At last I am given a glass of lemonade, which turns out to be unhygienic, since it is made with old, stagnant water from my sister's canteen. Nor is there any water in the thermos flask, and I almost drank Sidol by mistake. I awaken in a deep depression, which lasts all day.

This is a dream (recently published by one of us[1]) of a patient who had regressed orally and who had an orally determined ejaculatory disturbance. The starting point of the dream is the stimulus of thirst. But how differently the patient elaborates this wish from the normal person who would perhaps comfort himself with the dream that he was drinking from a spring. The word "thirst" is the cue which releases in our patient a whole witch's brew of super-ego reproaches which are heaped on the intimidated ego: oral wishes directed toward his sister and mother (who was in the habit of sending the sister to the office every day with a thermos bottle of coffee for the patient). The last phase of the dream is to be equated with a suicide: Sidol is a poisonous, white metal polish. It is as though the *dæmon* wished to embitter the ego against every oral wish, as though it had said to the resigned ego, "What can life mean to you? Give it up and die; you will never fulfil your true wishes".

[1] *Cf.* Bergler, Edmund: *Some Special Varieties of Ejaculatory Disturbances Not Hitherto Described.* Int. J. Ps-A., XVI, 1935, pp. 84-95; and Chapter C of the monograph: Bergler, Edmund: *Die Psychische Impotenz des Mannes.* Berne: Verlag Hans Huber, 1937.

In this dream, too, the day's residue is a reproach of the ego ideal. The sister's canteen, out of which the patient had repeatedly drunk during a mountain climbing trip on the preceding day, and the mother's thermos bottle are both symbolic representations of the breast or of the female penis which are held up to the patient as reminders, and which represent to a certain extent the derisive answer of the *dæmon* to the patient's apparently harmless wish to drink.[1]

Between these extremes, the wish dream and the resignation dream, lie great possibilities of variation. Someone with an inclination for classifying and systematising could pick out the two sharply characterised dream types from the wealth of compromise possibilities on the erotic and thanatotic parts of the scale; on the erotic side: aggression against the ego ideal and the dream of "undisguised acknowledgment"; on the thanatotic side, the anxiety dream and the punishment dream.

Let us begin with the dream of aggression against the ego ideal. One of the possibilities of defence of Eros against the advances of the *dæmon* is aggression against the bothersome ego ideal.[2] Examples of such aggression against the ego ideal are: mania, wit, comedy,[3] hypocrisy,[4] humour.[5] Each of these techniques is employed according to its nature by Eros, to wrest from the *dæmon* its instrument of torture, the ego ideal.

The showing up of the fragility and hypocrisy of the ego ideal also takes place in the dream, and is indispensable for the psychic economy of many people. This is shown by the following dream:

> The patient appears at the office of the analyst. In the waiting room he asks a gentleman whether the analyst is the right doctor for his wife who has a disease of the eyes. The gentleman says yes, and relates that the analyst in a few treatments has cured a woman with drooping and puckered eyelids. Suddenly the door to the doctor's office opens, and the analyst says to the gentleman, "Dorli, don't disturb us now; leave us alone". Instead of the elegant couch in the office there is a shabby,, dirty sofa. The analyst resembles Dr. Rake (German=*Greif*).

---

[1] The attainment of the repressed id wish fails, unless we take the white colour of the suicide potion, Sidol, a milk substitute, to be a triumph of Eros, paid for, indeed, with death.

[2] *Cf.* the chapter *The Development of the Super-ego*, p. 180 ff.

[3] Cf. *On the Psychology of Comedy*, p. 97.

[4] Bergler, Edmund: Address before the Vienna Psycho-analytic Association, 9th May, 1934.

[5] Bergler, Edmund: *A Clinical Contribution to the Psychogenesis of Humour.* Psa. Rev., XXIV, 1937.

The dreamer is an hysteric with vomiting and flatulence. Both symptoms appeared when the wife of the patient insisted upon a pregnancy against his will. The patient denies his illness (feminine identification) since not he but his wife needs treatment for adhesions (puckering) in the tubes, and a fallen uterus (drooping eyelids). This accorded with the facts and had long made pregnancy impossible. The patient has a strong unconscious feminine identification. His symptoms are wish and defence fantasies of an orally perceived and anally achieved pregnancy and birth. Dorli is the name of his sister's girl friend. The analyst accordingly has a masculine girl friend, and the patient may hope for the gratification of his passive homosexual rape fantasy. Dr. Rake is the director of an insurance company (analysis=assured success; arguments regarding the duration of the treatment and the uncertainty of the prognosis were a constant form of resistance). He is a lady-killer who is worthy of his name ("rake"). With the shabby divan the patient associated the furniture of a *brothel*.

The reproach of the ego ideal is: you have passive homo-sexual feminine wishes—the wish of the id, to have intercourse with your father. The wish of the id is realised by means of debasing the ego ideal. The analyst is a prostitute and is him-self feminine, or bisexual, like the patient. In self-defence the patient accuses the analyst (whom he identifies with his sister) of being a prostitute whom anyone can buy (fee). Don't pretend to be so noble. You are a swindler like Dr. Rake, the insurance expert (the analysis is a promise of health, insuring recovery). Therefore, fulfil my wishes".[1]

A step further in the defence against the *dæmon* is taken in those rare dreams in which the ego ideal is entirely shaken off and the ego in manic elation takes over the id wish undis-guised (dream of undisguised acknowledgment). These dreams most frequently occur after a period of distressing dreams.

The anxiety dream too lies on the border between the erotic and thanatotic sections of the scale. We know from experi-ence that it appears when the ego is pressed too hard by the *dæmon*. It is an erotic attempt at rescue and prevention. In agreement with a number of authors, we are of the opinion that anxiety is the reaction of the ego to the destructive instinct

---

[1] In this dream, too, the day's residue corresponds to the reproaches of the ego ideal, as is shown by the dream elements—Dorli, Rake, gynecological illness.

which has been turned back against the individual. Certainly anxiety can be secondarily misused by Thanatos for purposes of torment.

Punishment dreams are not identical with the previously discussed resignation dreams. Both are thanatotic, but they differ from each other in their effect. Fundamentally the punishment dream still serves the pleasure principle since its solution is, "Expiation to achieve release", and it generally extracts some masochistic pleasure from its misery. In the true resignation dream this is not the case to any appreciable degree.

In summarising, let us emphasise that we ascribe to the second component of *every* wish dream (the above described refutation of the reproach of the *dæmon*, held up to the ego in the form of the day's residues through the mediation of the ego ideal) *the same psychic valence as the repressed infantile id wish which is hallucinatorily fulfilled.* It is this dualism, the combination of both tendencies, which finally creates the dream which thus emerges as a typical example of instinct fusion. According as the two basic instincts succeed in gaining control of the undifferentiated psychic energy of the ego ideal, there arises one of the many possible variations between the wish and resignation dreams.

Freudian psycho-analysis derives from the discovery of the dynamic effect of repression. That is why Freud first came on the meaning of the id wishes in the dream. The super-ego aspect was first described by Freud as the "censor". Only the more recent disclosures of his studies—dualism of instinct, Eros and Thanatos—have enabled us to find the second constituent of the dream—the *reproach of the dæmon*, which we submit as the *equal partner of the id wish,* and whose substantiation with clinical dream material should be sought. We are well aware that it will take time to overcome difficulties that stand in the way of an acceptance of our assumptions, should these prove correct. Nor do we underestimate the objection that during the last forty years millions of dreams in thousands of analyses have been successfully solved without these new ideas. Finally, our conception underscores much more heavily the element of guilt feelings in the dream, with the result that a large part of the libido, even in the "ordinary" wish dream, is consumed in protection against and the overcoming of unconscious guilt feelings, that is, the death instinct.

TRANSFERENCE AND LOVE*

*"The greatest difficulties lie precisely
where we are not looking for them".*

Goethe

THE MIRACLE OF OBJECT CATHEXIS

"NARCISSISTIC or ego libido seems to be the great reservoir from which the object cathexes are sent out and into which they are withdrawn once more; the narcissistic libidinal cathexis of the ego is the original state of things, realised in earliest childhood, and is merely screened by the later extrusions of libido, but in essentials persists behind them".[1]

This statement of Freud raises a number of questions. That the ego relinquishes a part of its libido in favour of an alien ego is anything but a matter of course which would make superfluous inquiry into basic causes; rather is it a miracle which urgently requires explanation. Why does the ego act in this manner? What are its motives? Does it gain advantages by this process—as seems very likely—and if so, what advantages?

As far as we know, there is in psycho-analytic literature only one direct clue to this puzzle: Freud[2] says that the ego employs object cathexis in order to avoid an increased damming-up of the libido in the ego, which might be experienced as unpleasant. This explanation cannot be denied a certain degree of correctness. It is our purpose to investigate beyond this, and to seek the psychological motives which may explain this miracle of object cathexis which is ordinarily taken so much as a matter of course.

THE WISH TO BE LOVED

A forty-year-old married woman made a confession to her analyst which was very painful for her to make because it

* Translated by Henry Alden Bunker, M.D. First published in *Imago*, XX, 1934, pp. 5-31. First published in English in *The Psychoanalytic Quarterly*, XVIII, 3, 1949. Read before the Vienna Psycho-analytic Society, 8th November, 1933.

[1] Freud: *Three Essays on the Theory of Sexuality*. London: Imago Publishing Co., Ltd., 1949, p. 95.

[2] Freud: *On Narcissism: An Introduction*. Coll. Papers, IV. London: The Hogarth Press.

conflicted with her moral standards.[1] During the following session she told the doctor between sobs: "Yesterday evening I had the feeling that you had deserted me. I felt that I no longer had you, that I didn't know where you were, that I was not good enough for you". Every analyst can cite an abundance of similar examples. The patient's reaction leaves no doubt that the substance of her fear is that she may be deserted by her analyst who represents her super-ego. This fear of being separated from one's super-ego is rightly interpreted in psychoanalysis as the fear of the threatened loss of love. The narcissistic identification with the analyst[2] doubtless also serves to prevent fear of loss of love. From the frequency with which a patient repeats the doctor's views almost verbatim without any recollection of their source, this unconscious plagiarism in analysis, this identification, is to be regarded as a defence against anxiety, that is, as a desire to be loved, which may be formulated: "I am like you, and since you love yourself, you must love me also". Beside this fear of loss of love, we must also note that this anxiety is almost always unequivocally expressed by the idea of separation in space. It scarcely requires more precise observation to establish this.

This state of affairs deserves attention all the more in that Freud, in *The Problem of Anxiety*, describes anxiety as the reaction to a loss, to a separation. According to Freud, the anxiety of infants, and young children no less, has as its sole condition the missing or loss of the object. This object toward which longing is directed and whose absence causes anxiety is, according to prevailing opinion, the beloved and yearned-for mother, or her substitute. The child is believed to experience this for an economic reason, as a consequence of the increase in tension arising out of need. This explanation is based upon the fact that the presence of an externally perceived object can end the danger implicit in the situation.

This summary provides us with a framework for the detailed analysis of the psychic experience, through the minute observation of which we hope to gain an understanding of object relationship in its earliest beginnings. It is our conclusion that spatial separation as an expression of anxiety is based—

---

[1] Cf. *The Sense of Guilt*, p. 74 ff.

[2] Bergler, Edmund: *Das Plagiat*. Psa. Bewegung, IV, 1932. (See fifteenth and sixteenth forms of unconscious plagiarism.)

far beyond the object-libidinal relationship to the mother—fundamentally upon the feeling of the threat to narcissistic unity. One corroboration of this is the fact that feelings of guilt and anxiety have their source in not being loved by the super-ego which is the fear of being unloved. This brings us directly to the problem of love. In order, however, to throw light upon this phenomenon in its complete psychological sense, it is essential to consider first the structure and function of the super-ego.

The Development of the Super-Ego

The modifications which the concept of the super-ego has undergone since its formulation clearly mirror the development of the freudiàn instinct psychology. This "stage of the ego" was discovered at a time when the libido alone was recognised, and the ego instincts seemed in no way demonstrable. This differentiation in the ego was then called the ego ideal: "Man does not want to forego the narcissistic completeness of childhood, and when he cannot hold on to it . . . he tries to regain it in the new form of the ego ideal".[1] Seven years later it was conceived of as ". . . the sum of all the restrictions to which the ego is supposed to submit".[2] Following replacement of this instinct dualism by the antithesis of Eros and Thanatos, and to the extent to which in general the importance of aggression was increasingly taken into account, there occurred a shift, in favour of the latter, in the conception of the content and character of the institution now called super-ego, till the current degree of exclusiveness was reached: "The super-ego seems to have made a one-sided selection, to have chosen only the harshness and severity of the parents, their preventive and punitive functions, while their loving care is not taken up and continued by it".[3] This super-ego, however, retained also the

[1] Freud: *On Narcissism: An Introduction. Op. cit.*
[2] Freud: *Group Psychology and the Analysis of the Ego.* London: The Hogarth Press. New York: Liveright Publishing Co.
[3] Freud: *New Introductory Lectures on Psycho-analysis.* London: The Hogarth Press, p. 85. New York: W. W. Norton & Co. pp. 89-90.

character and the function of the former ego ideal: "It is also the vehicle of the ego ideal, by which the ego measures itself, toward which it strives, and whose demands for ever-increasing perfection it is always striving to fulfil. No doubt this ego ideal is a precipitation of the old idea of the parents, an expression of the admiration which the child felt for the perfection which it at that time ascribed to them".[1]

Despite these definite statements, there exists considerable confusion, as a survey of the literature shows. Nunberg, for example, states: "If, furthermore, the ego ideal is supposed to be a replica of the loved objects in the ego, and the super-ego an image of the hated and feared objects, how is it that these two concepts were confused, and used interchangeably?"[2]

We believe that, with the concept of the struggle between Eros and Thanatos which we here use, Freud's view of the super-ego will gain in clarity and sharpness by a precise understanding of details, especially in the relationship between super-ego and ego ideal.

We conceive the ego ideal to be a "neutral zone", lying between two countries. We believe further that, just as in war every effort is made by neighbouring belligerents to occupy at the outset any neutral strip of land, here too the possession of the ego ideal is the real goal and object of the seesaw struggle between the two great opponents, Eros and Thanatos. This conception of the neutral character of the ego ideal is, in our view, a very gradual development, traversing a number of preliminary stages. In every state of this development we find the two basic drives to be at work, and from this point of view one may, very schematically, speak of two roots of ego ideal development. One of these consists of the attempt of the ego to redirect upon objects the aggression of the death instinct, which is aimed against the ego, whereby these objects become something to be feared. There is thus an attempted exchange of an inner for a projected external danger which, however, miscarries. This consummation of the instinct of destruction is parried by Eros by the incorporation of these fearsome objects into the ego, where they become the subject of one's own narcissism.

[1] *Ibid.*, p. 88.   N.Y. edn. pp. 89-90.
[2] Nunberg, Herman: *Allgemeine Neurosenlehre auf psychoanalytischer Grundlage.* Bern: Hans Huber Verlag, 1932, p. 124.

The following process may be regarded as the second root. The child's feeling of omnipotence is undermined by the demands of external reality, such as hunger, weaning, toilet training. After a series of unsuccessful attempts to restore its feeling of omnipotence, the child is faced with the alternative of relinquishing it or of maintaining it at the price of a compromise. Such a compromise is described by Freud: "We may say that the one . . . has set up an ideal in himself . . . To this ideal ego is now directed the self-love which the real ego enjoyed in childhood. The narcissism seems to be now displaced on to this new ideal ego, which, like the infantile ego, deems itself the possessor of all perfections. As always where the libido is concerned, here again man has shown himself incapable of giving up a gratification he has once enjoyed. He is not willing to forego his narcissistic perfection in his childhood; and if, as he develops, he is disturbed by the admonitions of others and his own critical judgment is awakened, he seeks to recover the early perfection, thus wrested from him, in the new form of an ego ideal".[1]

If Eros were to succeed in this defence against Thanatos through setting up the ego ideal, this would be exclusively the place of love, which in reality it is not. Thanatos does not admit defeat, but on the contrary sharpens this weapon which Eros has created. It is well known that the formation of an ideal is based upon identifications which begin very early and are demonstrable at all stages of organisation. We know, however, that desexualisation runs parallel with every identification.

Desexualisation, which is the achievement of Thanatos, is a subject hitherto little touched upon by psycho-analysis. Desexualisation is commonly considered equivalent to sublimation—incorrectly so, in our opinion, because desexualisation is more inclusive, and sublimation a special case of desexualisation. The latter we imagine as a continual process, following the libido like its shadow, a process active in all stages of its development. Under the influence of the destructive instinct, the ego tries in the pregenital stages to preserve the oral, anal, and urethral functions from sexual amphimixis, and to change them into pure ego functions—ingestion, intestinal and urinary excretions. Even here, as we know, only a partial success is

[1] Freud: *On Narcissism: An Introduction. Op. cit.*, p. 51.

attained, one completely denied the ego in the phallic-genital stage. This is comprehensible when we reflect that the genital does not possess any ego function and only serves the sexual one. Thus desexualisation—as is proven by the latent period in which it happens—would equal an extinction of sexuality altogether, would mean throwing out the baby with the bath water.

It is well known that neurosis leads to the opposite result: the sexualisation of the functions of the ego. But as far as the phallic-genital phase is concerned, sexualisation, usually occurring after the termination of the latent period, is subjected to a renewed desexualisation by the neurotic process (impotence, frigidity). The ego's attempts at desexualisation are crowned with complete success only after the resolution of the Oedipus complex because desexualisation here concerns the organ specific to, and exclusively serving, sexuality; also perhaps after so many unsuccessful attempts, an occasional resigned giving-over of attempts to satisfy the libido directly may supervene. All the preceding explanations, especially with reference to the developmental history of the ego ideal, its derivation from the process of identification, and the attendant desexualisation, serve to support the conception of the ego ideal as a neutral zone. We believe that with this statement, and with the arguments set forth to prove it, we have come very close to one of the problems stated by Freud which gives a more general and deeper meaning to our views. We refer to that much discussed and variously commented upon passage in *The Ego and the Id*, in which there is given a hypothetical explanation of the direct change (independent of the behaviour of the object) of love into hate, as, for example, in cases of paranoia persecutoria; also of hate into love in some cases of homosexuality in which love was preceded by hostile rivalry. Such a direct change of affect, Freud believes, makes the differentiation of the two kinds of drive very questionable or impossible, since this change is based on the assumption of "contrary physiological processes". There is, however, also another possibility of explaining this phenomenon of the transformation of affect into its opposite which does not contradict postulating two kinds of drive. This would be the concept if this change of affect were based merely on the economic motive of a more favourable possibility of discharge. Of course, Freud continues, this hypothesis is based merely upon the assumption: "We have reckoned as though there existed in the mind—whether in the ego or in the id—a displaceable energy, which is in itself neutral, but is able to join forces either with an erotic or with a destructive impulse, differing qualitatively as they do, and augment its total cathexis. Without assuming the existence of a displaceable energy of this kind we can make no headway. The only question is where it comes from, what it belongs to, and what it signifies".[1]

We believe it possible to strengthen Freud's hypothesis, to lend it added proof, by referring—on the basis of our con- clusions—to the ego ideal as that displaceable neutral energy postulated by Freud. This is the less contradictory because the ego ideal has those characteristics which Freud presupposes for that neutral energy: it stems from the narcissistic reserves of the libido, and is desexualised Eros.

Here, however, arises an apparent contradiction; for it is not easy to join narcissism with a neutral state of energy. This contradiction loses much of its point when one remembers that Eros has here undergone desexualisation. Little more than its shadow remains. One might say that there is about it a tinc- ture of the death instinct, since desexualisation is, in fact, the work of Thanatos; furthermore, the introjected persons were fearsome till the intervention of Eros, which greatly modified this fear. All in all, the ego ideal presents itself as an unhomo- geneous, and hence very incomplete institution, a barely suc- cessful alloy of two unequal substances—of the extremely resistant, almost invincible original narcissism with the images of the introjected persons to whom one cannot attribute nearly the same resistance.

Little wonder, in view of this nature of the ego ideal, that the two instincts have no difficulty in taking possession of this energy which thus becomes the alternating prey of now the one, now the other, and then wears the colours—one thinks of black and red—of the victor of the moment. Like Homer's heroes who wake to new life in Hades after they have drunk blood, so can this shadow, the desexualised Eros, be revived through the infusion of the energy of one of the two drives.

This changing play of the instincts makes it understandable that the super-ego is founded on a double principle, which

[1] Freud: *The Ego and the Id.* London: The Hogarth Press, 1927, pp. 61-62.

Freud characterised by the two formulas: "You ought to", and "You must not". The two currents differ both genetically and from the standpoint of instinct psychology. The "you ought to" corresponds to the ego ideal. The "you must not" has its genesis in the aggression of Thanatos directed against the ego, an aggression which the ego attempts at all costs to redirect to external objects, so that it may not itself be annihilated. But this redirection can be successful only to a small degree because of the helplessness of the child, which cannot express such considerable aggressions. The irreconcilability of self-aggression with the narcissistic position of the ego results in a projection of this aggression in such wise that it is felt as coming from without as an external threat. However, these persons in the environment originally felt to be dangerous are later on incorporated into the ego ideal, a fact which has as its consequence a radical change in their evaluation as dangerous. There they have become invested with narcissism, so that the ego's aggression against them must be greatly reduced and modified; otherwise it would in a certain sense become self-aggression. This in turn results in a damming-up of aggression, and therewith the danger of its being turned against the subject's own ego, a danger which is signalised by anxiety.

The derivation of the "you must not" of the super-ego—in which the emphasis seems to lie with the intensity of the death instinct, whereas its conditioning by the object and its connection with the latter is regarded as a very loose one—finds support in the striking fact that the severity of the super-ego is comparatively rarely derived from the severity of the parents. Usually there is, rather, no relationship, or an antithesis between the two. The decisive factor seems to us the presence of a greater outpouring of instinctual energy which the ego is hindered in directing upon objects. The ultimate aggression of the death instinct, turned against the subject's own ego, is reflected in mythology and ancient religion in the daimon, and for purposes of easier reference we shall use this term to designate the anxiety-creating you-must-not part of the super-ego. The non-homogeneity of the ego ideal furthers the strivings of the daimon to an extraordinary degree. It is possible for the daimon to use the ego ideal and its neutral energy as a sort of silent example which is constantly held up to the intimidated ego, thus giving rise to feelings of guilt; thus it happens that the persons of the environment who have been incorporated into the ego ideal turn out to be extremely uncertain allies of the ego. They attack the ego behind its back, and become indirectly helpers of Thanatos in that they alleviate the aggression of the ego and are themselves full of contradictions—an echo of the inconsistency of all upbringing. This explains why the daimon can dictate the most contradictory and therefore entirely unachievable demands to the ego. On the one hand, the daimon is opposed to every object cathexis because this conducting-off of aggression relieves the ego; on the other hand, it urges the ego toward object cathexis, in constantly holding up to it the silent example of the ego ideal which also is a residue of objects; finally the daimon also turns against the self-sufficient narcissism as an expression of Eros.

By using the ego ideal for his own purposes, the daimon mobilises Eros against Eros, defeats him with his own weapons, and thus renders at naught the purposes of Eros which the latter pursued in the creation of the ego ideal.

Nevertheless, Eros is by no means finally defeated; he is constantly attempting to parry Thanatos's onslaughts, and to shake the ego ideal out of its neutrality. The aggression directed against the ego (originally it had no relationship at all to the objects of the external world) is experienced by way of projection as coming from the external world to relieve the narcissistic threat involved. Even the need for punishment may be conceived of as a *praevenire*, whose motive is also to be found in the striving for narcissistic unity. Perhaps this is the true meaning of Nietzsche's conception of guilt: the will to power against one's own helplessness.

While, however, these processes may be regarded as protective and thus merely defence measures of Eros, the possibility of a complete triumph is vouchsafed only if Eros succeeds in erotising punishment, in making it a source of masochistic pleasure. Thus masochism is a triumph of Eros, but certainly not an isolated one because, as one of us noted in an earlier paper,[1] guilt not only is a consequence of but also an incentive toward renewed efforts on the part of Eros in its fight against the death instinct; efforts not only to restrain aggression, but even to use it as a means to its own ends. The hard-pressed ego does not shrink from attack in its despairing defence. There

[1] Jekels, Ludwig: *The Sense of Guilt*.

is no lack of visible evidence of these offensive tactics of the ego which is usually regarded as only passive in this struggle. Witness, for example, the psycho-dynamics of wit, comedy,[1] humour, and especially of mania. These are all—with the exception of mania—more or less veiled eruptions of the ego's aggression against the ego ideal. They represent attempts to wrest from the daimon the weapons used to torture the ego. For this, the narcissistic ego mobilises aggression against the daimon's aggression; the daimon is to be conquered with his own weapons. In this case aggression seems to have been placed in the service of Eros; the complete antithesis to the use of the ego ideal by the daimon. Eros pitted against Eros, Thanatos against Thanatos—what complete revenge!

LOVE AND GUILT

Despite the fact that from ancient times there have been numberless investigations of the subject, little progress was made in elucidating the psychology of love. In his *Metaphysik der Geschlechtsliebe*, Schopenhauer wrote: "One should be surprised . . . that a thing which in human lives plays such an important rôle throughout has been regarded so little by philosophers, and is still an uninvestigated subject today. Plato perhaps was the only one to treat the subject to any extent, as he did, especially in the Symposium and in the Phaedrus, but what he has to say remains in the field of mythology, fable and jest, and mostly concerns only the Greek love of boys. The little which Rousseau in his *Discours sur l'Inégalité* has to say on our subject is incorrect, and insufficient. Kant's discussion of the subject, in the third part of his *Über das Gefühl des Schönen und Erhabenen*, is very superficial and without knowledge of the subject, therefore also partly incorrect".

M. Rosenthal, a contemporary writer who is not a psychoanalyst, states in a book entitled *Die Liebe, Ihr Wesen und Wert:* "To discover and explain the spiritual currents which partly flow deeply below the surface, and which have determined the

[1] *Cf.* Jekels, Ludwig: *On the Psychology of Comedy.*

development of sexual love from its beginnings, to the modern idealistic view . . . is a difficult and hitherto unsolved task".

In psycho-analysis we are again indebted to Freud for giving us the most far-reaching, most comprehensive illumination of the psychology of love. From his paper on Instincts and Their Vicissitudes we gather that the relations of the ego to the object, carried by pregenital libido, can at most be regarded as preliminary stages of love. This is true not only of the object relations of the oral stage, but especially of anal-sadistic relationships, which are hard to differentiate from hate. One can speak of love only when the relation of the whole ego to the object stems from the already developed genital organisation of the libido. This relationship to the object cannot be separated from genital organisation, is conditioned by it, and formed by it into the antithesis of hate.

These are accepted as psycho-analytic axioms; however, when these formulations were made, Freud had not as yet developed two of his greatest concepts: Eros and Thanatos, the two powers dominating the mind and the metapsychological structure of the personality.

In our discussion of the super-ego we have sketched the struggle between these two primal instincts, and we believe that love also is an expression of this struggle. For here, too, the problem is to make the daimon powerless by taking away its implement of torture, the ego ideal, and adding the erotic striving to the neutral energy of the ego ideal. This accounts for the often startling similarity of love to the exalted mood of the manic and of the unquestionable psychological relationship of the two. The difference is the use of another method of disarming the daimon. In mania the daimon is disarmed by aggression, in love by projecting the ego ideal on to the object. This is the ideal state in which there is no tension between the ego and the ego ideal. We believe, nevertheless, that the search for love has as its prerequisite a certain degree of tension between ego and ego ideal. Love, for the ego, has the significance of incontestable proof that the unbearable tension between ego and ego ideal does *not* exist; thus love is an attempted denial which, in contrast to mania, is successful. It is self-evident that where in the normal states there is no appreciable tension of this sort, this mechanism of denial is unnecessary.

The disarming of the daimon, as well as the great narcissistic satisfaction given by the proof of being loved by one's own ego ideal, are the sources of the manic ecstasy of love.

The projection of the ego ideal on the object, under pressure of the daimon, springs from a tendency of the ego to renew the ego ideal out of the endopsychic perception that the old ego ideal has proved itself insufficiently effective against the daimon's aggression, and that its projection has been felt to be insufficient. This projection ("cathexis of the object with libido") is the attempt to set up an agreement between the object and the ego ideal, such as the subject desires in his hard-pressed state.

This projection is followed by a partial reintrojection of the projected ego ideal into the ego, which by implication means that the object was cathected with narcissistic libido. This reintrojection exhibits, by comparison with the initial projection, the essential element of love. One can speak of love only when such a reintrojection has taken place.

In love the ego ideal is, then, projected on the object and, thus "strengthened", is reintrojected—the daimon is thereby disarmed. The consequence of this is the pre-eminence of Eros, which also has taken to itself the neutral energy of the ego ideal. This is the explanation of the disregard of all logical and rational considerations so often observed as characteristic of almost all love, and of the overestimation of the love object, sometimes almost delusional in degree. Behind the beloved object there is one's own ego—basking in the manic intoxication of being loved—which the object has deemed worthy to replace the most treasured thing on earth, the ego ideal.

This concept of ours leads finally to the conclusion that love is an attempt at recapturing narcissistic unity, the complete wholeness of the personality, which the ego considers endangered, seriously threatened by the daimon, by guilt feeling which constitutes a considerable disturbance to narcissistic unity.

Is love then a consequence of a feeling of guilt? This opinion may seem peculiar, but we maintain it. We also believe that it is substantiated by the phenomenon of transference. Let us emphasise at this point the decisive characteristic which distinguishes the latter from love. We are sure of the assent of

N

all experienced analysts when we emphasise the following symptoms of transference as especially striking and characteristic: (1) the infallibility of its occurrence despite the absence of choice as regards the object, manifesting itself with a complete disregard of age or sex, and disregarding every personal quality or its absence; (2) its impetuosity which, though often veiled, betrays itself in some instances before the patient has met the physician.

In contrast to the indiscriminateness and inevitability of transference, how greatly and how closely is love conditioned by circumstances; how touchy and changeable in its early stages if conditions do not conform to at least a minimum extent.

This phenomenological difference reveals to a large extent the psychological one. What do these characteristics of transference, the inevitability of its occurrence under practically all circumstances and its impetuosity, denote? Are these not the characteristics of an attitude of "cost what it may", and the expression of the fact that the transference is an act of despair arising from a mood of panic—born out of the intuitive realisation of the power of love to protect against the daimon, as in the case of the person in love? But what a difference! Like the provident fighter, the person in love knew how to wrest from the daimon at his first approach the weapon of the ego ideal even before he could successfully grasp it.

There is an almost grotesque contrast between the neurotic, capable of hardly more than years of passivity without initiative (the intermediate state of the transference neurosis), and the activity and initiative of the person in love who in wooing the object projects his ego ideal with unceasing efforts to remodel the object to accord with his wishful fantasy, and to attribute to it as much reality as possible. There is no more effective force in human motivation than love. The mature lover is a victorious fighter.

Is guilt the only difference between transference and love? Psycho-analytically, the difference is that in the case of love, only the ego ideal is projected on to the object, whereas in transference the super-ego, the ego ideal and the daimon, are projected. Transference is also very different from love in that the object is not only the object of love but perhaps to an even greater extent an object of anxiety.

While the ego ideal is capable of a complete projective cathexis—possibly due to the plasticity and displaceability of the erotic drives—the daimon can apparently be only partially projected. The recurrent depressions and complaints of patients in analysis, long after projection has been completed, speak in favour of this.

All loving is the equivalent of being loved. In the last analysis there is only the wish to be loved; it depends only on the mechanism whether the wish to be loved is infantile (pregenital) or mature (genital). Either the object coincides with the ego ideal which the subject in love feels as ego, or the situation is reversed and the person himself acts his ego ideal and reduces the object to the ego.

These two mechanisms have a special place in the phenomena of love. On the one hand there is a type of person in love who looks up to the object, stands in subjection to it, demands and enjoys the object's care, demands emphatically to be loved in return. The other extreme is exemplified by him who is concerned primarily with patronising, benevolent ruling, caring for, and spending upon, and who cares much less for the return of affection.

For purposes of differentiation we call the first type feminine love, the second masculine love. These designations result from a general impression, and we do not maintain that these forms of love always coincide with the respective sexes.[1]

It is superfluous to emphasise that the psychological difference between the two types of love does not conflict with the statement that the meaning of love is the disarmament of the daimon. Only the method is different. While the masculine type arrogates the attributes of the ego ideal to annihilate all tension between it and the ego, the feminine type succeeds through the illusion of satisfying the ego ideal by being loved by it. A confirmation of the correctness of this explanation of the process of love is the fact that it resolves a contradiction in the psychology of narcissism. While in Freud's *On Narcissism: An Introduction*, the essential feature in relation to the object is the desire to be loved, the opposite is stated in *Libidinal Types*, where it is said that the active desire to love is characteristic of the narcissistic type. The two types discussed by Freud seem

[1] This noncorrespondence is largely conditioned by fixations: in the male on the oral, in the female on the phallic level (penis envy).

to correspond wholly with what we call feminine and masculine loving whereby, as already mentioned, both lead back to the deep desire to be loved.[1]

The narcissistic intoxication of love requires that the object fulfil the wishful rôle which the ego ideal projects. In requited love, this strengthens the feeling of being loved. While nothing happens to destroy the illusion, there obtains the possibility of astonishing deception. The more completely the object conforms, the more happy and intense the love. This seems to apply especially in instances of "love at first sight". As an example, one recalls young Werther who at the very first meeting falls deeply in love with Lotte, who appears as a loving mother surrounded by children to whom she is giving bread.

Occasionally very little agreement between the desire of the ego ideal and the reaction of the object is necessary to produce the feeling of requited love. Gross indifference or repulse from the object causes the lover to fall prey to a more or less profound depression, a severe narcissistic injury with marked reduction of self-esteem. The narcissistic ego has failed in the drive against the daimon who now basks in his victory over the ego. The ego ideal which had been wrested from the daimon again becomes subservient to its aims. The discrepancy between the fantasied and the realisable ego ideal is inescapable, and the ego is plunged into an abyss of guilt, to the point of a feeling of complete worthlessness.

The preservation of self-esteem observed in mature personalities, which despite disappointments enables them to invest new objects with love, stems from an ego that—to escape the daimon —can prove to itself that it is after all loved by its ego ideal. After a disappointment in love the ego may regress through homosexuality to narcissistic withdrawal or suicidal masochism.

The correctness of the interpretation of love as a reintrojection—following its projection—of the ego ideal is gauged by its utility, by its illumination for us of much that was hitherto unclear. To illustrate this point we choose a phenomenon which Freud indicated as hitherto unexplained, and which seems without doubt of the greatest importance both for the comprehension of psycho-pathology and for the understanding of character formation: the substitution of object cathexis by identification, which Freud first established in homosexuality,

---

[1] *Cf.* Spinoza: *"Amor est titillatio concomitante idea causae externae"*.

later in melancholia, and finally, in *The Ego and the Id,* he attributed to normal character development.

"When it happens that a person has to give up a sexual object, there quite often ensues a modification in his ego which can only be described as a reinstatement of the object within the ego, as it occurs in melancholia; the exact nature of this substitution is as yet unknown to us. It may be that by under-taking this introjection, which is a kind of regression to the mechanism of the oral phase, the ego makes it easier for an object to be given up or renders that process possible. It may even be that this identification is the sole condition under which the id can give up its objects. At any rate the process, especially in the early phases of development, is a very frequent one, and it points to the conclusion that the character of the ego is a precipitate of abandoned object cathexes and that it contains a record of past object choices".[1]

We believe that Freud's reservation, "the exact nature of this substitution is as yet unknown to us", is no longer justified in the light of our conception of the love process; for this identification, replacing object love (reintrojection), is not a phenomenon arising *de novo*, but occurs at the very beginning of the love process and is an integral part of it. Our concept of reintrojection and of its pre-eminent importance in the process of love is, moreover, greatly strengthened by Freud's conception in *Instincts and Their Vicissitudes:* "It is primarily narcissistic, is then transferred to those objects which have been incor-porated in the ego, now much extended . . ."[2]

The conflicts and complications arising out of love in many instances continue a sort of atonement through the chronic suffering which greatly outlasts the state of being in love, an appeasement of the daimon, who thus takes revenge at com-pound interest for his temporary helplessness. When a love relationship terminates, the ego treats the object with the same severity and criticism with which it is itself dominated by the daimon. This makes understandable the aggressions against a former love object; they are attempts of the ego to transfer the punishment of the daimon on to the object. This represents at the same time a *captatio* of the daimon, according to the formula: I don't love the object.

[1] Freud: *The Ego and the Id.* London: Hogarth Press, 1927, p. 36.
[2] Coll. Papers, IV, p. 81.

The Autarchic Fiction

At the beginning of extrauterine life the infant is ignorant of any sources of pleasure other than in itself, a state falling within the scope of the "period of unconditional omnipotence", described by Ferenczi. According to Freud, the maternal breast is for a time regarded by the child as part of its own body. This conception of Freud has hitherto been insufficiently appreciated in its fundamental significance, indeed hardly recognised. The familiar controversy about when the ego is discovered must much more correctly and fruitfully be replaced by the more important question: when is the object discovered?

This stage of infantile omnipotence is an "autarchic fiction" of the infant. A substantiation of this is the frequency with which an infant reacts to weaning with masturbation—demonstrating how unwillingly the infantile ego orients itself to objects, and how, clinging to its feeling of omnipotence, it first of all disavows objects.

How enduring this autarchic fiction is, is illustrated by the psycho-analysis of coitus. Stärcke's paper on the castration complex[1] deserves first mention because he was the first to call attention to oral castration through weaning. Ferenczi[2] observed that infants of both sexes play the double rôle of child and mother with their own bodies.[3] Coitus is characterised as a "trace of maternal regression" in which there is a threefold identification: of the whole organism with the genitals; with the partner; with the genital secretion. The rhythm of sucking is retained as an important part of all adult erotic activity, whereby considerable quantities of oral and anal erotism are transferred to the vagina. In the transformation of instincts, the female infant's pleasure in sucking the nipple is displaced to the woman's vaginal pleasure in receiving the penis in coitus.[4]. For her this re-creation of her first relationship to an external object is an "oral" incorporation which represents a mastering of the trauma of weaning. According to Bernfeld, the hand of the male infant at first replaces the mouth, and is

[1] Stärcke, August: *The Castration Complex.* Int. J. Psycho-Anal., II, 1921, pp. 179-201.
[2] Ferenczi, Sandor: *Thalassa: A Theory of Genitality.* New York: Psa. Quarterly, Inc., 1938.
[3] *Cf.* also Rank, Otto: *The Genesis of Genitality.* Psa. Rev., XIII, 1926, pp. 129-144.
[4] Deutsch, Helene: *Psychology of Women.* Two Vols. New York: Grune & Stratton, 1944 and 1945.

later characterised by equating milk and semen. Adult coitus thus would not only be a substitute for the breast but a sadistic revenge for weaning. Bergler and Eidelberg[1] observed clinically that children have the repetitive compulsion to reproduce actively in play what once they had to endure passively, in attempts to master the trauma of weaning. The severe narcissistic injury caused by withdrawal of the breast is partially compensated by masturbation which helps restore the feeling of omnipotence. The authors assume a cathexis of the penis with an instinct fusion of Eros and Thanatos, and believe that the position of this fusion, stemming from the death instinct, has undergone such extensive change in the sex act that its gratification can be accomplished without danger to the ego. In coitus the male, in identification with the phallic mother, overcomes the trauma of weaning through becoming the active rather than the passive participant.

Thus, in the opinion of all the authors cited, coitus has the significance of a repetition of infantile sexuality. Beyond this assumption of coitus as an echo of the child-mother relationship is our conviction of the deeply narcissistic character of the sex act. The emphasis placed on the relationship to the object seems not to be what is of importance, especially since by identification with the object the infantile gratification is also recaptured. What is fundamental is that the desire to be loved —the nucleus of the later demand of the ego upon the ego ideal—is based on the desire never to be separated from the lactating maternal breast. This longing is not really directed to the object, the maternal breast; rather it represents an attempt at narcissistic restitution, for it was directed to the breast when this was still perceived as part of the subject's ego—the basis of the later ego ideal. Of what great consequence this "cardinal error of the infant" becomes—*sit venia verbo*—regarding the "allocation" of the giving breast, we have outlined in connection with the process of love. Grotesque as it may sound, the object cathexis in the process of love stems in the last analysis from this, its purpose being to recapture for the individual his lost narcissistic completeness. Freud's well-known statement supports this thesis.[2]

---

[1] Bergler, Edmund and Eidelberg, Ludwig: *Der Mammakomplex des Mannes.* Int. Ztschr. f. Psa., XIX, 1933, pp. 547-583.
[2] See the first paragraph of this paper.

When we keep in mind how the ego continually endeavours by means of the attempts at restitution outlined above to make sure of its narcissistic unity, the behaviour of the neurotic in the transference at last becomes clear. It is based primarily on the fear of literal spatial separation.

The truly surprising fact—usually dismissed with a reference to the instinct of reproduction—that love so imperatively urges sexual union and satisfaction now also becomes comprehensible. We believe that there must exist precise psychic determinants, the discovery of which seems essential for the comprehension of the psychology of love. To Freud's formulation that love stems from the capacity of the ego to satisfy part of its drives autoerotically, through the gain of organic pleasure, we would pose the question: for what purpose, then, does the ego follow the roundabout way through objects, only to return again to itself?

In the final analysis both tender and sensual love have the same aim. Both are by nature narcissistic attempts at restitution which occur under the pressure of the repetitive compulsion.

Coitus expresses physically what tenderness does emotionally; for what in tenderness is expressed through reintrojection of the object, substituted for the ego ideal, is revealed in sensual love through the pure impulse to "contractation", this hitherto puzzling urge which so dominates people in love, the need to cling together as closely, as inseparably as possible.

It is alone the combination of both parts of love—the maximum expression of unity—that becomes the strongest negation of the feeling of separateness, of incompleteness, of narcissistic damage—a maximal expression of unity perhaps only surpassed by the creating of a child, that materialisation of the fantasy of unity.

THE TRANSFERENCE

In *Observations on Transference Love*, Freud says that no difference exists between transference and love. Transference is merely love under special conditions (of analysis and resistance), and thus represents merely a special case of love.

Repeating and supplementing our earlier discussion of love in transference, we believe that the difference between the two lies in the fact that while in love the object is put in the place of the ego ideal through projection, in transference the physician unites in his person via projection the super-ego, ego ideal and daimon. In the last, anxiety predominates. With the former there is overestimation of the object, the work of love. Dread of the physician, or the desire to be loved by him, are thus the characteristic attitudes of transference.

In the positive transference the patient wants to be loved by the doctor as his ego ideal. The consequence of this desire to be loved by the physician and of the fear of him is a narcissistic identification with him. The nucleus of all positive transference, as in the case of love, is the narcissistic phenomenon of wanting to be loved. Equally, what has previously been said about active loving and the passive desire to be loved applies also to transference: the actively loving person represents his ego in the object, while he himself imitates his ego ideal. For the person wanting passively to be loved, the object represents the ego ideal by which he wants to be loved, and he himself represents the ego.

In the negative transference the hatred directed against the physician (the parents) is also directed against the ego. This hatred often disguises love (positive transference under the guise of negative transference), or the aggression of the patient is merely an attempt to test the love of the physician. Sometimes the discharge of the aggressions of the person's own ego upon the object has been unsuccessful. This is the difference between "normal" and neurotic hatred; in the former, the directing of Thanatos on to the object has been successful. Neurotic hatred is directed against the ego through anxiety and guilt.

This leads to the psycho-pathology of ambivalence. According to the conception here outlined, love is the desire to be loved by the ego ideal which has been projected on to the object: hate is the attempt to transfer Thanatos on to the object. The attempt is unsuccessful; the aggression is inhibited because the object is the person's own ego ideal, so that the aggression is after all again directed against the ego.

Thus, in positive and negative transference narcissistic elements are as predominant as they are in love. What distinguishes it from love is the extent of the participation of the super-ego which is projected on to the object (in love, only the ego ideal; in transference, the ego ideal and the daimon). Progress in analytic treatment lies in overcoming the projection of the daimon upon the doctor in the interest of projecting the ego ideal upon him, in order to resolve this too at the end of treatment. Thus, the patient learns to "love". Identification as a defence against anxiety gives way also to that identification which we have previously designated as an integral part of love.

NARCISSISTIC RESTITUTION AND THE DISCHARGE OF AGGRESSION

First the ego turns toward objects only reluctantly; in the stage of fictitious autarchy its own body is also an object. Only after attempts to maintain this fiction have failed, does it resort to other mechanisms to reinstate the lost feeling of omnipotence. This is the most basic function and use of objects for the ego. This is the origin of the ego ideal, of the libidinal cathexis of objects.

Adult love has been described as a special instance of object cathexis, dependent upon feelings of guilt. The infant, however, first invests the objects which ministered to its instinct of self-preservation and which become sources of pleasure. This seems to reverse our view of the close tie of love with guilt, since it would seem that there is no place for feelings of guilt in this instance; however, insufficiently discharged forces of self-aggression exclude complete freedom from feelings of guilt.

Anna Freud, in connection with a report by Dorothy Burlingham on the urge for communication in children—according to which, apart from its exhibitionistic aim, it is also an invitation to partnership in mutual sexual pleasure—made some observations which seem to be extremely important. Anna Freud believes that in view of this concept, the uninhibiting form of upbringing does not differ in its result from the orthodox, prohibiting form because the expectation of sexual partnership by the child is not attained. This may account for instances in which the most complete tolerance toward infantile masturbation has not the anticipated effect. The child may feel in the adult's failure to participate in its sexual activity an actual rejection.

From here, it is only a short step to assuming feelings of guilt in the infant. The young child does not remain ignorant of the fact that its desires are at variance with the attitudes of adults, that it therewith remains far behind its developing ego ideal.

The objection that this assumption of guilt in the child contradicts psycho-analytic theory is met by the statement that we are speaking here only of the preliminary stages—however far-reaching in their consequences—of the super-ego which will finally emerge only after the complete resolution of the Oedipus complex; moreover, let us not overlook the fact that in the question of guilt feeling we are dealing, in the last analysis, with the problem of anxiety, and let us take stock of the intimate psychological relationship between these two phenomena. One may then justly state that as guilt feelings act as a motive for love in the adult, so anxiety acts in the child. Freud's conclusion is basically that this anxiety is an expression of the fear of separation. But we do not regard this postulated desire not to be separated from the mother as the ultimate and deepest motive, but rather regard the threat to the infant's narcissistic unity as the ultimate danger. The autarchic fiction gives us a clear hint that fundamentally anxiety is based on the threat to this fictitious unity, which seems to be paradigmatic for psychic life; thus, a disturbing of this fiction may be evaluated as the most severe violation of narcissism, whose restitution is at the root of object cathexis, the almost compulsive pertinacity of which it explains.

The way in which the object is made to serve this narcissistic restoration has already been sufficiently emphasised in the discussion of the phenomenon of love. Let us mention the familiar psycho-analytic concept according to which the ego withdraws from objects the libido with which the id has cathected them in order to grow and expand at the cost of these objects. Let us also add that reintrojection is not only a weapon against the daimon, but likewise, through the expansion and strengthening of the ego, renders considerable support to the fiction of omnipotence. This seems an additional proof that love may be counted among those narcissistic efforts at restitution which occur under the pressure of the repetitive compulsion. As can be seen from the foregoing, we do not consider justified a far-reaching distinction in principle—let alone an antithesis—between narcissistic and object-libidinal cathexes, however great the heuristic value of such differentiation might be. Object cathexes have no other significance than of a statement concerning the state of the narcissistic libido; hence nothing more than an indicator. We are thus in complete agreement with Freud's original contention, unchanged through five decades, as expressed in the New Introductory Lectures: "There is therefore a constant transformation of ego libido into object libido, and object libido into ego libido" (p. 141).

The second function of objects for the ego—the discharge of the aggression of Thanatos originally directed against the ego itself—is certainly as important for the psychic economy as the first. It, also, serves narcissistic intactness. However apt it might be, we are not malicious enough to state that object relationship in the service of the discharge of aggression is the most respectable of which the human being is capable.

Here again we find a cause why real objects are necessary in the automatic repetitions previously described. Why does man not stick to masturbation which has been familiar and comfortable to him since childhood? Surely all this could also have been partially expressed in masturbation. Simply, there is not enough possibility in the subject's own ego for discharge of so important aggressive elements, which in part form the substratum of these tendencies, such as revenge, hostile feeling tones, etc., unless one chooses the masochistic and hence neurotic way out. It is practically the stigma of neurotics, with their insufficient and inhibited directing of aggression from their own egos upon objects, that they have to resort to masturbation. The insufficient discharge of aggression in masturbation seems to us a circumstance of which the importance should not be underrated.[1] It is one which seems important to us for two reasons: first, it explains the inadequacy of satisfaction through masturbation; second, it makes highly

[1] Nunberg, Herman: *Allgemeine Neurosenlehre auf psychoanalytischer Grundlage.* Op. cit., p. 168.

questionable the frequently alleged harmlessness of masturbation, if it does not contradict it outright.

The autarchic fiction is the paradigm of the striving for narcissistic completeness which man, with the aid of objects, pursues throughout his life. Possibly the intuitive realisation of this is reflected—however distortedly—in those philosophical systems which teach that the world exists only as idea. Much more attractive is the thought that the autarchic fiction may in the last analysis be why man's whole life is interwoven with fictions, and is hardly possible without them.